PENGUIN CLASSICS

AN AUTOBIOGRAPHY

ANTHONY TROLLOPE was born in London in 1815 and died in 1882. On the bankruptcy of his barrister father, the family was maintained by his mother, Frances, who in middle age launched a successful career as a writer. It appears that nobody held out any hopes of worldly success for Anthony, who was an awkward and miserable schoolboy and youth, until the Post Office, in which he was a clerk, posted him to Ireland, and after a while he turned to novel-writing.

Trollope enjoyed considerable acclaim during his lifetime, writing forty-seven novels, eight travel books and many short stories, while pursuing his career as a senior civil servant. *The Warden* (1855), his earliest novel to achieve success, was the first of the immensely popular *Chronicles of Barsetshire*: *Barchester Towers* (1857), *Doctor Thorne* (1858), *Framley Parsonage* (1860–61), *The Small House at Allington* (1862–4) and *The Last Chronicle of Barset* (1866–7). Equally famous were the six 'Palliser' novels: *Can You Forgive Her?* (1864–5), *Phineas Finn* (1867–9), *The Eustace Diamonds* (1871–3), *Phineas Redux* (1873–4), *The Prime Minister* (1875–6) and *The Duke's Children* (1879–80). Of his many other novels, *He Knew He Was Right* (1868–9) and *The Way We Live Now* (1874–5) are most frequently cited among the greatest mid-Victorian novels. In his day his fiction was regarded as presenting the most convincing picture ever of the lives of the landed and professional classes.

DAVID SKILTON was educated at King's College, Cambridge, and at the University of Copenhagen. After holding posts at the universities of Stockholm, Glasgow and Lampeter, he is now Professor of English at Cardiff, where he has been Head of the School of English Studies, Communication and Philosophy, and Pro Vice-Chancellor. His books include *Anthony Trollope and His Contemporaries* (1972; 1996), *Defoe to the Victorians* (Penguin, 1985), *The Early and Mid-Victorian Novel* (1993) and editions of numerous Victorian novels. For the Penguin Classics he has also edited Hardy's *Tess of the d'Urbervilles* and Trollope's *The Prime Minister*, and he has co-edited *Framley Parsonage*.

Valparaiso Public Library
103 Jefferson St.
Valparaiso, IN 46383

ANTHONY TROLLOPE

———————

AN AUTOBIOGRAPHY

EDITED WITH AN INTRODUCTION
BY DAVID SKILTON

PORTER COUNTY PUBLIC LIBRARY SYSTEM

921 TROLLOPE   VAL
Trollope, Anthony,
An autobiography /
33410004178416

MAY 0 8 1997

PENGUIN BOOKS

Valparaiso Public Library
103 Jefferson St.
Valparaiso, IN 46383

PENGUIN BOOKS

Published by the Penguin Group
Penguin Books Ltd, 27 Wrights Lane, London w8 5tz, England
Penguin Books USA Inc., 375 Hudson Street, New York, New York 10014, USA
Penguin Books Australia Ltd, Ringwood, Victoria, Australia
Penguin Books Canada Ltd, 10 Alcorn Avenue, Toronto, Ontario, Canada m4v 3b2
Penguin Books (NZ) Ltd, 182–190 Wairau Road, Auckland 10, New Zealand

Penguin Books Ltd, Registered Offices: Harmondsworth, Middlesex, England

Published in Penguin Classics 1996
1 3 5 7 9 10 8 6 4 2

Introduction and notes copyright, © David Skilton, 1996
All rights reserved

The moral right of the editor has been asserted

Set in 10/12.5pt Monotype Janson
Typeset by Datix International Limited, Bungay, Suffolk
Printed in England by Clays Ltd, St Ives plc

Except in the United States of America, this book is sold subject
to the condition that it shall not, by way of trade or otherwise, be lent,
re-sold, hired out, or otherwise circulated without the publisher's
prior consent in any form of binding or cover other than that in
which it is published and without a similar condition including this
condition being imposed on the subsequent purchaser

CONTENTS

INTRODUCTION

Trollope's *Autobiography* is an indispensable book for every reader of his fiction. It tells the story of an exceptional man who made immense efforts to appear as unremarkable as possible, and whose artistic talent was backed by prodigious physical stamina and strength of mind. The story of the author's eventual triumph over a miserable childhood and undistinguished youth has achieved almost mythic status, equal in renown to Dickens's narrative of his childhood suffering when he was sent to work in Warren's Blacking Warehouse after his father's bankruptcy. Trollope's story too centres on financial failure and social disgrace, each stage of the family's downward progress bringing with it a new phase of suffering for this friendless boy, 'big, and awkward, and ugly ... ill-dressed and dirty' (Chapter 1). His father's impracticality and intractability led to debt and the family's flight to Belgium, so that the father could escape the imprisonment which was the fate of Mr Dickens senior. Set adrift in London without advice, discipline or support, and constantly in debt, Trollope remembers himself as perpetually on the edge of the social precipice which divided the socially 'respectable' from those below, and in constant risk of falling over it. The subsequent story of how belated literary success led to his acceptance in London clubland and to friendships with the rich and famous, makes emotive telling and has been used by generations of critics as the explanation for his down-to-earth attitude to his art, as well as the importance he attaches to being a lady or a gentleman, and hence qualified to belong to those circles from which the young Anthony Trollope felt himself excluded.

Practical his attitudes certainly were. No novelist was ever more convinced that he owed his social position to his professionalism, was more businesslike about the process of composition, more experienced in negotiating with publishers, or less inclined to claim for himself the status of an inspired artist. In order to separate himself from the myth of the writer as aesthetic hero, he claimed that writing was a trade, carried on honestly or dishonestly, but in its conduct much resembling the work of an artisan, such as a shoemaker. In 1861, years before *An Autobiography* was written, James Russell Lowell heard him make this comparison in Boston, Massachusetts: 'I dined the other day with Anthony Trollope ... He says he goes to work on a novel "just like a shoemaker on a shoe, only taking care to make honest stitches".'[1] The analogy becomes the object of sarcasm in the *Saturday Review*, which frequently accuses Trollope of lacking imagination and producing mechanical art.[2] Characteristically, he defies ridicule and continues to use the comparison: 'My belief of book writing is much the same as my belief as to shoemaking. The man who will work the hardest at it, and will work with the most honest purpose, will work the best.'[3] When the by now notorious shoemaker makes his appearance in *An Autobiography*, Trollope is making his usual points, but this time attacking those

who think that the man who works with his imagination should allow himself to wait till – inspiration moves him. When I have heard such doctrine preached I have hardly been able to repress my scorn. To me it would not be more absurd if the shoemaker were to wait for inspiration, or the tallow-chandler for the divine moment of melting. If the man whose business it is to write has eaten too many good things, or has drunk too much, or smoked too many cigars, – as men who write sometimes will do, – then his condition may be unfavourable for work; but so will be the condition of a shoemaker who had been similarly imprudent. I have sometimes thought that the inspiration wanted has been the remedy which time will give to the evil results of such imprudence (Chapter 7).

1. See Lowell to an unknown correspondent, 20 September 1861, in H. E. Scudder, *James Russell Lowell: A Biography*, 2 vols. (Macmillan & Co, 1901), ii, pp. 82–3.
2. See David Skilton, *Anthony Trollope and His Contemporaries: A Study in the Theory and Conventions of Mid-Victorian Fiction* (London: Longman; New York: St Martin's, 1972; new edition, Macmillan, 1996), pp. 53–7.
3. Letter to Mrs Catherine Gould, in N. John Hall (ed.), *The Letters of Anthony Trollope* (Stanford, Calif.: Stanford University Press, 1983), pp. 100–101.

On the face of it *An Autobiography* stands as the record of a phenomenally fertile creative life which pays no attention to the process of creativity itself, and readers accustomed to narratives of genius suffering agonies and ecstasies in the cause of art wonder what Trollope is doing, and why he is writing his story at all if he cannot summon up raptures of perinatal enthusiasm. Is *An Autobiography* simply an account of the triumph of Victorian practicality over Romantic or Aesthetic self-consciousness, and if so, how can it be judged in the end anything but a record of a bourgeois philistinism which denies the very art it creates? If possessed of Trollope's robust trust in common sense one might reply that no man who devoted his life to aesthetic experiment in the way he did could in fact despise his art, and that he must be doing something else with his life story. One possibility is that he truly lacked imagination and had no creative struggles to recall. Another is that he deliberately played down his individual talent because he thought it ungentlemanly to parade oneself as blatantly as contemporaries like Dickens and Bulwer Lytton. Yet another – based on the belief that such an uncomplicated triumph as Trollope records after such heart-rending adversity is not in nature – is that the book deliberately presents a stolid façade in order to conceal a problematic psychology which early trauma, including rejection by his mother, is presumed to have produced.

Whichever reading is chosen, the question of interpretation arises. We are used to accepting Trollope's fictional versions of the world almost as though they were true, as though he was the 'giant' Nathaniel Hawthorne compared him to, hewing out a great piece of the English countryside and putting it on display without its inhabitants being aware of what was happening to them (Chapter 8). Hawthorne's compliment turned out, intentionally or unintentionally, to have a barb. The implication that what seems to be the accurate reproduction of life implies a weakness of creative imagination has dogged Trollope's reputation ever since. Despite the fact that the gruff social exterior for which Trollope was famous accords ill with the delicate psychological analysis which is the speciality of his fiction, critics have frequently invited us to see him as a novelist who was a great realist because – and this can be paraded as an artistic weakness – he was completely and

uncomplicatedly honest in real life. Yet our evidence for his simplicity
is flimsy. We have the word of some of his contemporaries as to how
straightforward he appeared to them, and of course we have his own
word in *An Autobiography*. But what sort of credence should we give to
this or any other aspect of Trollope's narrative of his own life? In any
case, his own presentation of himself as trustworthy – even if true in
the most literal sense – should not be applied uncritically to his narrative art, whether fictional or non-fictional. Even non-fictional narrative
is invention, and all invention is unreliable to some degree. All nar-
rators are liars, like the proverbial Cretans, and never less to be believed
than when claiming to tell the truth.

Trollope himself comments on non-fictional writing when giving an
account of his travel books: 'There are two kinds of confidence which a
reader may have in his author, – which two kinds the reader who
wishes to use his reading well should carefully discriminate. There is a
confidence in facts, and a confidence in vision' (Chapter 7). The question which arises for us as readers of *An Autobiography* is which kind of
confidence we should have in our author on this occasion. Trollope
himself expands on his original distinction: the author who relies on
carefully researched fact in non-fictional writing, he informs us, 'tells
you accurately what has been', while '[t]he other suggests to you what
may, – or perhaps what must have been or what ought to have been'.
One is the purveyor of raw data requiring unquestioning belief from
readers, while the other is the presenter of more general visions which
allow readers to develop their own conclusions. He himself, he claims,
is to be trusted for his overall vision of his subject, and not for any
'rock of fact' on which his accounts are based. And his vision of the
world is to be trusted by his fellows because of his education, experience and social standing.

An Autobiography seems to be an exception to this approach. When
we see the sheer quantity of information Trollope gives in it about his
dealings with his publishers, about the prices and publication dates of
his many works, and about the history of the periodicals with which he
was associated, we are inclined to think that as far as writers of lives are
concerned he must be an author who concentrates on facts and aims to
tell 'accurately what has been'. Moreover our inclination is confirmed

when at the end of the book he disclaims any attempt to present states of mind or psychological motivation: 'It will not, I trust, be supposed by any reader that I have intended in this so-called autobiography to give a record of my inner life' (Chapter 20). This autobiographer claims not to go beyond the narration of ascertainable fact in telling his story, and proposes that no larger significance can be extracted from it. This conclusion is strengthened when Trollope asserts that 'Rousseau probably attempted' to give a record of his 'inner life' but in the event only revealed 'the thoughts and convictions rather than the facts of his life' (Chapter 20). It seems that even a psychological account of one's life – even one's 'confessions' – should seek to tie the happenings of the 'inner life' firmly to the established facts of one's career. Reliability of historical narration seems to be the quality Trollope most prizes in an autobiography, and few writers are more persuasive when they ask us to trust their account of things.

This has not stopped commentators wondering whether even at a factual level Trollope's narrative of his life is accurate, and in particular whether his childhood and youth were 'really' as dreadful as he conveys.[4] Other readers have caught glimpses of this 'inner life' at odd moments through the interstices of this apparently 'objective' work, and those given to psychoanalysis have a ready-made way of expanding on these hints. A miserable childhood and troubled youth were the prelude to Trollope's professional life, and the post-Freudian mind is forced to conclude that the balanced tone of *An Autobiography* results from the suppression of psychologically troubling material. The moments in question are short passages which show Trollope as an adult brooding for hours on end over his father's unhappy fate (Chapter 1), or confessing his lifelong desire 'to be liked by those around me' (Chapter 9), or revealing that there had clung to him throughout his life '[s]omething of the disgrace of my school days' (Chapter 1), so that he regarded himself as 'something of a Pariah' (Chapter 9). Large psychoanalytic structures can be and have been built on these slight hints.

4. See, for example, T. H. S. Escott, *Trollope: His Work, Associates and Literary Originals* (John Lane, 1913), James R. Kincaid, *The Novels of Anthony Trollope* (Oxford: Clarendon Press, 1977), R. H. Super, *The Chronicler of Barsetshire: A Life of Anthony Trollope* (Ann Arbor: University of Michigan Press, 1988).

The few moments of confession have seemed to many readers momentarily to open up a hidden life, so that the rest of *An Autobiography* is seen by them as a fiction carefully constructed to conceal inner torment. For example, it is often assumed that he must have nursed a bitter hurt at his mother's neglect of him as a child when she disappeared to America, and this resentment must have been either unconsciously suppressed or deliberately censored in the narrative of his life. On this reading, the reference to Rousseau is no more than a device for distracting attention from Trollope's own involuntary lapses into psychological revelation; his pride in his measurable achievement in earning so and so much money by writing so and so many volumes is the psychological or literary screen he puts up; and his writing of his many books is an obsessive behaviour deriving from early trauma.

Such conjectures sound plausible, but cannot be sustained in detail. Admittedly the memory of his former misery remained with him, not like Dickens's agonizing and involuntary memory of his childish misery, which would make him forget he was a grown man, 'and wander desolately back to that time of my life',[5] but as an awareness of 'unhappiness so great that the very fear of it is an alloy to happiness' (Chapter 4). Thus even Trollope's fears received reasonable expression, and were used as spurs to further professional efforts. There is little evidence from other sources to support the hypothesis of an abnormal state of mind, and we are forced to the conclusion that all we really know is that Trollope was an exceptionally energetic man, who espoused the Victorian work ethic to an almost egregious degree, and who, whatever may have been the deep psychological roots of this behaviour, gave no outward signs of morbid psychopathology. He was only happy when working or hunting or playing whist, but there were no periods of depression, long or short, as we might have expected if he had had to recruit his strength for the next burst of compulsive activity. The twentieth century has found it hard to accept such a life without psychoanalytic accreditation. Perhaps the twenty-first will be able to believe an alternative version: the story of a man who made and sustained his life by act of will; who was – in all but the class sense – a 'self-

5. John Forster, *The Life of Charles Dickens* 3 vols. (Chapman & Hall, 1872–4), i, p. 32.

made man'. It may also become possible to see the book as a literary work, with all the formal conventionality and artificiality that implies.

His granddaughter, Muriel Trollope, recalled in her old age an occasion when 'a working-man' who had asked to borrow a copy of *An Autobiography*, returned it with the words: 'Every young man should read it! Your grandfather always made the best of everything.'[6] The term 'working-man' is significant. For Muriel Trollope it probably meant a member of the working-classes, but it clearly connects this 'working-man' across barriers of time and social class with that other working man, Anthony Trollope. 'Every young man should read it' because it shows what energy, dedication and honest application to one's trade could do to raise the individual in the world. In fact it was an aid to self-reliance, and a supplement to Samuel Smiles's famous manual on self-advancement, *Self-Help*, which had been published in 1859, and quickly become one of the most important mid-Victorian guides to the conduct of life.

Indeed *An Autobiography* becomes clear when it is seen as following the pattern of the exemplary life-story, and no effort is made to shoehorn it into a genre of self-revelation or confession. The journey from adversity to prosperity is at least as old as Defoe, who added a secular progress to the spiritual journeys recounted by Bunyan and other Puritan writers in both first- and third-person narratives. For the increasingly secular mind, spiritual prosperity or grace was replaced by possession of a worldly competence, a family, social status and contentment – this last based on a moral satisfaction with the means by which the others had been achieved. The most famous collection of such exemplary lives in the mid-Victorian period was of course *Self-Help*. Drawing on his own resources of strength (the subject was of course male), and aspiring at all times to be a 'gentleman', our hero succeeded in establishing himself as an example for others to follow. It was in this pattern that Anthony Trollope cast his autobiography. So important was this pattern indeed that it is difficult to see how It was to be avoided. Practically any life-story could be seen in the mid-Victorian period as exemplary, displaying things to be

6. Muriel Trollope, 'What I was told', *Trollopian* 2 (March 1948), 223–35.

courted or avoided, and examples to be followed or shunned. The more prominent the life, the more potent the examples, and the greater the influence of the story of that life on writers of subsequent lives.

The most prominent literary biography when Trollope sat down to write in October 1875 was John Forster's *Life of Charles Dickens*, which had been published in three volumes from 1872 to 1874, and Trollope's autobiography makes a good number of references to this life of his inimitable contemporary. His reaction to Forster's subject was at best equivocal. Dickens was a faulty stylist, whose characters could not be recognized as in any degree 'real' people. Yet Dickens was also the most popular writer of his day, and the verdict of the public when so clearly expressed could not be ignored. None the less Trollope was warning aspiring authors against following the example of Dickens, whose exceptional degree of creativity and popularity made him an unsafe model, likely to lure a lesser talent to destruction. Thus we find Trollope proudly pointing out that *he* didn't read his work to a circle of admirers before publication, as he mentions that Dickens did, and that no professional man of letters could say of *his* writing what Forster did of Dickens's: 'There was nothing written by him after this date which I did not see before the world did, either in manuscript or proofs . . .' Trollope claimed never to have missed a publisher's deadline, as Forster reports Dickens did on a number of occasions.[7] Unlike Dickens he applied himself with mechanical regularity to his work; and unlike Dickens again he had no improper dealings with his critics. Indeed he snubbed the literary critic of *The Times*, Eneas Sweetland Dallas, who had hinted that Trollope should thank him for a series of enthusiastic notices of *The West Indies and the Spanish Main*. Dickens on the other hand presented the same critic with a bound copy of the manuscript of *Our Mutual Friend*, in gratitude for a good review in *The Times*.[8] The dangerous effect of the adoration of Dickens's circle of

7. *The Life of Charles Dickens*, i, pp. 99 and 105. See ii, pp. 41–9 and 62–5 for further examples of un-Trollopian working habits and disappointing deals made with publishers.
8. See F. X. Roellinger, 'E. S. Dallas in Trollope's *Autobiography*', *Modern Language Notes* 55 (June 1940), 422–4. Forster (i, p. 160) makes great play of Dickens's generosity in writing an approving notice of Lockhart's *Life of Scott* even before he knew that Lockhart had reviewed *Oliver Twist* positively in the *Quarterly Review*.

admirers seems often to be in Trollope's mind, for it seemed to be this worship that sustained the myth of the creative artist who was above the considerations of everyday morality. Trollope's very practical attitude to his earnings is in marked and possibly deliberate contrast to Dickens's frequent alternation between the pose of being superior to financial considerations and complaints that his genius was not adequately paid for, while others were making money by him.[9] Trollope knew that Dickens was happy to use and discard people, most notably his wife, whom he humiliated by advertising their separation in the public press, while by the same act he showed himself not to be what Trollope would have considered a gentleman. Trollope was certainly aware of the whole affair, since his brother Thomas Adolphus was married to the sister of Dickens's mistress, but whether he knew about other disreputable acts of the Dickens circle, such as the attempt to dispose of Bulwer Lytton's wife by having her certified and locked away as a lunatic when quite sane, though understandably rebellious at her husband's treatment of her, is not known.[10] Trollope naturally thought himself a better example to the young, and moreover a gentleman. Even Forster had had to worry at one point whether Dickens's reputation as a gentleman would suffer from his public readings of his work.[11]

Although this is only one note in *An Autobiography*, it reinforces the exemplary pattern of the life, and we do well to read the book as though Trollope was doing something other than recording the mere facts relating to his life and works, or writing at the prompting of his tormented soul. His own formulation of what he is doing is simple:

[I]t will not be so much my intention to speak of the little details of my private life, as of what I, and perhaps others round me, have done in

9. See, for example, Forster, i, pp. 139–40.

10. See John Sutherland, *Victorian Fiction: Writers, Publishers, Readers* (Macmillan, 1995), pp. 71–4. Had Trollope known of the involvement of Robert Bell in the plot he might perhaps have written less warmly of him in *An Autobiography*. He shows no personal liking for another of the conspirators, John Forster, whose *Life of Charles Dickens* was advertised as by 'One of Her Majesty's Commissioners in Lunacy'.

11. Forster, iii, p. 165: 'it had so much of the character of a public exhibition for money as to raise, in the question of respect for his calling as a writer, a question also of respect for himself as a gentleman'.

literature, of my failures and successes such as they have been, and their causes, and of the opening which a literary career offers to men and women for the earning of their bread' (Chapter 1).

The story of his life in general fits the pattern of the achievement of prosperity out of adversity. In addition, that story is to be laced with careful advice on whether to choose a literary career, and how to pursue it, once chosen. It had earlier been his intention to establish 'some rules for the writing of novels, – or I might perhaps say with more modesty, to offer some advice on the art to such tyros in it as might be willing to take advantage of the experience of an old hand' (Chapter 12). His would not have been the first book to give such advice. Trollope's friend and George Eliot's closest advisor, George Henry Lewes, wrote *The Principles of Success in Literature*, which ran in the *Fortnightly Review* in 1865, and advocated the new practice of 'realism', while adumbrating what would later be called 'creative writing' courses on the novel, complete with suggestions of exercises such as describing a brick wall. As the title of the work suggests, Lewes was aiming to advise neophytes on how to achieve financial as well as aesthetic success, as was appropriate at a time when novel-writing seemed to hold out the promise of an income to many literate people with no other means of support. Lewes was highly responsible in the advice he gave and encouraged no false hopes, but with evidence about him of many self-deluded scribblers who had the example of Dickens and his circle of admirers before them, it is no wonder that Trollope stressed the hard work involved in writing novels, and advocated pursuing another profession in parallel, as he himself did so successfully in the Post Office.

Other career guidance was available which compared the life of letters to the Church, the army and the law, in terms of necessary investment and probable rewards. H. Byerley Thomson's book of advice to young men and their fathers, *The Choice of a Profession* (1857), advises on just the kind of career choices Trollope had had to make and which lie at the centre of the stories of his fictional characters. This book of career guidance devotes serious discussion to the chances of making a decent income from literature, concluding that if ... the aspiring author unhastily and carefully prepares himself for his literary labour, in the same manner as he would consider himself bound to prepare himself for following the law, or practising medicine, he can promise himself some measure of success and reward. Even if he has the misfortune to be a dull writer, he may bring forth a work of great value in other respects, that will find favour with some classes of readers.[12]

 Books advising on a career in literature were highly practical and arguably much needed, since the profession of letters required 'no special education', and was often, in Thomson's words, 'an occupation ... entered upon by chance rather than by design'. A remark of George Eliot's in 1856 explains why the guidance Trollope offered was recognized as necessary:

Every art which has its absolute technique is, to a certain extent, guarded from the intrusions of mere left-handed imbecility. But in novel-writing there are no barriers for incapacity to stumble against, no external criteria to prevent a writer from mistaking foolish facility for mastery.[13]

 A later generation of writers, less inclined to compare writing to shoemaking, as Trollope did, or calico-making, as George Eliot did, or even the pastry-cook's art, as Thackeray did,[14] would establish aesthetic codes of professional conduct, rather than commercial ones, and would insist on the separateness of writers from the world of trade, rather than their nearness to it. A closer look at Trollope's position on this subject will draw two strands of *An Autobiography* together, so that his advice on the conduct of a moral, professional life through the

12. H. Byerley Thomson, *The Choice of a Profession. A Concise Account and Comparative Review of the English Professions* (Chapman & Hall, 1857), pp. 336–8. For a more extended context, see David Skilton, *The Early and Mid-Victorian Novel: Criticism in Context* (Routledge, 1993), pp. 265–7.
13. George Eliot, 'Silly Novels by Lady Novelists', *Westminster Review* 66 (October 1856), 461.
14. See George Eliot, 'Leaves from a Note-Book', in *Essays and Leaves from a Note-Book* (*Standard Edition*, Edinburgh: William Blackwood, 1883), p. 290; and, as an example of Thackeray's habit, his letter to Trollope, printed in the present volume, page 91.

exemplary story of his own success will not appear to be divorced from the far more personal and psychological note he strikes from time to time.

The secret is that in the mid-Victorian period there briefly existed an alliance between the ethos of trade and the practice of literature. In the 1860s, trading successfully as an author was regarded by a majority of significant novelists as a major purpose of their artistic lives. The contrast with an author like George Gissing, who was born in 1857, is clear from a comment of his in 1885 on George Meredith:

> It is amazing that such a man is so neglected. For the last thirty years he has been producing work unspeakably above the best of any living writer and yet no one reads him outside a small circle of highly cultivated people. Perhaps that is better than being popular, a hateful word.[15]

For Trollope, to become popular – at least in the social circle to which he aspired – was one of his motives of writing, and he counted his first success from the time when he became recognized as an author by his social equals:

> The novel reading world did not go mad about *The Warden*, but I soon felt that it had not failed as the others had failed. There were notices of it in the press, and I could discover that people around me knew that I had written a book (Chapter 5).

Later, when he began to frequent the Garrick Club, his yearning to belong began to be gratified, and authorship was the route to acceptance:

> I think that I became popular among those with whom I associated. I have long been aware of a certain weakness in my own character which I may call a craving for love. I have ever had a wish to be liked by those around me, – a wish that during the first half of my life was never gratified (Chapter 9).

15. *Letters of George Gissing to Members of His Family* (Constable, 1927), pp. 171–2.

A state like his earlier social and economic estrangement – that feeling of being 'something of a Pariah' – would be the very stuff of the artistic life of many a later author, but was precisely what Trollope spent half a lifetime fleeing from. His aim of 'belonging' was triumphantly achieved during the 1860s, a period when he was an acknowledged leader among 'realistic' novelists, and sought after by the editors and publishers of London.

There is an amusing essay composed by Robert Louis Stevenson in 1887–8 and published posthumously under the significant title 'On the Choice of a Profession', in which Stevenson shows how awful it would be to an artist thought successfully middle-class. 'You are now come to that time of life,' writes Stevenson's typical bourgeois father to his son, 'and have reason within yourself to consider the absolute necessity of making provision for the time when it will be asked, Who is this man? Is he doing any good in the world? Has he the means of being "One of us?"'[16] For Stevenson and many of his contemporaries, nothing worse could be contemplated than this 'being "One of us"'. In contrast, Trollope's dearest wish, and one of his obvious motives in writing fiction, was exactly to be considered respectably bourgeois. Indeed, as Trollope's reviewers often make clear, the novelist's claim to authority as a realistic author derived from his belonging to the bourgeois world and understanding it from the inside.

The poignant story of miserable childhood which Trollope presents in *An Autobiography* is scarcely mirrored in his fiction. *The Landleaguers* contains the only significant child character in his work, which displays almost nothing that could be termed 'developmental psychology', although the problems of youthful awkwardness or 'hobbledehoydom' are vividly presented in several of the novels. On the other hand analogues of the latter part of his secular progress to his worldly paradise are amply present in the many tales of characters who are either painfully excluded from 'belonging', like Ferdinand Lopez in *The Prime Minister*, or who are eventually admitted or recognized as belonging, like the Reverend Josiah Crawley in *The Last*

16. R. L. Stevenson, 'On the Choice of a Profession', *Essays Literary and Critical* (*Tusitala Edition*, William Heinemann, 1923), p. 17.

Chronicle of Barset. These stories act out dramas that happened in his non-fictional world: the drama of the Trollope family in general, as it nearly lost its genteel status, and that of Anthony in particular, as he risked slipping over the precipice to social perdition, but finally fought his way to respectability and social recognition. The central decision in fiction as in life was the choice of a profession and the moral seriousness with which to pursue it. The emotional charge attached to these subjects in his fiction undoubtedly derived from his own experience.

Meanwhile the plausibility of his fictional presentation of the mid-Victorian landed and professional classes stems from the clarity with which he understood the society from which he felt so long excluded. In *Studies in Early Victorian Literature* (1895), Frederic Harrison explains that he recognizes the world of Trollope's fiction because he himself lived in it and knew the people.[7] Trollope too lived in this world, and the strength of his fiction is that he belonged to it, joyfully, while retaining enough of that feeling of being 'a Pariah' to provide a critical perspective on it, even while he celebrated it. He was acutely sensitive to shifts in social status, so that his fictional world is a dynamic one, and the heroes are those who manage or stoically endure change. *An Autobiography* makes it clear to us how this came about, and convincingly explains whence this major novelist derived the vision which is still so powerful today.

DAVID SKILTON

17. Frederic Harrison, *Studies in Early Victorian Literature* (1895), p. 201, quoted in R. C. Terry (ed.), *Trollope: Interviews and Recollections* (Macmillan, 1987), p. 188.

Most books on Trollope's fiction contain some treatment of *An Auto-biography*. Those dealing specifically with his life and career include: Bradford A. Booth, *Anthony Trollope: Aspects of His Life and Art* (Bloomington, Indiana: Indiana University Press, 1958); Walter M. Kendrick, *The Novel Machine: The Theory and Fiction of Anthony Trollope* (Baltimore and London: Johns Hopkins University Press, 1980); Michael Sadleir, *Trollope: A Commentary* (London: Constable, 1927); C. P. Snow, *Trollope: His Life and Art* (London: Macmillan; New York: Scribners, 1975); L. P. and R. P. Stebbins, *The Trollopes: The Chronicle of a Writing Family* (London: Secker and Warburg, 1946); Andrew Wright, *Anthony Trollope: Dream and Art* (Chicago: Chicago University Press; London: Macmillan, 1983).

The most scholarly biographies are N. John Hall, *Trollope: A Biography* (Oxford: Oxford University Press, 1991), and R. H. Super, *The Chronicler of Barsetshire: A Life of Anthony Trollope* (Ann Arbor: University of Michigan Press, 1988), while Richard Mullen, *Anthony Trollope: A Victorian in His World* (London: Duckworth, 1990), gives a more opinionated account. Victoria Glendinning's *Anthony Trollope* (London: Hutchinson, 1992) is exceptionally readable, and contains very plausible speculations about unknown aspects of the author's life, including his marriage. R. H. Super, *Trollope in the Post Office* (Ann Arbor: University of Michigan Press, 1982) provides a full account of Trollope's career as a civil servant.

Trollope's letters are admirably collected in N. John Hall (ed.), *The Letters of Anthony Trollope* (Stanford, Calif.: Stanford University Press, 1983). Also useful in the study of Trollope as a public and private figure is R. C. Terry (ed.), *Trollope: Interviews and Recollections* (London: Macmillan, 1987). Other sources for a study of Trollope's life and career include: R. C. Terry, *A Trollope Chronology* (London: Macmillan, 1989), and Thomas Adolphus Trollope, *What I Remember*, 2 vols. (London: Richard Bentley & Son, 1887).

Articles on *An Autobiography* include: James Kincaid, 'Trollope's Fictional Autobiography', *Nineteenth Century Fiction* 37 (1982); A.L. Rowse, 'Trollope's *Autobiography*', in J. Halperin (ed.), *Trollope: Centenary Essays* (London: Macmillan, 1982); Sarah Gilead, 'Trollope's *Autobiography*: The Strategies of Self-Production', *Modern Languages Quarterly* 47 (1986); N.John Hall, 'Seeing Trollope's *An Autobiography* through the Press: The Correspondence of William Blackwood and Henry Merivale Trollope', *Princeton University Library Chronicle*, 47 (1986); Robert Tracy, 'Stranger than Truth: Fictional Autobiography and Autobiographical Fiction', *Dickens Studies Annual* 15 (1986); John Sutherland, 'Trollope, Publishers and the Truth', *Prose Studies* 10 (1987); R.H. Super, 'Truth and Fiction in Trollope's *Autobiography*', *Nineteenth Century Literature* 48 (1993); John Sutherland, 'Trollope's Lives', *Trollopiana* 20 (February 1993).

Trollope's reception by his contemporaries and the factors influencing mid-Victorian understanding of his fiction are analysed in David Skilton, *Anthony Trollope and His Contemporaries: A Study in the Theory and Conventions of Mid-Victorian Fiction* (London: Longman, 1972; 2nd edn, London: Macmillan, 1996). Despite a number of serious bibliographical errors, Donald Smalley (ed.), *Anthony Trollope: The Critical Heritage* (London: Routledge and Kegan Paul, 1969), contains a useful collection of Victorian criticism of Trollope's fiction. An annotated bibliography of later criticism is found in J.C. Olmsted and J.E. Welch, *The Reputation of Trollope: An Annotated Bibliography 1925–1975* (New York and London: Garland, 1978), and a fuller listing of Trollope editions as well as selected secondary works is found in *Anthony Trollope: A Collector's Catalogue 1847–1990* (London: Trollope Society, 1992). The standard descriptive bibliography of Trollope's works in their original editions is Michael Sadleir, *Trollope: A Bibliography* (London: Constable, 1928).

Trollope started *An Autobiography* on a voyage from New York in late October 1875, left it until the New Year, and completed the main body of the work on 11 April 1876. He returned to it to make some changes at some point late enough for him to be able to list the sums earned and the year of publication for each of *South Africa* (1878) and *John Caldigate* (1879), the last books on his schedule in Chapter 20, but too soon to list *Cousin Henry* (1879). The cover bears the inscription, 'An Autobiography / by / Anthony Trollope / April. 11. 1876 ætat LXI'.

He presented the manuscript to his son, Henry, in 1878, probably in June of that year,[1] accompanied by a letter dated 30 April 1876. The manuscript was in a wrapper labelled: 'An Autobiography – / Begun 1 January 1876 / Finished 11 April 1876'.

Henry Trollope reprints the first paragraph and postscript of the letter in his Preface to the first edition of 1883. In his letter Trollope asks Henry to have 'Fred Chapman' publish the book, but by 1882 Chapman was no longer an independent publisher, and with Thomas Adolphus Trollope's approval Henry arranged publication with Blackwood, for the price of £1000 for the first 4000 copies, and two-thirds profits thereafter.[2]

The manuscript is in Anthony Trollope's own hand, except for Chapter 1, which is in the hand of his niece and amanuensis, Florence Bland, and is very lightly corrected in Trollope's hand, and three passages quoted from a letter by Thackeray, a criticism by Nathaniel

1. See letter of Henry Trollope to John Blackwood, 19 January 1883. This and the other letters quoted are in the Blackwood Papers in the National Library of Scotland. See also N. John Hall, 'Seeing Trollope's *An Autobiography* through the Press: The Correspondence of William Blackwood and Henry Merivale Trollope', *Princeton University Library Chronicle* 47 (1986), 189–223.
2. See *The Letters of Anthony Trollope*, ed. N. John Hall (Stanford, Calif.: Stanford University Press, 1983), pp. xiii and 685–6.

Hawthorne, and his own preface to *The Vicar of Bullhampton*, which are in the hand of his wife, Rose. The manuscript is now in the British Library, as ADDITIONAL MS 42856.

Henry Trollope himself copied his father's manuscript for the publisher,[3] and we do not know how many of the variants between Anthony Trollope's original manuscript and the 1883 edition are due to Henry Trollope, and how many to Blackwood's printer. The rendering of book titles in italics was Henry's doing, and he told Blackwood, 'I do believe the habit is coming to England from France, and therefore it is a foreign habit; – but I believe equally that the mind of the reader is thus more quickly and more surely informed than by the other process' – i.e. inverted commas.[4]

According to the Preface, Henry Trollope 'suppressed some few passages, but not more than would amount to two printed pages has been omitted'. These are the passages concerning W.H. Russell and Charles Reade which are mentioned in the Textual Notes as having been omitted from Chapters 8 and 13 of the first edition. Henry Trollope reports to Blackwood that Langford would look at the proofs 'with a view to suggesting any little things that might perhaps be omitted', and that he himself thought certain remarks on 'Billy Russell would be hurtful', and that there was 'too much ... about the wrong-headedness of Charles Reade'.[5] Blackwood himself requested the removal at proof of some words in Chapter 11 relating to his reluctance to go on publishing Trollope's anonymous works, in which Trollope suggested that he 'no doubt would have done so had I continued it without any price'. Henry Trollope claimed that they were not offensive, but conceded: 'Your suggestion shall be complied with. I read my father's words merely as a little joke, a satire against himself'.[6]

There are other very numerous changes, often small, between the manuscript and the first edition of 1883, and the most significant of

3. Letters to Blackwood dated 19 and 26 January 1883.
4. Letter of 20 February 1883.
5. *Ibid.*; J.M. Langford (1809–84) was the head of Blackwood's London office.
6. Henry Trollope to Blackwood, 29 August 1883.

these are also recorded in the Textual Notes. There are many examples of the familiar kinds of copyist's or printer's errors, including misreadings, omissions and transpositions of words, and the mistaken printing of an insertion as a footnote. Between them Henry Trollope and the printer imposed their own punctuation, which is no more regular than Anthony Trollope's own. As usual, the spelling of that edition follows house style and not the manuscript. A few errors of fact and slips in the spelling of proper names were corrected in 1883.

The edition prepared by Frederick Page for the Oxford Trollope, and published in 1950, reprints in an Appendix those major omissions which were made by Henry Trollope, corrects the 1883 text in very many instances against the manuscript, and lists a large number of variants between the manuscript and the 1883 edition. It also perpetuates a significant number of the bad readings from 1883, and introduces a number of new errors of its own, some in the spelling of proper names, which are wrong often enough in the manuscript for additional variation to be superfluous. (For example, Trollope spells 'Becky Sharp' in a number of different ways, and Page exaggerates this looseness by spelling it wrong even on those occasions when Trollope got it right.) The largest single cause of variation between 1950 and the manuscript is that the 1950 edition follows the punctuation of 1883, which varies from that of the manuscript in very many instances, certainly in excess of one thousand. Page also follows 1883 in printing an insertion as a footnote.

The present edition derives from a working version of the text which follows the manuscript as closely as possible. From that an acceptable reading version has been prepared, which varies from the manuscript as little as would be found tolerable by the reader who reads for pleasure and by a commercial publisher. A few dozen misreadings in 1950 are corrected, and a few extra short deletions, almost certainly made by Trollope while writing or correcting his manuscript, are transcribed in the Textual Notes. Significant variants between this 1996 text and the 1950 and 1883 texts, and between 1996 and the manuscript, are recorded in the Textual Notes. Almost every textual note records an alternative reading, indicating which of the three other versions contain it. A note of the form 'MS and 1883: xxx' indicates that

1996 follows an amendment made in 1950, while '1883 and 1950: yyy' indicates that 1996 alone follows the manuscript.

The following conventions operate in the present edition:

Spelling: I have retained irregular spelling in letters and quotations, but in the main text, where there is variation, have changed the less frequently occurring forms to the dominant form. Where there are equal numbers of occurrences of alternative spellings, I have chosen the form which is now more usual. I have retained a number of antiquated spellings, some of them already old-fashioned in Trollope's day, such as 'encrease', 'holyday', 'idiotcy' and 'oeconomical'. The abbreviation 'MS' is expanded to 'manuscript' on each occurrence. I have normalized all proper names, many of which appear in more than one mutation, since erroneous spelling does not help the modern reader to recognize the bearers of the names, and because it would in any case be strange to regularize the spelling to an erroneous rendering.

Capital Letters: Trollope uses capitals erratically, and sometimes writes initial letters in a fashion which makes it impossible to determine whether they are capitals or not. Moreover he has more than one way of forming a number of capital letters, with some of his capital A's resembling enlarged lower-case a's, and leaving a large number of indeterminate cases which may be slightly outsize lower-case initials. Thus, while it is clear that he often uses the habits of his childhood and youth, when eighteenth-century usage persisted, it is far from clear that he was deliberate in this, or that we can find any rationale for the capitalization of one word rather than another, or one occurrence of a given word rather than another. The present edition has therefore not reproduced the capitals on the small minority of occasions when such words as 'Art' and 'Literature' enjoy this distinction, but has retained those on 'Post Office Surveyor', 'Letter Carrier' and 'Secretary', for example, which Trollope nearly always capitalizes. The one respect in which this edition slavishly follows the capitalization of the manuscript is in the words 'liberal' and 'conservative' when used politically. Trollope is very clear when he declares in the manuscript that he is 'an advanced but still a conservative Liberal', and the distinction between the lower-case of 'conservative' and the upper-case of 'Liberal' seems deliberate. I have therefore deemed it unwise to tamper with other occurrences of these two words, for fear of discarding a set of distinctions which may be consistently meaningful.

Titles: Trollope sometimes includes the definite article in titles, but the present edition has adopted the common modern practice of excluding the definite article from most titles, and has hence not followed the manuscript in such usage as 'Mr Seward was at that time The Secretary of State', or in 'The Argosy' or 'The Spectator'. Strangely, considering that '*The Times*' is a form frequently met with today, this is the only title from which Trollope on all but one occasion excludes the article, rendering it as 'the "Times" ' in eight instances and 'the "Times" newspaper' on six occasions. The titles of Trollope's novels have been put into their normal forms, with the accent put back on *La Vendée*, but not on *The Golden Lion of Granpere*, since the latter novel was published without a grave accent. On all but one occurrence, Trollope writes 'The Small House of Allington', which has been changed to *The Small House at Allington*, and a textual note written. 'Dr Thorne' is expanded to *Doctor Thorne*, and *Can You Forgive Her?* gets back the question mark which Trollope rarely gives it.

Punctuation: Minor changes have silently been made to the punctuation in a few dozen places, but otherwise the manuscript's punctuation is followed throughout. The 1950 edition follows the punctuation of the 1883 first edition, where the copyist and compositor did as they pleased, and were at least as erratic as the manuscript itself. We know that Trollope paid great attention to the way his writing sounded when read – he weighed the words as he read over what he had written – and consequently it is not surprising that much of his punctuation is rhetorical, designed to make various passages read at differing speeds, to produce pauses for effect, or to distinguish between lists with commas between the items, and those which are to be read without pauses. Trollope's texts are in a sense performance scripts, and I have sought to preserve this quality in *An Autobiography*. It is therefore not appropriate to insist, as some editors do, on the grammatical/syntactic use of commas in all cases, and I have allowed some phrases to remain separated off by a comma from the rest of the sentence at only one end – but never to the detriment of sense.

NOTE ON THE EDITORIAL APPARATUS

There are two sets of notes to the text of the present edition. The Explanatory Notes are placed for convenience at the back of the volume, and are signalled by numerical superscript cues, with a new sequence for each chapter. These notes give further details about the people Trollope mentions, explain certain facts that are not now common knowledge, and identify literary quotations and allusions. The Textual Notes, which are signalled by alphabetical superscript cues and are located before the Explanatory Notes, list many of the variants between the present editor's reading of the manuscript and the two previous principal editions: the first edition of 1883 and the Oxford University Press edition of 1950. Only variants which significantly affect sense have been listed. The editorial procedures involved are explained in the Note on the Text. Where matter which is included in a textual note requires elucidation, an explanatory note is printed at the end of the textual note concerned.

ACKNOWLEDGEMENTS

I am grateful to the British Library for access to the manuscript of *An Autobiography*, and to the National Library of Scotland for access to the letters of Henry Trollope to Blackwood, which are in the Blackwood Papers. I also wish to thank the staff of the British Library, the London Library, Princeton University Library and Cardiff University Library for their unfailing help. I am also deeply indebted to Hugh Osborne for his considerable contribution to this edition, and to Dean Burnett, Claire Connolly, Peter Garside, N. John Hall, Stuart Lyons, John Percival, Line Pouchard, Christopher Skelton-Foord, Donald Thomas, Sir Aubrey Trotman-Dickenson and J. B. Wynn for assistance of various kinds.

Facsimile of the title page of the first volume edition of *An Autobiography* (1883)

AN AUTOBIOGRAPHY

BY

ANTHONY TROLLOPE

IN TWO VOLUMES

VOL. I.

WILLIAM BLACKWOOD AND SONS
EDINBURGH AND LONDON
MDCCCLXXXIII

All Rights reserved

It may well be that I should put a short preface to this book. In the summer of 1878 my father told me that he had written a memoir of his own life. He did not speak about it at length, but said that he had written me a letter, not to be opened until after his death, containing instructions for publication.

This letter was dated 30th April 1876.[1] I will give here as much of it as concerns the public: 'I wish you to accept as a gift from me, given you now, the accompanying pages which contain a memoir of my life. My intention is that they shall be published after my death, and be edited by you. But I leave it altogether to your discretion whether to publish or to suppress the work; – and also to your discretion whether any part or what part shall be omitted. But I would not wish that anything should be added to the memoir. If you wish to say any word as from yourself, let it be done in the shape of a preface or introductory chapter.' At the end there is a postscript: 'The publication, if made at all, should be effected as soon as possible after my death.' My father died on the 6th of December 1882.

It will be seen, therefore, that my duty has been merely to pass the book through the press conformably to the above instructions. I have placed headings to the right-hand pages throughout the book, and I do not conceive that I was precluded from doing so. Additions of any other sort there have been none; the few footnotes are my father's own additions or corrections. And I have made no alterations. I have suppressed some few passages, but not more than would amount to two printed pages has been omitted.[2] My father has not given any of his own letters, nor was it his wish that any should be published.

I see from my father's manuscript, and from his papers, that the first two chapters of this memoir were written in the latter part of 1875, that he began the third chapter early in January 1876, and that he finished the record before the middle of April in that year. I state this, though there are indications in the book by which it might be seen at what time the memoir was being written.

So much I would say by way of preface. And I think I may also give in a few words the main incidents in my father's life after he completed his autobiography.

He has said that he had given up hunting; but he still kept two horses for such riding as may be had in or about the immediate neighbourhood of London. He continued to ride to the end of his life: he liked the exercise, and I think it would have distressed him not to have had a horse in his stable. But he never spoke willingly on hunting matters. He had at last resolved to give up his favourite amusement, and that as far as he was concerned there should be an end of it. In the spring of 1877 he went to South Africa, and returned early in the following year with a book on the colony already written. In the summer of 1878, he was one of a party of ladies and gentlemen who made an expedition to Iceland in the *Mastiff,* one of Mr John Burns' steamships.[3] The journey lasted altogether sixteen days, and during that time Mr and Mrs Burns were the hospitable entertainers. When my father returned, he wrote a short account of *How the 'Mastiffs' went to Iceland.* The book was printed, but was intended only for private circulation.

Every day, until his last illness, my father continued his work. He would not otherwise have been happy. He demanded from himself less than he had done ten years previously, but his daily task was always done. I will mention now the titles of his books that were published after the last included in the list which he himself has given at the end of the second volume –

An Eye for an Eye	1879
Cousin Henry	1879
Thackeray	1879
The Duke's Children	1880
Life of Cicero	1880
Ayala's Angel	1881
Doctor Wortle's School	1881
Frohmann Frohmann and other Stories	1882

At the time of his death he had written four-fifths of an Irish story, called *The Landleaguers*, shortly about to be published; and he left in manuscript a completed novel, called *An Old Man's Love*, which will be published by Messrs Blackwood & Sons in 1884.

In the summer of 1880 my father left London, and went to live at Harting, a village in Sussex, but on the confines of Hampshire. I think he chose that spot because he found there a house that suited him, and because of the prettiness of the neighbourhood. His last long journey was a trip to Italy in the late winter and spring of 1881; but he went to Ireland twice in 1882. He went there in May of that year, and was then absent nearly a month. This journey did him much good, for he found that the softer atmosphere relieved his asthma, from which he had been suffering for nearly eighteen months. In August following he made another trip to Ireland, but from this journey he derived less benefit. He was much interested in, and was very much distressed by, the unhappy condition of the country. Few men knew Ireland better than he did. He had lived there for sixteen years,[4] and his Post Office work had taken him into every part of the island. In the summer of 1882 he began his last novel, *The Landleaguers* which, as stated above, was unfinished when he died. This book was a cause of anxiety to him. He could not rid his mind of the fact that he had a story already in the course of publication, but which he had not yet completed. In no other case, except *Framley Parsonage*, did my father publish even the first number of any novel before he had fully completed the whole tale.[5]

On the evening of the 3rd of November 1882 he was seized with paralysis on the right side, accompanied by loss of speech. His mind also had failed, though at intervals his thoughts would return to him. After the first three weeks these lucid intervals became rarer, but it was always very difficult to tell how far his mind was sound or how far astray. He died in the evening of the 6th of December following, nearly five weeks from the night of his attack.

I have been led to say these few words, not at all from a desire to supplement my father's biography of himself, but to mention the main incidents in his life after he had finished his own record. In what I have here said I do not think I have exceeded his instructions.

HENRY M. TROLLOPE.

September 1883.

CHAPTER I^a

My Education.
1815–1834.

In writing these pages, which, for the want of a better name, I shall be fain to call the autobiography of so insignificant a person as myself, it will not be so much my intention to speak of the little details of my private life, as of what I, and perhaps others round me, have done in literature, of my failures and successes such as they have been, and their causes, and of the opening which a literary career offers to men and women for the earning of their bread. And yet the garrulity of old age, and the aptitude of a man's mind to recur to the passages of his own life, will I know tempt me to say something of myself; – nor without doing so should I know how to throw my matter into any recognised and intelligible form. That I, or any man, should tell everything of himself, I hold to be impossible. Who could endure to own the doing of a mean thing? Who is there that has done none? But this I protest; – that nothing that I say shall be untrue. I will set down naught in malice;[1] nor will I give to myself, or others, honour which I do not believe to have been fairly won.

My boyhood was I think as unhappy as that of a young gentleman could well be, my misfortunes arising from a mixture of poverty and gentle standing on the part of my father, and from an utter want on my own part of that juvenile manhood which enables some boys to hold up their heads even among the distresses which such a position is sure to produce.

I was born in 1815, in Keppel Street, Russell Square, and while a baby, was carried down to Harrow where my father had built a house on a large farm which, in an evil hour, he took on a long lease from Lord Northwick.[2] That farm was the grave of all my father's hopes, ambition, and prosperity, the cause of my mother's sufferings, and of those of her children, and perhaps the director of her destiny and of ours. My father had been a Wykamist and a fellow of New College, and Winchester was the destination of my brothers and myself; but as he had friends among the masters at Harrow, and as the school offered an education almost gratuitous to children living in the parish, he, with a certain aptitude to do things differently from others which accompanied him throughout his life, determined to use that august seminary as a 't'other school' for Winchester,[3] and sent three of us there, one after the other, at the age of seven. My father at this time was a Chancery barrister practising in London, occupying dingy, almost suicidal chambers, at No. 23 Old Square,[b] Lincoln's Inn, – chambers which on one melancholy occasion did become absolutely suicidal.* He was, as I have been informed by those quite competent to know, an excellent and most conscientious lawyer, but plagued with so bad a temper that he drove the attorneys from him. In his early days he was a man of some small fortune and of higher hopes. These stood so high at the time of my birth that he was felt to be entitled to a country house, as well as to that in Keppel Street; – and in order that he might build such a residence, he took the farm. This place he called Julians, and the land runs up to the foot of the hill on which the school and church stand, – on the side towards London. Things there went much against him, the farm was ruinous, and I remember that we all regarded the Lord Northwick of those days as a cormorant who was eating us up. My father's clients deserted him. He purchased various dark gloomy chambers in and about Chancery Lane, and his purchases always went wrong. Then as a final crushing blow an old uncle, whose heir he was to have been, married and had a family! The house in London was let; – and also the house he built at Harrow, from whence he descended to a farm house on the land, which I have endeavoured to make known to some readers under the name of Orley Farm. This place, just as it was when we lived there, is to be seen in the frontispiece to the first edition of that novel, having had the good fortune to be delineated by no less a pencil than that of John Millais.[4]

My two elder brothers had been sent as day boarders to Harrow school from the bigger House, and may probably have been received among the aristocratic crowd, – not on equal terms, because a day-boarder at Harrow in those days was never so received, – but at any

* A pupil of his destroyed himself in the rooms.

rate as other day boarders. I don't suppose that they were well treated, but I doubt whether they were subjected to the ignominy which I endured. I was only seven, and I think that boys at seven are now spared among their more considerate seniors. I was never spared; – and was not even allowed to run to and fro between our house and the school without a daily purgatory. No doubt my appearance was against me. I remember well, when I was still the junior boy in the school, Dr Butler, the head master, stopping me in the street, and asking me, with all the clouds of Jove upon his brow, and all the thunder in his voice, whether it was possible that Harrow school was disgraced by so disreputably dirty a little boy as I! Oh what I felt at that moment! But I could not look my feelings. I do not doubt that I was dirty; – but I think that he was cruel. He must have known me, had he seen me as he was wont to see me, for he was in the habit of flogging me constantly. Perhaps he did not recognise me by my face.

At this time I was three years at Harrow; and as far as I can remember, I was the junior boy in the school when I left it.

Then I was sent to a private school at Sunbury kept by Arthur Drury. This I think must have been done in accordance with the advice of Henry Drury who was my tutor at Harrow School and my father's friend, – and who may probably have expressed an opinion that my juvenile career was not proceeding in a satisfactory manner at Harrow. To Sunbury I went, and during the two years that I was there, though I never had any pocket-money and seldom had much in the way of clothes, I lived more nearly on terms of equality with other boys than at any other period during my very prolonged school days. Even here I was always in disgrace. I remember well how on an occasion four boys were selected as having been the perpetrators of some nameless horror. What it was, to this day I cannot even guess; – but I was one of the four, innocent as a babe, but adjudged to have been the guiltiest of the guilty. We each had to write out a sermon, and my sermon was the longest of the four. During the whole of one term-time we were helped last at every meal. We were not allowed to visit the playground till the sermon was finished. Mine was only done a day or two before the holydays. Mrs Drury, when she saw us, shook her head with pitying horror. There were ever so many other punishments

9

accumulated on our heads. It broke my heart, knowing myself to be innocent, and suffering also under the almost equally painful feeling that the other three, no doubt wicked boys, were the curled darlings of the school,[5] who would never have selected me to share their wickedness with them. I contrived to learn from words that fell from Mr Drury that he condemned me because I, having come from a public school, might be supposed to be the leader of wickedness! On the first day of the next term he whispered to me half a word that perhaps he had been wrong. With all a stupid boy's slowness, I said nothing; – and he had not the courage to carry reparation further. All that was fifty years ago, and it burns me now as though it were yesterday. What lily-livered curs[6] those boys must have been not to have told the truth – at any rate as far as I was concerned! I remember their names well and almost wish to write them here.

When I was twelve there came the vacancy at Winchester College which I was destined to fill. My two elder brothers had gone there, and the younger had been taken away, being already supposed to have lost his chance of New College. It had been one of the great ambitions of my father's life that his three sons, who lived to go to Winchester, should all become fellows of New College. But that suffering man was never destined to have an ambition gratified. We all lost the prize which he struggled with infinite labour to put within our reach. My eldest brother all but achieved it, and afterwards went to Oxford, taking three exhibitions from the school, though he lost the great glory of a Wykamist.[7] He has since made himself well known to the public as a writer in connexion with all Italian subjects.[8] He is still living as I now write. But my other brother died early.

While I was at Winchester my father's affairs went from bad to worse. He gave up his practice at the bar, and, unfortunate that he was, took another farm. It is odd that a man should conceive, – and in this case a highly educated and a very clever man, – that farming should be a business in which he might make money without any special education or apprenticeship. Perhaps of all trades it is the one in which an accurate knowledge of what things should be done and the best manner of doing them, is most necessary. And it is one also for success in which a sufficient capital is indispensable. He had no knowledge, and, when he took this second farm, no capital. This was the last step preparatory to his final ruin.

Soon after I had been sent to Winchester, my mother went to America, taking with her my brother Henry and my two sisters, who were then no more than children. This was, I think, in 1827. I have no clear knowledge of her object, or of my father's; but I believe that he had an idea that money might be made by sending goods, – little goods such as pincushions, pepper-boxes, and pocket-knives, – out to the still unfurnished States, and that she conceived that an opening might be made for my brother Henry by erecting some bazaar or extended shop in one of the Western cities. Whence the money came I do not know; but the pocket-knives and the pepper-boxes were bought and the bazaar was built. I have seen it since in the town of Cincinnati, – a sorry⁣ᶜ building! But I have been told that in those days it was an imposing edifice. My mother went first with my sisters and second brother. Then my father followed them, taking my elder brother before he went to Oxford. But there was an interval of some year and a half during which he and I were at Winchester together.

Over a period of forty years, since I began my manhood at a desk in the Post Office, I and my brother, Thomas Adolphus, have been fast friends. There have been hot words between us, for perfect friendship bears and allows hot words. Few brothers have had more of brother-hood. But in those school days he was of all my foes the worst. In accordance with the practice of the college, which submits, or did then submit, much of the tuition of the younger boys to the elder, he was my tutor; and in his capacity of teacher and ruler, he had studied the theories of Draco.⁹ I remember well how he professed to exact obedience after the manner of that lawgiver. Hang a little boy for stealing apples, he used to say, and other little boys will not steal apples. The doctrine was already exploded elsewhere, but he stuck to it with conservative energy. The result was that, as a part of his daily exercise he thrashed me with a big stick. That such thrashings should have been possible at a school as a continual part of one's daily life, seems to me to argue a very ill condition of school discipline.

At this period I remember to have passed one set of holydays – the midsummer holydays – in my father's chambers in Lincoln's Inn. There was often a difficulty about the holydays, – as to what should be done with me. On this occasion my amusement consisted in wandering about among those old deserted buildings, and in reading Shakespeare out of a bicolumned edition which is still among my books. It was not that I had chosen Shakespeare, but that there was nothing else.

After a while my brother left Winchester and accompanied my father to America. Then another and a different horror fell to my fate. My college bills had not been paid, and the school tradesmen who administered to the wants of the boys were told not to extend their credit to me. Boots, waistcoats, and pocket handkerchiefs which with some slight superveillance were at the command of other scholars, were closed luxuries to me. My schoolfellows of course knew that it was so, and I became a Pariah. It is the nature of boys to be cruel. I have sometimes doubted whether among each other they do usually suffer much, one from the other's cruelty; – but I suffered horribly! I could make no stand against it. I had no friend to whom I could pour out my sorrows. I was big, and awkward, and ugly, and, I have no doubt, skulked about in a most unattractive manner. Of course I was ill-dressed and dirty. But, ah, how well I remember all the agonies of my young heart; how I considered whether I should always be alone; – whether I could not find my way up to the top of that college tower, and from thence put an end to everything! And a worse thing came than the stoppage of the supplies from the shopkeepers. Every boy had a shilling a week pocket money, which we called battels, and which was advanced to us out of the pocket of the second master. On one awful day the second master announced to me that my battels would be stopped. He told me the reason, – the battels for the last half year had not been repaid; – and he urged his own unwillingness to advance the money. The loss of a shilling a week would not have been much, – even though pocket money from other sources never reached me; – but that the other boys all knew it! Every now and again, perhaps three or four times in a half year, these weekly shillings were given to certain servants of College, in payment, it may be presumed, for some extra services. And now, when it came to the turn of any servant, he received sixty nine shillings instead of seventy, and the cause of the defalcation was explained to him. I never saw one of those servants without feeling that I had picked his pocket.

When I had been at Winchester something over three years my father returned to England and took me away. Whether this was done because of the expense or because my chance of New College was supposed to have passed away, I do not know. As a fact, I should, I believe, have gained the prize, as there occurred in my year an exceptional number of vacancies. But it would have served me nothing, as there would have been no funds for my maintenance at the University till I should have entered in upon the fruition of the founder's endowment, and my career at Oxford must have been unfortunate.

When I left Winchester I had three more years of school before me, having as yet endured nine. My father at this time having left my mother and sisters with my younger brother in America, took himself to live at a wretched tumble-down farm house on the second farm he had hired! And I was taken there with him. It was nearly three miles from Harrow, at Harrow Weald, but in the parish; – and from this house I was again sent to that school as a day boarder. Let those who know what is the usual appearance and what the usual appurtenances of a boy at such a school consider what must have been my condition among them, with a daily walk of twelve miles through the lanes added to the other little troubles and labours of a school life!

Perhaps the eighteen months which I passed in this condition, walking to and fro on those miserably dirty lanes was the worst period of my life. I was now over fifteen, and had come to an age in which I could appreciate at its full the misery of expulsion from all social intercourse. I had not only no friends but was despised by all my companions. The farm house was not only no more than a farm house, but was one of those farm houses which seem always to be in danger of falling into the neighbouring horse pond. As it crept downwards from house to stables, from stables to barns, from barns to cowsheds, and from cowsheds to dungheaps, one could hardly tell where one began and the other ended! There was a parlour in which my father lived, shut up among big books, but I passed my most jocund hours in the kitchen, making innocent love to the bailiff's daughter. The farm kitchen might be very well through the evening, when the horrors of the school were over; but it all added to the cruelty of the days. A Sizar at a Cambridge college, or a Bible clerk at Oxford,[10] has not pleasant days, or used not to have them half a century ago; – but his position was recognised and the misery was measured. I was a Sizar at a fashionable school, a condition never premeditated. What right had a wretched farmer's boy, reeking from a dunghill, to sit next to the sons of peers, – or much worse still, next to the sons of big tradesmen who had made their ten thousand a year? The indignities I endured are not to be described. As I look back it seems to me that all hands were turned against me, – those of masters as well as boys. I was allowed to join in no plays. Nor did I learn anything, – for I was taught nothing. The only expense, except that of books, to which a house boarder was then subject was the fee to a tutor, amounting I think to ten guineas. My tutor took me without the fee; – but when I heard him declare the fact in the pupil-room before the boys I hardly felt grateful for the charity. I was never a coward, and cared for a thrashing as little as any boy; – but one cannot make a stand against the acerbities of 300 tyrants without a moral courage of which at the time I possessed none. I know that I skulked and was odious to the eyes of those I admired and envied. At last I was driven to rebellion, and there came a great fight; – at the end of which my opponent had to be taken home for a while. If these words be ever printed I trust that some schoolfellow of those days may still be left alive who will be able to say that in claiming this solitary glory of my school days, I am not making a false boast.[11]

I wish I could give some adequate picture of the gloom of that farm house. My elder brother, – Tom as I must call him in my narrative, though the world I think knows him best as Adolphus, – was at Oxford. My father and I lived together, he having no means of living except what came from the farm. My memory tells me that he was always in debt to his landlord and to the tradesmen he employed. Of self-indulgence no one could accuse him. Our table was poorer I think than that of the bailiff who still hung on to our shattered fortunes. The furniture was mean and scanty. There was a large rambling kitchen garden, but no gardener; and many times verbal incentives were made to me, – generally, I fear, in vain, – to get me to lend a hand at digging and planting. Into the hayfield on holydays I was often compelled to go, – not I fear with much profit. My father's health was very bad. During the last ten years of his life, he spent nearly half of his time in bed suffering agony from sick head aches. But he was never idle unless when suffering. He had at this time commenced a work, – an Encyclopedia Ecclesiastica as he called it, – on which he laboured to the moment of his death. It was his intention to describe all ecclesiastical terms, including the denominations of every fraternity of monks and every convent of nuns, with all their orders and subdivisions. Under crushing disadvantages, with few or no books of reference, with immediate access to no library, he worked at his most ungrateful task with unflagging industry. When he died, three numbers out of eight had been published by subscription; – and are now I fear unknown and buried in the midst of that huge pile of futile literature, the building up of which has broken so many hearts![12]

And my father, though he would try, as it were by a side wind, to get a useful spurt of work out of me, either in the garden or the hayfield, had constantly an eye to my scholastic improvement. From my very babyhood, before those first days at Harrow, I had had to take my place along side of him as he shaved at six o'clock in the morning, and say my early rules from the Latin Grammar or repeat the Greek alphabet; and was obliged at these early lessons to hold my head inclined towards him, so that in the event of guilty fault, he might be able to pull my hair without stopping his razor or dropping his shaving brush. No father was ever more anxious for the education of his children, though I think none ever knew less how to go about the work. Of amusement, as far as I can remember, he never recognised the need. He allowed himself no distraction, and did not seem to think it was necessary to a child. I cannot bethink me of aught that he ever did for my gratification; but for my welfare, – for the welfare of us all, – he was willing to make any sacrifice. At this time, in the farm house at Harrow Weald, he could not give his time to teach me for every hour that he was not in the fields was devoted to his monks and nuns; but he would require me to sit at a table with Lexicon and Gradus[13] before me. As I look back on my resolute idleness and fixed determination to make no use whatever of the books thus thrust upon me, or of the hours, and as I bear in mind the consciousness of great energy in afterlife, I am in doubt whether my nature is wholly altered or whether his plan was wholly bad. In those days he never punished me, though I think I grieved him much by my idleness; but in passion he knew not what he did and he has knocked me down with the great folio Bible which he always used. In the old house were the two first volumes of Cooper's novel, called *The Prairie*, a relic – probably a dishonest relic, – of some subscription to Hookham's library.[14] Other book of the kind there was none. I wonder how many dozen times I read those two first volumes.

It was the horror of those dreadful walks backwards and forwards which made my life bad. What so pleasant, what so sweet, as a walk along an English lane, when the air is sweet and the weather fine, and when there is charm in walking? But here were the same lanes four times a day, in wet and dry, in heat and summer, with all the accompanying mud and dust, and with disordered clothes. I might have been known among all the boys, at a hundred yards' distance, by my boots and trousers, – and was conscious at all times that I was so known. I remembered constantly that address from Dr Butler when I was a little boy. Dr Longley might with equal justice have said the same thing any day, – only that Dr Longley never in his life was able to say an ill-natured word. Dr Butler only became Dean of Peterborough, but his successor lived to be Archbishop of Canterbury.[15]

I think it was in the autumn of 1831 that my mother, with the rest of the family, returned from America. She lived at first at the farm house, but it was only for a short time. She came back with a book written about the United States, and the immediate pecuniary success which that work obtained enabled her to take us all back to the house at Harrow; – not to the first house which would still have been beyond her means, but to that which has since been called Orley Farm, and which was an Eden as compared to our abode at Harrow Weald. Here my schooling went on under somewhat improved circumstances. The three miles became half a mile, and probably some salutary changes were made in my wardrobe. My mother and my sisters, too, were there. And a great element of happiness was added to us all in the affectionate and life enduring friendship of the family of our close neighbour, Colonel Grant. But I was never able to overcome, – or even to attempt to overcome, – the absolute isolation of my school position.

Of the cricket ground, or racket court, I was allowed to know nothing. And yet I longed for these things with an exceeding longing. I coveted popularity with a coveting that was almost mean. It seemed to me that there would be an Elysium in the intimacy of those very boys whom I was bound to hate because they hated me. Something of the disgrace of my school days has clung to me all through life. Not that I have ever shunned to speak of them as openly as I am writing now, but that when I have been claimed as schoolfellow by some of those many hundreds who were with me either at Harrow or at Winchester, I have felt that I had no right to talk of things from most of which I was kept in estrangement.

Through all my father's troubles he still desired to send me either to Oxford or Cambridge. My elder brother went to Oxford, and Henry to Cambridge. It all depended on my ability to get some scholarship that would help me to live at the University. I had many chances. There were exhibitions from Harrow – which I never got. Twice I tried for a sizarship at Clare Hall, – but in vain. Once I made a futile attempt for a scholarship at Trinity, Oxford, but failed again. Then the idea of a University career was abandoned. And very fortunate it was that I did not succeed, for my career with such assistance only as a scholarship would have given me, would have ended in debt and ignominy.

When I left Harrow I was all but nineteen, and I had at first gone there at seven. During the whole of those twelve years no attempt had been made to teach me anything but Latin and Greek, and very little attempt to teach me those languages. I do not remember any lessons either in writing or arithmetic. French and German I certainly was not taught. The assertion will scarcely be credited, but I do assert that I have no recollection of other tuition except that in the dead languages. At the school at Sunbury there was certainly a writing master and a French master. The latter was an extra, and I never had extras. I suppose I must have been in the writing master's class, but though I can call to mind the man I cannot call to mind his ferule. It was by their ferules that I always knew them, and they me. I feel convinced in my mind that I have been flogged oftener than any human being alive. It was just possible to obtain five scourgings in one day at Winchester, and I have often boasted that I obtained them all. Looking back over half a century, I am not quite sure whether the boast is true; but if I did not, nobody ever did.

And yet when I think how little I knew of Latin or Greek on leaving Harrow at nineteen, I am astonished at the possibility of such waste of time. I am now a fair latin scholar; – that is to say I read and enjoy the latin classics, and could probably make myself understood in latin prose. But the knowledge which I have, I have acquired since I left school, – no doubt aided much by that groundwork of the language which will in the process of years make its way slowly, even through the skin. There were twelve years of tuition in which I do not remember that I ever knew a lesson! When I left Harrow I was nearly at the top of the school, being a monitor, and I think the seventh boy. This position I achieved by gravitation upwards.[d] I bear in mind well with how prodigal a hand prizes used to be showered about; but I never got a prize.[16] From the first to the last there was nothing satisfactory in my school career, – except the way in which I licked the boy who had to be taken home to be cured.

CHAPTER 2

My Mother.

Though I do not wish in these pages to go back to the origin of all the Trollopes I must say a few words of my mother; – partly because filial duty will not allow me to be silent as to a parent who made for herself a considerable name in the literature of her day, and partly because there were circumstances in her career well worthy of notice. She was the daughter of the Rev William Milton Vicar of Heckfield, who, as well as my father, had been a fellow of New College. She was nearly thirty when in 1809 she married my father. Six or seven years ago a bundle of love letters from her to him fell into my hand in a very singular way, having been found in the house of a stranger who with much courtesy sent them to me. They were then about sixty years old, and had been written some before and some after her marriage over the space of perhaps a year. In no novel of Richardson's or Miss Burney's have I seen a correspondence at the same time so sweet, so graceful, and so well expressed. But the marvel of these letters was in the strange difference they bore to the love letters of the present day. They are, all of them, on square paper, folded and sealed, and addressed to my father on circuit; but the language in each, though it almost borders on the romantic, is beautifully chosen and fit without change of a syllable, for the most critical eye. What girl now studies the words with which she shall address her lover, or seeks to charm him with grace of diction? She dearly likes a little slang, and revels in the luxury of entire familiarity with a new and strange being. There is something in that, too, pleasant to our thoughts, but I fear that this phase of life does not conduce to a taste for poetry among our girls. Though my mother was a writer of prose and revelled in satire the poetic feeling clung to her to the last.

In the first ten years of her married life she became the mother of six children four of whom died of consumption at different ages. My elder sister married and had children of whom one still lives, but she was one of the four who followed each other at intervals during my mother's life time. Then my brother Tom and I were left to her, – with the destiny before us three of writing more books than were probably ever before produced by a single family.* My married sister added to the number by one little anonymous high-church story called *Chollerton.*¹

From the date of their marriage up to 1827, when my mother went to America, my father's affairs had always been going down in the world. She had loved society, affecting a somewhat liberal rôle, and professing an emotional dislike to tyrants which sprung from the wrongs of would-be regicides and the poverty of patriot exiles. An Italian Marquis who had escaped with only a second shirt from the clutches of

---

* The family of Estienne,² the great French printers of the fifteenth and sixteenth centuries, of whom there were at least nine or ten, did more perhaps for the production of literature than any other family. But they, though they edited, and not unfrequently translated the works which they published, were not authors in the ordinary sense.

some Arch Duke whom he had wished to exterminate, or a French *prolétaire* with distant ideas of sacrificing himself to the cause of liberty, were always welcome to the modest hospitality of her house. In after years, when Marquises of another caste had been gracious to her, she became a strong Tory, and thought that Arch Duchesses were sweet. But with her, politics were always an affair of the heart, – as, indeed, were all her convictions. Of reasoning from causes I think that she knew nothing. Her heart was in every way so perfect, her desire to do good to all around her so thorough, and her power of self-sacrifice so complete, that she generally got herself right in spite of her want of logic; – but it must be acknowledged that she was emotional. I can remember now her books and can see her at her pursuits. The poets she loved best were Dante and Spenser. But she raved also of him of whom all such ladies were raving then, and rejoiced in the popularity and wept over the persecution of Lord Byron. She was among those who seized with avidity on the novels as they came out of the then unknown[a] Scott and who could still talk of the triumphs of Miss Edgeworth.[3] With the literature of the day she was familiar, and with the poets of the past. Of other reading I do not think she had mastered much. Her life I take it, though latterly clouded by money troubles,[b] was easy, luxurious, and idle, till my father's affairs and her own aspirations sent her to America. She had dear friends among literary people of whom I remember Mathias, Henry Milman, and Miss Landon;[4] but till long after middle life she never herself wrote a line for publication.

In 1827 she went to America having been partly instigated by the social and communistic ideas of a lady whom I well remember, – a certain Miss Wright[5] who was I think the first of the American female lecturers. Her chief desire, however, was to establish my brother Henry; – and perhaps joined with that was the additional object of breaking up her English home without pleading broken fortunes to all the world. At Cincinnati in the State of Ohio she built a bazaar, and I fancy lost all the money which may have been embarked in that speculation. It could not have been much, and I think that others also must have suffered. But she looked about her, at her American cousins, and resolved to write a book about them. This book she brought back with her in 1831, and published[c] early in 1832. When she did this she was already fifty. When doing this she was aware that unless she could so succeed in making money, there was no money for any of the family. She had never before earned a shilling. She almost immediately received a considerable sum from the publishers, – if I remember rightly amounting to two sums of £400 each within a few months; and from that moment till nearly the time of her death,[6] at any rate for more than twenty years, she was in the receipt of a considerable income from her writings. It was a late age at which to begin such a career.

The Domestic Manners of the Americans was the first of a series of books of travels, of which it was probably the best and was certainly the best known. It will not be too much to say of it that it had a material effect upon the manners of the Americans of the day and that that effect has been fully appreciated by them. No observer was certainly ever less qualified to judge of the prospects or even of the happiness of a young people. No one could have been worse adapted by nature for the task of learning whether a nation was in a way to thrive. Whatever she saw she judged, as most women do, from her own standing point. If a thing were ugly to her eyes, it ought to be ugly to all eyes, – and if ugly it must be bad; what though people had plenty to eat and clothes to wear, if they put their feet upon the tables and did not reverence their betters? The Americans were to her rough, uncouth, and vulgar, – and she told them so. Those communistic and social ideas, which had been so pretty in a drawing-room, were scattered to the winds. Her volumes were very bitter; – but they were very clever, and they saved the family from ruin.

Book followed book immediately, – first two novels and then a work on Belgium and Western Germany.[7] She refurnished the house which I have called Orley Farm, and surrounded us again with moderate comforts. Of the mixture of joviality and industry which formed her character it is almost impossible to speak with exaggeration. The industry was a thing apart; – kept to herself. It was not necessary that any one who lived with her should see it. She was at her table at four in the morning and had finished her work before the world had begun to be aroused. But the joviality was all for others. She could dance with other people's legs, eat and drink with other people's palates, be proud with the lustre of other people's finery. Every mother can do that for her own daughters; but she could do it for any girl whose look and voice and manners pleased her. Even when she was at work the laughter of those she loved was a pleasure to her. She had much, very much to suffer. Work sometimes came hard to her, so much being required – for she was extravagant and liked to have money to spend; but of all people I have known she was the most joyous, – or at any rate the most capable of joy.

We continued this renewed life at Harrow for nearly two years, during which I was still at school, and at the end of which I was nearly nineteen. Then there came a great catastrophe. My father who, when he was well, lived a sad life among his monks and nuns, still kept a horse and gig. One day in March 1834, just as it had been decided that I should leave the school then, instead of remaining as had been intended, till midsummer, I was summoned, very early in the morning, to drive him up to London. He had been ill, and must still have been very ill indeed when he submitted to be driven by any one. It was not till we had started that he told me that I was to put him on board the Ostend boat. This I did, driving him through the city down to the docks. It was not within his nature to be communicative, and to the last he never told me why he was going to Ostend. Something of a general flitting abroad I had heard before, but why he should have flown the first, and flown so suddenly I did not in the least know till I returned. When I got back with the gig, the house and furniture were all in the charge of the Sheriff's officers.

The gardener who had been with us in former days stopped me as I drove up the road, and with gestures, signs, and whispered words gave me to understand that the whole affair, horse, gig, and harness, would be made prize of if I went but a few yards farther. Why they should not have been made prize of I do not know. The little piece of dishonest business which I at once took in hand and carried through successfully was of no special service to any of us. I drove the gig into the village and sold the entire equipage to the ironmonger for £17, the exact sum which he claimed as being due to himself. I was much complimented by the gardener who seemed to think that so much had been rescued out of the fire. I fancy that the ironmonger was the only gainer by my smartness.

When I got back to the house a scene of devastation was in progress, which still was not without its amusement. My mother through her various troubles had contrived to keep a certain number of pretty-pretties which were dear to her heart. They were not much, for in those days the ornamentation of houses was not lavish as it is now; but there was some china, and a little glass, a few books and a very moderate supply of household silver. These things and things like them were being carried down surreptitiously, through a gap between the two gardens, on to the premises of our friend Colonel Grant. My two sisters, then sixteen and seventeen, and the Grant girls who were just younger, were the chief marauders. To such forces I was happy to add myself for any enterprise, and between us we cheated the creditors to the extent of our powers amidst the anathemas, but good-humoured abstinence from personal violence, of the men in charge of the property. I still own a few books that were thus purloined.

For a few days the whole family bivouacked under the Colonel's hospitable roof, cared for and comforted by that dearest of all women, his wife. Then we followed my father to Belgium and established ourselves in a large house just outside the walls of Bruges. At this time and till my father's death everything was done with money earned by my mother. She now again furnished the house, this being the third that she had put in order since she came back from America two years and a half ago.

There were six of us went into this new banishment. My brother Henry had left Cambridge and was ill. My younger sister was ill. And though as yet we hardly told each other that it was so, we began to feel that that desolating fiend consumption was among us. My father was broken-hearted as well as ill, but, whenever he could sit at his table he still worked at his ecclesiastical records. My elder sister and I were in good health, but I was an idle, desolate hanger on, that most hopeless of human beings, a hobbledehoy of nineteen without any idea of a career, a profession, or a trade. As well as I can remember I was fairly happy, for there were pretty girls at Bruges with whom I could fancy that I was in love; and I had been removed from the real misery of school. But as to my future life I had not even an aspiration. Now and again there would arise a feeling that it was hard upon my mother that she should have to do so much for us, – that we should be idle while she was forced to work so constantly; but we should probably have thought more of that, had she not taken to work as though it were the recognised condition for life for an old lady of fifty five.

Then, by degrees, an established sorrow was at home among us. My brother was an invalid, and the horrid word, which of all words was, for some years after, the most dreadful to us, had been pronounced. It was no longer a delicate chest, and some temporary necessity for peculiar care, – but Consumption! The Bruges doctor had said so and we knew that he was right. From that time forth my mother's most visible occupation was that of nursing. There were two sick men in the house, and hers were the hands that tended them. The novels went on of course. We had already learned to know that they would be forthcoming at stated intervals, – and they always were forthcoming. The doctor's vials and the inkbottle held equal places in my mother's rooms. I have written many novels under many circumstances; but I doubt much whether I could write one when my whole heart was by the bedside of a dying son. Her power of dividing herself into two parts, and keeping her intellect by itself, clear from the troubles of the world and fit for the duty it had to do, I never saw equalled. I do not think that the writing of a novel is the most difficult task which a man may be called upon to do; but it is a task that may be supposed to demand a spirit fairly at ease. The work of doing it with a troubled spirit killed Sir Walter Scott.[8] My mother went through it unscathed in strength though she performed all the work of day nurse and night nurse to a sick household; – for there were soon three of them dying.

At this time there came from some quarter an offer to me of a commission in an Austrian Cavalry regiment; – and so it was apparently my destiny to be a soldier. But I must first learn German and French, – of which languages I knew almost nothing. For this a year was allowed me and in order that it might be accomplished without expense I undertook the duties of a classical usher to a school then kept by William Drury at Brussels.[9] Mr Drury had been one of the Masters of Harrow when I went there at seven years old, and is now after an interval of fifty three years even yet officiating as clergyman at that place.* To Brussels I went, and my heart still sinks within me as I reflect that any one should have entrusted^d to me the tuition of thirty boys. I can only hope that those boys went there to learn French, and that their parents were not particular as to their classical acquirements. I remember that on two occasions I was sent to take the school out for a walk, but that after the second attempt Mrs Drury declared that the boys' clothes would not stand any further experiments of that kind. I cannot call to mind any learning by me of other languages; but as I only remained in that position for six weeks, perhaps the return lessons had not been as yet commenced. At the end of the six weeks a letter reached me offering me a clerkship in the General Post Office, – and I accepted it. Among my mother's dearest friends she reckoned Mrs Freeling, the wife of Clayton Freeling, whose father Sir Francis Freeling then ruled the Post Office.[10] She had heard of my desolate position, and had begged from her father-in-law the offer of a berth in his own office.

I hurried back from Brussels to Bruges on my way to London and found that the number of invalids had been encreased. My younger sister, Emily, who when I had left the house, was trembling in the balance, – who had been pronounced to be delicate, but with that false-tongued hope which knows the truth but will lie lest the heart should faint,[11] had been called delicate, but only delicate, – was now ill. Of course she was doomed. I knew it of both of them, – though I had never heard the word spoken, or had spoken it to any one. And my father was very ill, – ill to dying though I did not know it. And my mother had decreed to send my elder sister away to England, thinking that the vicinity of so much sickness might be injurious to her. All this happened late in the autumn of 1834, in the spring of which year we had come to Bruges; – and then my mother was left alone in a big house outside the town, with two Belgian women servants, to nurse three dying patients – the patients being her husband and children, – and to write novels for the sustenance of the family! It was about this period of her career that her best novels were written.[12]

To my own initiation at the Post Office I will return in the next

* He died two years after these words were written.

chapter. Just before Christmas my brother died, and was buried at Bruges. In the following February my father died and was buried along side of him, – and with him died that tedious task of his which I can only hope may have solaced many of his latter hours. I sometimes look back, meditating for hours together, on his adverse fate. He was a man finely educated, of great parts, with immense capacity for work, physically strong very much beyond the average of men, addicted to no vices, carried off by no pleasures, affectionate by nature, most anxious for the welfare of his children, born to fair fortunes, – who when he started in the world may be said to have had everything at his feet. But everything went wrong with him. The touch of his hand seemed to create failure. He embarked in one hopeless enterprise after another, spending on each all the money he could at the time command. But the worse curse to him of all was a temper so irritable that even those whom he loved the best could not endure it. We were all estranged from him, and yet I believe that he would have given his heart's blood for any of us. His life as I knew it was one long tragedy.

After his death my mother moved to England and took and furnished a small house at Hadley near Barnet. I was then a clerk in the London Post Office, and I remember well how gay she made the place with little dinners, little dances, and little picnics while she herself was at work every morning long before others had left their beds. But she did not stay at Hadley much above a year. She went up to London where she again took and furnished a house, from which my remaining sister was married and carried away into Cumberland. My mother soon followed her, and on this occasion did more than take a house. She bought a bit of land, – a field of three acres near the town, – and built a residence for herself. This I think was in 1841, and she had thus established and re-established herself six times in ten years. But in Cumberland she found the climate too severe, and in 1844 she moved herself to Florence where she remained till her death in 1863. She continued writing up to 1856 when she was seventy six years old; – and had at that time produced 114 volumes of which the first was not written till she was fifty. Her career offers great encouragement to those who have not begun early in life but are still ambitious to do something before they depart hence.

She was an unselfish, affectionate and most industrious woman, with great capacity for enjoyment and high physical gifts. She was endowed too with much creative power, with considerable humour, and a genuine feeling for romance. But she was neither clear sighted nor accurate; and in her attempts to describe morals, manners, and even facts, was unable to avoid the pitfalls of exaggeration.

CHAPTER 3

The General Post Office.

While I was still learning my duty as an usher at Mr Drury's school at Brussels, I was summoned to my clerkship in the London Post Office, and on my way passed through Bruges. I then saw my father and my brother Henry for the last time. A sadder household never was held together. They were all dying, – except my mother, who would sit up night after night nursing the dying ones, and writing novels the while, – so that there might be a decent roof for them to die under. Had she failed to write the novels I do not know where the roof would have been found. It is now more than forty years ago and looking back over so long a lapse of time I can tell the story, though it be the story of my own father and mother, of my own brother and sister, almost as coldly as I have often done some scene of intended pathos in fiction; – but that scene was indeed full of pathos. I was then becoming alive to the blighted ambition of my father's life, and becoming alive also to the violence of the strain which my mother was enduring. But I could do nothing but go and leave them. There was something that comforted me in the idea that I need no longer be a burden, – a fallacious idea, as it soon proved. My salary was to be ninety pounds a year, and on that I was to live in London, keep up my character as a gentleman, and be happy. That I should have thought this possible at the age of nineteen and should have been delighted at being able to make the attempt does not surprise me now; – but that others should have thought it possible, friends who knew something of the world, does astonish me. A lad might have done so, then, no doubt, or might do so even in these days, who was properly looked after and kept under control, on whose behalf some law of life had been laid down. Let him pay so much a week for his board and lodging, so much for his clothes, so much for washing, and then let him understand that he has, – shall we say sixpence a day – left for pocket money and omnibuses. Any one making the calculation will find the sixpence far too much. No such calculation was made for me or by me. It was supposed that a sufficient income had been secured to me and that I should live upon it as other clerks lived.

But as yet the £90 a year was not secured to me. On reaching London I went to my friend Clayton Freeling who was then Secretary at the Stamp Office, and was taken by him to the scene of my future labours in St Martin's-le-Grand. Sir Francis Freeling was the Secretary, but he was greatly too high an official to be seen at first by a new junior clerk. I was taken therefore to his eldest son, Henry Freeling, who was the Assistant Secretary; and by him I was examined as to my fitness. The story of that Examination is given accurately in one of the opening chapters of a novel written by me many years afterwards called[a] *The Three Clerks*.[1] If any reader of this memoir would refer to that chapter and see how Charley Tudor was supposed to have been admitted into the Internal Navigation Office, that reader will learn how Anthony Trollope was actually admitted into the Secretary's office of the General Post Office in 1834. I was asked to copy some lines from the *Times* newspaper with an old quill pen, and at once made a series of blots and false spellings. 'That won't do you know,' said Henry Freeling to his brother Clayton. Clayton, who was my friend, urged that I was nervous, and asked that I might be allowed to do a bit of writing at home and bring it as a sample on the next day. I was then asked whether I was a proficient in arithmetic. What could I say? I had never learned the multiplication table, and had no more idea of the rule of three[2] than of Conic Sections. 'I know a little of it,' I said humbly. Whereupon I was sternly assured that on the morrow, should I succeed in showing my handwriting was all that it ought to be, I should be examined as to that little of arithmetic. If that little should not be found to comprise a thorough knowledge of all the ordinary rules together with practised and quick skill, my career in life could not be made at the Post Office. Going down the main stairs of the building, – stairs which[b] have I believe been now pulled down to make room for sorters and stampers, Clayton Freeling told me not to be too down-hearted. I was myself inclined to think that I had better at once go back to the school in Brussels. But nevertheless I went to work and under the surveillance of my elder brother made a beautiful transcript of four or five pages of Gibbon. With a faltering heart I took these on the next day to the office. With my calligraphy I was contented but was certain that I should come to the ground among the figures. But when I got to 'The Grand' as we used to call our office in those days, – from its site, in St Martin's-le-Grand, – I was seated at a desk without any further reference to my competency. No one condescended even to look at my beautiful penmanship.

That was the way in which candidates for the Civil Service were examined in my young days. It was, at any rate, the way in which I was examined. Since that time there has been a very great change indeed;[c] – and in some respects a great improvement. But, in regard to the absolute fitness of the young men selected for the public service, I doubt whether more harm has not been done than good. And I think that good might have been done without the harm. The rule of the present day is that every place shall be open to public competition, and that it shall be given to the best among the comers. I object to this that at present there exists no known mode of learning who is best, and that the method employed has no tendency to elicit the best. That method pretends only to decide who among a certain number of lads will best answer a string of questions for the answering of which they are prepared by tutors who have sprung up for the purpose since this fashion of election has been adopted. When it is decided in a family that a boy shall 'try the Civil Service', he is made to undergo a certain amount of cramming. But such treatment has, I maintain, no connexion whatever with education. The lad is no better fitted after it than he was before for the future work of his life. But his very success fills him with false ideas of his own educational standing, and so far unfits him. And, by the plan now in vogue, it has come to pass that no one is in truth responsible either for the conduct, the manners, or even for the character of the youth. The responsibility was perhaps slight before; – but existed,[d] and was on the encrease.

There might have been, – in some future time of still encreased wisdom, there yet may be, – a department established to test the fitness of acolytes without recourse to the dangerous optimism of competitive choice. I will not say but that there should have been someone to reject me, – though I will have the hardihood to say that had I been so rejected the Civil Service would have lost a valuable public servant. This is a statement that will not, I think, be denied by those who, after I am gone, may remember anything of my work. Lads, no doubt, should not be admitted who have none of the small acquirements that are wanted. Our offices should not be schools in which writing and early lessons in geography, arithmetic, or French should be learned. But all that could be ascertained without the perils of competitive examination.

The desire to examine[e] the efficiency of the young men selected has not been the only object; – perhaps not the chief object; – of those who have yielded in this matter to the arguments of the reformers. There had arisen in England a system of patronage, under which it had become gradually necessary for politicians to use their influence for the purchase of political support. A member of the House of Commons, holding office, who might chance to have five clerkships to give away in a year, – found himself compelled to distribute them among those who sent him to the House. In this there was nothing pleasant to the distributer of patronage. Do away with the system altogether, and he would have as much chance of support as another. He bartered his patronage only because another did so also. The beggings, the refusings, the jealousies, the correspondence, were simply troublesome. Gentlemen in office were, therefore, not indisposed to rid themselves of the curse of patronage. I have no doubt their hands are the cleaner, and their hearts are the lighter; – but I do doubt whether the offices are on the whole better manned.

As what I now write will certainly never be read till I am dead, I may dare to say what no one does dare to say in print, – though some of us whisper it occasionally into our friends' ears. There are places in life which can hardly be well filled except by 'gentlemen'. The word is one the use of which almost subjects one to ignominy. If I say that a judge should be a gentleman, or a bishop, I am met with a scornful allusion to Nature's Gentlemen. Were I to make such an assertion with reference to the House of Commons, nothing that I ever said again would receive the slightest attention. A man in public life could not do himself a greater injury than by saying in public that commissions in the army or navy or berths in the Civil Service should be given exclusively to gentlemen. He would be defied to define the term, – and would fail should he attempt to do so. But he would know what he meant, and so very probably would they who defied him. It may be that the son of the butcher in the village shall become as well fitted for employments requiring gentle culture[f] as the son of the parson. Such is often the case. When such is the case no one has been more prone to give the butcher's son all the welcome he has merited than I myself; – but the chances are greatly in favour of the parson's son. The gates of the one class should be open to the other; – but neither to one class nor to the other can good be done by declaring that there are no gates, no barrier, no difference. The system of competitive examination is I think based on a supposition that there is no difference.

I got into my place without any examining. Looking back now I think I can see with accuracy what was then the condition of my own mind and intelligence. Of things to be learned by lessons I knew almost less than could be supposed possible after the amount of schooling I had received. I could read neither French, Latin, nor Greek. I could speak no foreign language, – and I may as well say here as elsewhere that I never acquired the power of really talking French. I have been able to order my dinner and take a railway ticket, but never got much beyond that. Of the merest rudiments of the sciences I was completely ignorant. My handwriting was in truth wretched. My spelling was imperfect. There was no subject, as to which examination would have been possible on which I could have gone through an examination otherwise than disgracefully. And yet, I think, I knew more than the average of young men of the same rank who had begun life at nineteen. I could have given a fuller list of the names of the poets of all countries, with their subjects and periods, – and probably of historians than many others; and had, perhaps, a more accurate idea of the manner in which my own country was governed. I knew the names of all the bishops, all the judges, all the Heads of Colleges and all the Cabinet Ministers, – not a very useful knowledge, indeed, but one that had not been acquired without other matter which was more useful. I had read Shakespeare and Byron and Scott and could talk about them. The music of the Miltonic line was familiar to me. I had already made up my mind that *Pride and Prejudice* was the best novel in the English language, – a palm which I only partially withdrew after a second reading of *Ivanhoe* and did not completely bestow elsewhere till *Esmond* was written.[3] And though I would occasionally break down in my spelling, I could write a letter. If I had a thing to say I could so say it in written words that the reader should know what I meant, – a power which is by no means at the command of all those who come out from these competitive examinations with triumph. Early in life, at the age of fifteen, I had commenced the dangerous habit of keeping a journal, and this I maintained for ten years. The volumes remained in my possession unregarded, – never looked at, – till 1870, when I examined them and with many blushes destroyed them. They convicted me of folly, ignorance, indiscretion, idleness, extravagance, and conceit, – but they had habituated me to the rapid use of pen and ink and taught me now to express myself with facility.

I will mention here another habit which had grown upon me from still earlier years, – which I myself often regarded with dismay when I thought of the hours devoted to it, – but which I suppose must have tended to make me what I have been. As a boy, even as a child, I was thrown much upon myself. I have explained, when speaking of my school days, how it came to pass that other boys would not play with me. I was therefore alone and had to form my plays within myself. Play of some kind was necessary to me then, – as it has always been. Study was not my bent, and I could not please myself by being all idle.[g] Thus it came to pass that I was always going about with some castle-in-the-air firmly built within my mind. Nor were these efforts in architecture spasmodic, or subject to constant change from day to day. For weeks, for months, if I remember rightly, from year to year I would carry on the same tale, binding myself down to certain laws, to certain proportions and proprieties and unities.

Nothing impossible was ever introduced,[h] – nor even anything which from outward circumstances would seem to be violently improbable. I myself was of course my own hero. Such is a necessity of castle-building. But I never became a king, or a duke, – much less, when my height and personal appearance were fixed, would I be an Antinous,[4] or six feet high. I never was a learned man, nor even a philosopher. But I was a very clever person, and beautiful young women used to be fond of me. And I strove to be kind of heart and open of hand and noble in thought, despising mean things; and altogether I was a very much better fellow than I have ever succeeded in being since. This had been the occupation of my life for six or seven years before I went to the Post Office, and was by no means abandoned when I commenced my work. There can, I imagine, hardly be a more dangerous mental practice; but I have often doubted whether, had it not been my practice, I should ever have written a novel. I learned in this way to maintain an interest in a fictitious story, to dwell on a work created by my own imagination, and to live in a world altogether outside the world of my own material life. In after years I have done the same, – with this difference, that I have discarded the hero of my early dreams, and have been able to lay my own identity aside.

I must certainly acknowledge that the first seven years of my official life were neither creditable to myself nor useful to the public service. These seven years were passed in London, and during this period of my life it was my duty to be present every morning at the office, punctually at 10 am. I think I commenced my quarrels with the authorities there by having in my possession a watch which was always ten minutes late. I know that I very soon achieved a character for irregularity, and came to be regarded as a black sheep by men around me who were not themselves, I think, very good public servants. From time to time rumours reached me that if I did not take care, I should be dismissed; – especially one rumour in my early days, through my dearly beloved friend Mrs Clayton Freeling,[i] – who as I write this is still living, – and who with tears in her eyes besought me to think of my mother. That was during the life of Sir Francis Freeling, who died, – still in harness, – a little more than twelve months after I joined the office. And yet the old man showed me signs of almost affectionate kindness, writing to me with his own hand more than once from his death bed.

Sir Francis Freeling was followed at the Post Office by Colonel Maberly,[5] who certainly was not my friend. I do not know that I deserved to find a friend in my new master, but I think that a man with better judgement would not have formed so low an opinion of me as he did. Years have gone by and I can write now, and almost feel, without anger; but I can remember well the keenness of my anguish when I was treated as though I were unfit for any useful work. I did struggle, – not to do the work for there was nothing which was not easy without any struggling, – but to show that I was willing to do it. My bad character nevertheless stuck to me, and was not to be got rid of by any efforts within my power. I do admit that I was irregular. It was not considered to be much in my favour that I could write letters, – which was mainly the work of our office, – rapidly, correctly and to the purpose. The man who came at ten and who was always still at his desk at half past four was preferred before me though when at his desk he might be less efficient. Such preference was no doubt proper; but with a little encouragement I also would have been punctual. I got credit for nothing and was reckless.

As it was, the conduct of some of us was very bad. There was a comfortable sitting room up stairs, devoted to the use of some one of our number who in turn was required to remain in the place all night. Hither one or two of us would adjourn after lunch, and play *écarté*[6] for an hour or two. I do not know whether such ways are possible now in our public offices. And here we used to have suppers and card parties at night, – great symposiums with much smoking of tobacco; for in our part of the building there lived a whole bevy of clerks. These were gentlemen whose duty it then was to make up and receive the foreign mails. I do not remember that they worked later or earlier than the other sorting clerks; – but there was supposed to be something special in foreign letters which required that the men who handled them should have minds undistracted by the outer world. Their salaries too were higher than those of their more homely brethren; – and they paid nothing for their lodgings. Consequently there was a somewhat fast set in those apartments, given to cards and to tobacco, who drank spirits and water in preference to tea. I was not one of them, but was a good deal with them.

I do not know that I should interest my readers by saying much of my Post Office experiences in those days. I was always on the eve of being dismissed and yet was always striving to show how good a public servant I could become, if only a chance were given me. But the chances went the wrong way. On one occasion in the performance of my duty I had put a private letter containing bank notes on the Secretary's table, – which letter I had duly opened as it was not marked private. The letter was seen by the Colonel, but had not been moved by him when he left his room. On his return it was gone. In the mean time I had returned to the room, – again in the performance of some duty. When the letter was missed I was sent for, and there I found the Colonel much moved about his letter, and a certain chief clerk who with a long face was making suggestions as to the probable fate of the money. 'The letter has been taken,' said the Colonel, turning to me angrily, 'and, by G— there has been nobody in the room but you and I.' As he spoke he thundered his fist down upon the table. 'Then,' said I, 'by G— you have taken it.' And I also thundered my fist down; – but, accidentally, not upon the table. There was there, a standing movable desk, at which I presume it was the Colonel's habit to write; and on this movable desk was a large bottle full of ink. My fist unfortunately came on the desk, and the ink at once flew up, covering the Colonel's face and shirt front. Then it was a sight to see that senior clerk as he seized a quire of blotting paper and rushed to the aid of his superior officer, striving to mop up the ink, and a sight also to see the Colonel, in his agony, hit right out through the blotting paper at that senior clerk's unoffending stomach. At that moment there came in the Colonel's private secretary with the letter and the money, and I was desired to go back to my own room. This was an incident not much in my favour, – though I do not know that it did me special harm.

I was always in trouble. A young woman down in the country had taken it into her head that[j] she would like to marry me, – and a very foolish young woman she must have been to entertain such a wish. I need not tell that part of the story more at length, – otherwise than by protesting that no young man in such a position was ever much less to blame than I had been in this. The invitation had come from her and I lacked the pluck to give it a decided negative, – but I had left the house within half an hour, going away without my dinner, and had never returned to it. Then there was a correspondence, – if that can be called a correspondence in which all the letters came from one side. At last the mother appeared at the Post Office. My hair almost stands on my head now as I remember the figure of the woman walking into the big room in which I sat with six or seven other clerks, – having a large basket on her arm and an immense bonnet on her head. The messenger had vainly endeavoured to persuade her to remain in the ante-room. She followed the man in and walking up the centre of the room addressed me in a loud voice. 'Anthony Trollope, when are you going to marry my daughter?' We have all had our worst moments, and that was one of my worst. I lived through it, however and did not marry the young lady.[7] These little incidents were all against me in the office.

And then a certain other phase of my private life crept into official view and did me a damage. As I shall explain just now I rarely at this time had any money wherewith to pay my bills. In this state of things a certain tailor had taken from me an acceptance for, I think £12, which found its way into the hands of a money lender. With that man, who lived in a little street near Mecklenburgh Square,[8] I formed a most heart-rending but a most intimate acquaintance. In cash I once received from him £4. For that and for the original amount of the tailor's bill, which grew monstrously under repeated renewals, I paid ultimately something over £200. That is so common a story as to be hardly worth the telling, but the peculiarity of this man was that he became so attached to me as to visit me every day at my office. For a long period he found it to be worth his while to walk up those stone steps daily, and come and stand behind my chair whispering to me always the same words, 'Now I wish you would be punctual. If you only would be punctual I would like you to have anything you want.' He was a little, clean, old man, who always wore a high starched white cravat, inside which he had a habit of twisting his chin as he uttered his caution. When I remember the constant persistency of his visits, I cannot but feel that he was paid very badly for his time and trouble. Those visits were very terrible and can hardly have been of service to me in the office.

Of one other misfortune which happened to me in those days I must tell the tale. A junior clerk in the Secretary's office was always told off to sleep upon the premises, and he was supposed to be the presiding genius of the establishment when the other members of the Secretary's department had left the building. On an occasion, when I was still little more than a lad, – perhaps one and twenty years old, – I was filling this responsible position. At about seven in the evening, word was brought to me that the Queen of, – I think Saxony, but I am sure it was a Queen, – wanted to see the night mails sent out. At this time when there were many mail coaches this was a show, and august visitors would sometimes come to see it. But preparation was generally made beforehand, and some pundit of the office would be at hand to do the honours. On this occasion we were taken by surprise and there was no pundit. I therefore gave the orders and accompanied Her Majesty round the building, – walking backwards as I conceived to be proper, and often in great peril as I did so, up and down the stairs. I was, however, quite satisfied with my own manner of performing an unaccustomed and most important duty. There were two old gentlemen with Her Majesty who no doubt were German Barons, and an ancient Baroness also. They had come and, when they had seen the sights, took their departure in two glass coaches. As they were preparing to go, I saw the two Barons consulting together in deep whispers, and then as the result of that conversation, one of them handed me half a crown! That also was a bad moment.

I came up to town, as I said before, purporting to live a jolly life upon £90 per annum. I remained seven years in the General Post Office and when I left it my income was £140. During the whole of this time I was hopelessly in debt. There were two intervals, amounting together to nearly two years, in which I lived with my mother, and therefore lived in comfort, – but even then I was overwhelmed with debt. She paid much for me, – paid all that I asked her to pay, and all that she could find out that I owed. But who in such a condition ever tells all and makes a clean breast of it? The debts of course were not large, but I cannot think now how I could have lived, and sometimes have enjoyed life, with such a burden of duns as I endured. Sheriff's officers with uncanny documents, of which I never understood anything, were common attendants on me. And yet I do not remember that I was ever locked up, though I think I was twice a prisoner. In such emergencies some one paid for me. And now, looking back at it, I have to ask myself whether my youth was very wicked. I did no good in it; – but was there fair ground for expecting good from me? When I reached London no mode of life was prepared for me; – no advice even given to me. I went into lodgings, and then had to dispose of my time. I belonged to no club, and knew very few friends who would receive me into their houses. In such a condition of life a young man should no doubt go home after his work and spend the long hours of the evening in reading good books and drinking tea. A lad brought up by strict parents and without having had even a view of gayer things might perhaps do so. I had passed all my life at public schools, where I had seen gay things but had never enjoyed them. Towards the good books and tea no training had been given me. There was no house in which I could habitually see a lady's face and hear a lady's voice. No allurement to decent respectability came in my way. It seems to me that in such circumstances the temptations of loose life will almost certainly prevail with a young man. Of course if the mind be strong enough, and the general stuff knitted together of sufficiently stern material, the temptations will not prevail. But such minds and such material are I think uncommon. The temptation at any rate prevailed with me.

I wonder how many young men fall utterly to pieces from being turned loose into London after the same fashion. Mine, I think, was of all phases of such life the most dangerous. The lad who is sent to mechanical work has longer hours, during which he is kept from danger, and has not generally been taught in his boyhood to anticipate pleasure. He looks for hard work and grinding circumstances. I certainly had enjoyed but little pleasure, but I had been among those who did enjoy it and were taught to expect it. And I had filled my mind with the ideas of such joys. And now, except during official hours, I was entirely without control, – without the influences of any decent household around me. I have said something of the comedy of such a life, but it certainly had its tragic aspect. Turning it all over in my own mind, as I have constantly done in after years, the tragedy has always been uppermost. And so it was as the time was passing. Could there be any escape from such dirt, I would ask myself; and I always answered that there was no escape. The mode of life was itself wretched. I hated the office. I hated my work. More than all I hated my idleness. I had often told myself since I left school, that the only career in life within my reach was that of an author, and the only mode of authorship open to me that of a writer of novels. In the journal which I read and destroyed a few years since I found the matter argued out before I had been in the Post Office two years. Parliament was out of the question. I had not means to go to the bar. In official life, such as that to which I had been introduced, there did not seem to be any opening for real success. Pens and paper I could command. Poetry I did not believe to be within my grasp. The drama too, which I would fain have chosen, I believed to be above me. For history, biography, or essay-writing I had not sufficient erudition. But I thought it possible that I might write a novel. I had resolved very early that in that shape must the attempt be made. But the months and years ran on, and no attempt was made. And yet no day was passed without thoughts of attempting and a mental acknowledgment of the disgrace of postponing it. What reader will not understand the agony of remorse produced by such a condition of mind? The gentleman from Mecklenburgh Square was always with me in the morning, – always angering me by his hateful presence; but when the evening came I could make no struggle towards getting rid of him.

In those days I read a little, – and did learn to read French and Latin. I made myself familiar with Horace, and became acquainted with the works of our own greatest poets. I had my strong enthusiasms, and remember throwing out of the window in Northumberland Street where I lived a volume of Johnson's *Lives of the Poets*, because he spoke sneeringly of 'Lycidas'.[9] That was Northumberland Street, by the Marylebone Workhouse, on to the back door of which establishment my room looked out; – a most dreary abode at which I fancy I must have almost ruined the good-natured lodging-house keeper by my constant inability to pay her what I owed.

How I got my daily bread I can hardly remember; but I do

remember that I was often unable to get myself a dinner. Young men generally now have their meals provided for them. I kept house as it were. Every day I had to find myself with the day's food. For my breakfast I could get some credit at the lodgings, though that credit would frequently come to an end. But, for all that I had after breakfast, I had to pay[k] day by day; – and at your eating house credit is not given. I had no friends on whom I could sponge regularly. Out on the Fulham road I had an uncle, – but his house was four miles from the Post Office and almost as far from my own lodgings. Then there came borrowings of money, sometimes absolute want, and almost constant misery.

Before I tell how it came about that I left this wretched life I must say a word or two of the friendships with lessened its misfortunes. My earliest friend in life was John Merivale, which whom I had been at school at Sunbury and Harrow, and who was a nephew of my tutor, Harry Drury. Herman Merivale who afterwards became my friend was his brother, as is also Charles Merivale the historian and Dean of Ely. I knew John[l] when I was ten years old and am happy to be able to say that he is going to dine with me one day this week. I hope I may not injure his character by stating that in those days I lived very much with him. He too was impecunious, but he had a home in London, and knew but little of the sort of penury which I endured. For more than fifty years he and I have been close friends. And then there was one W.A., whose misfortunes in life will not permit me to give his full name, but whom I dearly loved. He had been at Winchester and at Oxford, and at both places had fallen into trouble. He then became a schoolmaster, – or perhaps I had better say usher, and finally he took orders. But he was unfortunate in all things, and died some years ago in poverty. He was most perverse; bashful to very fear of the rustle of a lady's dress; unable to restrain himself in anything, but yet with a conscience that was always stinging him; a loving friend, though very quarrelsome; and perhaps of all men I have known the most humorous. And he was entirely unconscious of his own humour. He did not know that he could so handle all matters as to create infinite amusement out of them. Poor W.A.! To him there came no happy turning point, at which life first loomed seriously on him and then became prosperous.

W.A., Merivale, and I formed a little club which we called the Tramp Society and subjected to certain rules in obedience to which we wandered on foot about the counties adjacent to London. Southampton was the furthest point we ever reached; but Buckinghamshire and Hertfordshire were dear to us. These were the happiest hours of my then life, – and perhaps not the least innocent, although we were frequently in peril from the village authorities whom we outraged. Not to pay for any conveyance, never to spend above 5/- a day, to obey all orders from the elected ruler of the hour, (this enforced under heavy fines) were among our statutes. I would fain tell here some of our adventures: how A. enacted an escaped madman and we his pursuing keepers, and so got ourselves a lift in a cart from which we ran away as we approached the lunatic asylum; how we were turned out of a little town at night, the towns folk frightened by the loudness of our mirth, and how we crept into a hay loft where we were[m] wakened in the dark morning by a pitchfork, – and how the juvenile owner of that pitchfork fled through the window when he heard the complaint[n] of the wounded man! But the fun was the fun of W.A., and would cease to be fun as told by me.

It was during these years that John Tilley who has now been for many years the permanent senior officer of the Post Office married my sister, – whom he took with him into Cumberland where he was stationed as one of our Surveyors. He has been my friend for more than forty years; – as has also Peregrine Birch,[10] a clerk in the House of Lords, who married one of those daughters of Colonel Grant who assisted us in the raid we made on the goods which had been seized by the Sheriff's officer at Harrow. These have been the oldest and dearest friends of my life; – and I can thank God that three of them are still alive.

When I had been nearly seven years in the Secretary's office of the Post Office, always hating my position there, and yet always fearing that I should be dismissed from it, there came a way of escape. There had latterly been created in the service a new body of officers called Surveyors' Clerks. There were at that time seven Surveyors in England, two in Scotland, and three in Ireland. To each of these officers a clerk had been lately attached whose duty it was to travel about the country under the Surveyor's orders. There had been much doubt among the young men in the office whether they should or should not apply for these places. The emoluments were good and the work alluring; – but there was at first supposed to be something derogatory in the position. There was a rumour that the first Surveyor who got a clerk, sent the clerk out to fetch his beer, and that another had called upon his clerk to send the linen to the wash. There was, however, a conviction that nothing could be worse than the berth of a Surveyor's clerk in Ireland. The clerks were all appointed, however. To me it had not occurred to ask for anything, nor would anything have been given me. But after a while there came a report from the far west of Ireland that the man sent there was absurdly incapable. It was probably thought then that none but a man absurdly incapable would go on such a mission to the west of Ireland. When the report reached the London office, I was the first to read it. I was at that time in dire trouble, having debts on my head and quarrels with our Secretary-Colonel, and a full conviction that my life was taking me downwards to the lowest pits. So I went to the Colonel boldly, and volunteered for Ireland if he would send me. He was glad to be so rid of me, and I went. This happened in August 1841, when I was twenty six years old. My salary in Ireland was to be but £100 a year; – but I was to receive 15/- a day for every day that I was away from home, and 6d for every mile that I travelled. The same allowances were made in England; but at that time travelling in Ireland was done at half the English prices. My income in Ireland after paying my expenses became at once £400. This was the first good fortune of my life.

CHAPTER 4

Ireland – My First Two Novels.
1841–1848.

In the preceding pages I have given a short record of the first twenty six years of my life – years of suffering, disgrace and inward remorse. I

fear that my mode of telling will have left an idea simply of their absurdities; – but in truth I was wretched, – sometimes almost unto
death, and have often cursed the hour in which I was born. There had
clung to me a feeling that I had been looked upon always as an evil, an
encumbrance, a useless thing, – as a creature of whom those connected
with him had to be ashamed, and I feel certain now that in my young
days I was so regarded. Even my few friends who had found with me a
certain capacity for enjoyment, were half afraid of me. I acknowledge
the weakness of a great desire to be loved, – of a strong wish to be
popular with my associates. No child, no boy, no lad, no young man
had ever been less so. And I had been so poor; – and so little able to
bear poverty! But from the day on which I set my foot in Ireland all
these evils went away from me. Since that time who has had a happier
life than mine? Looking round upon all those I know, I cannot put my
hand upon one. But all is not over yet. And, mindful of that, remembering how great is the agony of adversity, how crushing the despond-
ency of degradation,[a] how susceptible I am myself to the misery
coming from contempt, – remembering also how quickly good things
may go and evil things come, – I am often again tempted to hope,
almost to pray that the end may be near. Things may be going well
now;

> *Sin aliquem infandum casum, Fortuna, minaris;*
> *Nunc, oh nunc liceat crudelem abrumpere vitam.*[1]

There is unhappiness so great that the very fear of it is an alloy to
happiness. I had then lost my father and sister and brother, – have
since lost another sister and my mother; but I have never as yet lost a
wife or a child.

When I told my friends that I was going on this mission to Ireland
they shook their heads but said nothing to dissuade me. I think it must
have been evident to all who were my friends that my life in London
was not a success. My mother and elder brother were at this time
abroad and were not consulted; – did not even know my intention in
time to protest against it. Indeed I consulted no one, – except a dear
old cousin, our family lawyer,[2] from whom I borrowed £200 to help me

out of England. He lent me the money and looked upon me with pity-ing eyes, – shaking his head. 'After all you were right to go,' he said to me when I paid him the money a few years afterwards.

But nobody thought I was right to go then. To become clerk to an Irish Surveyor, in Connaught, with a salary of £100 a year, at twenty six years of age! I did not think it right even myself, – except that any-thing was right which would take me away from the General Post Office and from London.

My ideas of the duties I was to perform were very vague, as were also my ideas of Ireland generally. Hitherto I had passed my time, seated at a desk, either writing letters myself or copying into books those which others had written. I had never been called upon to do anything I was unable or unfitted to do. I now understood that in Ire-land I was to be a deputy-Inspector of country post offices and that among other things to be inspected would be the Postmasters' ac-counts! But as no other person asked a question as to my fitness for this work, it seemed unnecessary for me to do so.

On the 15th of September 1841, I landed in Dublin without an ac-quaintance in the country and with only two or three letters of intro-duction from a brother clerk in the Post Office. I had learned to think that Ireland was a land flowing with fun and whiskey,[b] in which ir-regularity was the rule of life, and where broken heads were looked upon as honourable badges. I was to live in a place called Banagher, on the Shannon, – which I had heard of because of its having once been conquered, though it had heretofore conquered everything, including the Devil.[3] And from Banagher my inspecting tours were to be made chiefly into Connaught, but also over a strip of country eastwards which would enable me occasionally to run up to Dublin. I went to a hotel which was very dirty, and after dinner I ordered some whiskey punch. There was an excitement in this, but when the punch was gone I was very dull. It seemed so strange to be in a country in which there was not a single individual whom I had ever spoken to or ever seen. And it was to be my destiny to go down into Connaught and adjust ac-counts, – the destiny of me who had never learned the multiplication table or done a sum in long division!

On the next morning I called on the Secretary of the Irish Post

Office[4] and learned from him that Colonel Maberly had sent a very bad character with me. He could not have sent a very good one, but I felt a little hurt when I was informed by this new master that he had been informed that I was worthless and must in all probability be dismissed. 'But,' said the new master, 'I shall judge you by your own merits.' From that time to the day on which I left the service I never heard a word of censure, nor had many months passed before I found that my services were valued. Before a year was over, I had acquired the character of a thoroughly good public servant.

The time went very pleasantly. Some adventures I had; – two of which I told in the *Tales of All Countries* under the names of 'The O'Conors of Castle Conor', and 'Father Giles of Ballymoy'.[c] I will not swear to every detail in these stories, but the main purport of each is true. I could tell many others of the same nature, were this the place for them. I found that the Surveyor to whom I had been sent, kept a pack of hounds, and therefore I bought a hunter. I do not think he liked it, but he could not well complain. He never rode to hounds himself, – but I did; and then and thus began one of the great joys of my life. I have ever since been constant to the sport, having learned to love it with an affection which I cannot myself fathom or understand. Surely no man has laboured at it as I have done, or hunted under such drawbacks as to distances, money, and natural disadvantages. I am very heavy, very blind, have been, – in reference to hunting – a poor man, and am now an old man. I have often had to travel all night outside a mail coach in order that I might hunt the next day. Nor have I ever been in truth a good horseman. And I have passed the greater part of my hunting life under the discipline of the Civil Service. But it has been for more than thirty years a duty to me to ride to hounds, and I have performed that duty with a persistent energy. Nothing has ever been allowed to stand in the way of hunting, – neither the writing of books, nor the work of the Post Office, nor other pleasures. As regarded the Post Office it soon seemed to be understood that I was to hunt; and when my services were re-transferred to England, no word of difficulty ever reached me on the subject.[d] I have written on very many subjects, and on most of them with pleasure; – but on no subject with such delight as on that of hunting. I have dragged it into many novels, – into too many, no doubt, – but I have always felt myself deprived of a legitimate joy when the nature of the tale has not allowed me a hunting chapter. Perhaps that which gave me the greatest delight was the description of a run on a horse, accidentally taken from another sportsman, – a circumstance which occurred to my dear friend Charles Buxton who will be remembered as one of the members for Surrey.[5]

It was altogether a very jolly life that I led in Ireland. I was always moving about, and soon found myself to be in pecuniary circumstances which were opulent in comparison with those of my past life. The Irish people did not murder me, nor did they even break my head. I soon found them to be good-humoured, clever, – the working classes very much more intelligent than those of England, – oeconomical,[e] and hospitable. We hear much of their spendthrift nature; but extravagance is not the nature of an Irishman. He will count the shillings in a pound much more accurately than an Englishman, and will with much more certainty get twelve pennyworths[f] from each. But they are perverse, irrational, and but little bound by the love of truth. I lived for many years among them, – not finally leaving the country until 1859; and I had the means of studying their character.

I had not been a fortnight in Ireland before I was sent down to a little town in the far west of County Galway to balance a defaulting Postmaster's accounts, find out how much he owed, and report upon his capacity to pay. In these days such accounts are very simple. They adjust themselves from day to day, and a Post Office Surveyor has nothing to do with them. At that time though the sums dealt with were small the forms of dealing with them were very intricate. I went to work, however, and made that defaulting Postmaster teach me the use of those forms. I then succeeded in balancing the account, and had no difficulty whatever in reporting that he was altogether unable to pay his debt. Of course he was dismissed; – but he had been a very useful man to me. I never had any further difficulty in the matter.

But my chief work was the investigating of complaints made by the public as to postal matters. The practice of the office was and is to send one of its servants to the spot to see the complainant and to enquire into the facts, when the complainant is sufficiently energetic or sufficiently big to make himself well heard. A great expense is often incurred for a very small object; but the system works well on the whole as confidence is engendered, and a feeling is produced in the country that the department has eyes of its own and does keep them open. This employment was very pleasant and to me always easy as it required at its close no more than the writing of a report. There were no accounts in this business, no keeping of books, no necessary manipulation of multitudinous forms. I must tell of one such complaint and enquiry, because, in its result, I think it was emblematic of many.

A gentleman in County Cavan had complained most bitterly of the injury done to him by some arrangement of the Post Office. The nature of his grievance has no present significance, but it was so unendurable that he had written many letters couched in the strongest language. He was most irate, and indulged himself in that scorn which is so easy to an angry mind. The place was not in my district, but I was borrowed, being young and strong, that I might encounter[g] the edge of his personal wrath. It was midwinter and I drove up to his house, – a squire's country seat, – in the middle of a snow storm just as it was becoming dark. I was on an open jaunting car, and was on my way from one little town to another, the cause of his complaint having reference to some mail conveyance between the two. I was certainly very cold and very wet and very uncomfortable when I entered his house. I was admitted by a butler, but the gentleman himself hurried into the hall. I at once began to explain my business. 'God bless me,' he said, 'you are wet through! John get Mr Trollope some brandy and water, – very hot.' I was beginning my story about the post again, when he himself took off my great-coat and suggested that I should go up to my bedroom before I troubled myself with business. 'Bedroom!' I exclaimed. Then he assured me that he would not turn a dog out on such a night as that, and into a bedroom I was shown, having first drunk[h] the brandy and water standing at the drawing-room fire. When I came down I was introduced to his daughter and the three of us went into dinner. I shall never forget his righteous indignation when I again brought up the postal question on the departure of the young lady. Was I such a Goth as to contaminate wine with business? So I drank my wine, and then heard the young lady sing while her father slept in his armchair. I spent a very pleasant evening, but my host was too sleepy to hear anything about the Post Office that night. It was absolutely necessary that I should go away the next morning after breakfast, and I explained that the matter must be discussed then. He shook his head and wrung his hands in unmistakeable disgust, – almost in despair. 'But what am I to say in my report?' I asked. 'Anything you please,' he said. 'Don't spare me if you want an excuse for yourself. Here I sit all the day, – with nothing to do; and I like writing letters.' I did report that Mr — was now quite satisfied with the postal arrangements of his district; and I felt a soft regret that I should have robbed my friend of his occupation. Perhaps he was able to take up the Poor Law Board or to attack the Excise. At the Post Office nothing more was heard from him.

I went on with the hunting Surveyor at Banagher for three years, during which, at Kingstown, the watering place near Dublin, I met Rose Heseltine,[6] the lady who has since become my wife. The engagement took place when I had been just one year in Ireland, but there was still a delay of two years before we could be married. She had no fortune, nor had I any income beyond that which came from the Post Office; and there were still a few debts, – which would have been paid off no doubt sooner, but for that purchase of the horse. When I had been nearly three years in Ireland we were married, – on 11 June 1844; – and perhaps I ought to name that happy day as the commencement of my better life rather than the day on which I first landed in Ireland.

For though during these three years I had been jolly enough, I had not been altogether happy. The hunting, the whiskey punch, the rattling Irish life – of which I could write a volume of stories were this the place to tell them, – were continually driving from my mind the still cherished determination to become a writer of novels. When I reached Ireland I had never put pen to paper; nor had I done so when I became engaged. And when I was married, being then twenty nine, I had only written the first volume of my first work. This constant putting off of the day of work was a great sorrow to me. I certainly had not been idle in my new berth. I had learned my work so that every one concerned knew that it was safe in my hands, and I held a position altogether the reverse of that in which I was always trembling while I remained in London. But that did not suffice, – did not nearly suffice. I still felt that there might be a career before me, – if I could only bring myself to begin the work. I do not think I much doubted my own intellectual sufficiency for the writing of a readable novel. What I did doubt was my own industry, and the chances of the market.

The vigour necessary to prosecute two professions at the same time is not given to every one, and it was only lately that I had found the vigour necessary for one. There must be early hours, and I had not as yet learned to love early hours. I was still, indeed, a young man; but hardly young enough to trust myself to find the power to alter the habits of my life. And I had heard of the difficulties of publishing, – a subject of which I shall have to say much should I ever bring this memoir to a close. I had dealt already with publishers on my mother's behalf and knew that many a tyro who could fill a manuscript lacked the power to put his matter before the public; – and I knew, too, that when the matter was printed how little had then been done towards the winning of the battle! I had already learned that many a book – many a good book

is born to blush unseen
And waste its sweetness on the desert air[7]

But still the purpose was strong within me and the first effort was made after the following fashion. I was located at a little town called Drumsna, – or rather village, – in the County Leitrim, where the Postmaster had come to some sorrow about his money; and my friend John Merivale was staying with me for a day or two. As we were taking a walk in that most uninteresting country we turned up through a deserted gateway, along a weedy grass-grown avenue, till we came to the modern ruins of a country house. It was one of the most melancholy spots I ever visited. I will not describe it here because I have done so in the first chapter of my first novel. We wandered about the place suggesting to each other causes for the misery we saw there, and while I was still among the ruined walls and decayed beams I fabricated the plot of *The Macdermots of Ballycloran*. As to the plot itself I do not know that I ever made one so good, – or, at any rate, one so susceptible of pathos. I am aware that I broke down in the telling, not having yet studied the art. Nevertheless *The Macdermots* is a good novel and worth reading by any one who wishes to understand what Irish life was before the potato disease, the famine, and the Encumbered Estates Bill.[8]

When my friend left me I set to work and wrote the first chapter or two. Up to this time I had continued that practice of castle-building of which I have spoken; but now the castle I built was among the ruins of that old house. The book, however, hung with me. It was only now and then that I found either time or energy for a few pages. I commenced the book in September 1843, and had only written a volume when I was married in June 1844.

My marriage was like the marriage of other people and of no special interest to any one except my wife and me. It took place at Rotherham in Yorkshire, where her father was the manager of a bank.[9] We were not very rich, having about £400 a year on which to live. Many people would say that we were two fools to encounter such poverty together. I can only reply that since that day I have never been without money in my pocket, and that I soon acquired the means of paying what I owed. Nevertheless more than twelve years had to pass over our heads before I received any payment for any literary work, which afforded an appreciable encrease to our income.

Immediately after our marriage, I left the west of Ireland and the hunting Surveyor, and joined another in the South. It was considered a better district and I was enabled to live at Clonmel, a town of some importance, instead of at Banagher which is little more than a village. I had not felt myself to be comfortable in my old residence as a married man. On my arrival there as a bachelor I had been received most kindly, but when I brought my English wife I fancied that there was a feeling that I had behaved badly to Ireland generally. When a young man has been received hospitably in an Irish circle, I will not say that it is expected of him that he should marry some young lady in that society; – but it certainly is expected of him that he shall not marry any young lady out of it. I had given offence and I was made to feel it.

There has taken place a great change in Ireland since the days in which I lived at Banagher, and a change so much for the better that I have sometimes wondered at the obduracy with which people have spoken of the permanent ill condition of the country. Wages are now nearly double what they were then. The Post Office at any rate is paying almost double for its rural labour, – 9/- a week when it used to pay 5/-, and 12/- a week when it used to pay 7/-. Banks have sprung up in almost every village. Rents are paid with more than English punctuality. And the religious enmity between the classes, though it is not yet dead, is dying out. Soon after I reached Banagher in 1841, I dined one evening with a Roman Catholic. I was informed next day by a Protestant gentleman who had been very hospitable to me that I must choose my party. I could not sit both at Protestant and Catholic tables. Such a caution would now be impossible in any part of Ireland. Home Rule no doubt is a nuisance, – and especially a nuisance because the professors of the doctrine do not at all believe it themselves. There are probably no other twenty men in England or Ireland who would be so utterly dumfounded and prostrated were Home Rule to have its way as the twenty Irish members[i] who profess to support it in the House of Commons. But it is not to be expected that nuisances such as these should be abolished at a blow. Home Rule is at any rate better and more easily managed than the rebellion at the close of the last century; it is better than the treachery of the Union, less troublesome than O'Connell's monster meetings, less dangerous than Smith O'Brien and the battle of the cabbage garden at Ballingary, and very much less bloody than Fenianism. The descent from O'Connell to Mr Butt has been the natural declension of a political disease which we had no right to hope could[j] be cured by any one remedy.[10]

When I had been married a year my first novel was finished. In July 1845 I took it with me to the north of England and intrusted the manuscript to my mother to do with it the best she could among the publishers in London. No one had read it but my wife; nor, as far as I am aware, has any other friend of mine ever read a word of my writing before it was printed. She, I think, has so read almost everything – to my very great advantage in matters of taste. I am sure I have never asked a friend to read a line; nor have I ever read a word of my own writing aloud, – even to her.[11] With one exception,[12] – which shall be mentioned as I come to it, I have never consulted a friend as to a plot or spoken to any one of the work I have been doing. My first manuscript I gave up to my mother agreeing with her that it would be as well that she should not look at it before she gave it to a publisher. I

knew that she did not give me credit for the sort of cleverness necessary for such work. I could see in the faces and hear in the voices of
those of my friends who were around me at the house in Cumberland,
– my mother, my sister, my brother-in-law, and I think my brother, –
that they had not expected me to come out as one of the family
authors. There were three or four in the field before me, and it seemed
to be almost absurd that another should wish to add himself to the number. My father had written much, – those long ecclesiastical descriptions, – quite unsuccessfully. My mother had become one of the popular authors of the day. My brother had commenced and had been fairly
well paid for his work. My sister, Mrs Tilley, had also written a novel
which was at the time in manuscript, – which was published afterwards
without her name and was called *Chollerton*. I could perceive that this attempt of mine was felt to be an unfortunate aggravation of the disease.

My mother, however, did the best she could for me and soon reported that Mr Newby[13] of Mortimer Street was to publish the book. It
was to be printed at his expense and he was to give me half the profits.
Half the profits! Many a young author expects much from such an
undertaking. I can with truth declare that I expected nothing. And I
got nothing. Nor did I expect fame, or even acknowledgment. I was
sure the book would fail; – and it did fail most absolutely. I never
heard of a person reading it in those days. If there was any notice taken
of it by any critic of the day, I did not see it.[14] I never asked any questions about it, or wrote a single letter on the subject to the publisher. I
have Mr Newby's agreement with me, in duplicate, and one or two
preliminary notes; but beyond that I did not have a word from Mr
Newby. I am sure that he did not wrong me in that he paid me nothing.
It is probable that he did not sell fifty copies of the work; – but of what
he did sell he gave me no account.

I do not remember that I felt in any way disappointed or hurt. I am
quite sure that no word of complaint passed my lips. I think I may say
that after the publication I never said a word about the book, even to
my wife. The fact that I had written and published it, and that I was
writing another did not in the least interfere with my life or with my
determination to make the best I could of the Post Office. In Ireland I
think that no one knew that I had written a novel.[15] But I went on writ-

ing. *The Macdermots* was published in 1847, and *The Kellys and the O'Kellys* followed in 1848. I changed my publisher but did not change my fortune. This second Irish story was sent into the world by Mr Colburn who had long been my mother's publisher, who reigned in Great Marlborough Street, and I believe created the business which is now carried on under the name of Messrs[k] Hurst & Blackett. He had previously been in partnership with Mr Bentley[16] in New Burlington Street. I made the same agreement as before as to half profits, and with precisely the same results. The book was not only not read but was never heard of, – at any rate in Ireland. And yet it is a good Irish story, – much inferior to the *Macdermots* as to plot, but superior in the mode of telling. Again I held my tongue, and not only said nothing, but felt nothing. Any success would I think have carried me off my legs, but I was altogether prepared for failure. Though I thoroughly enjoyed the writing of these books I did not imagine, when the time came for publishing them, that any one would condescend to read them.

But in reference to the *O'Kellys* there arose a circumstance which set my mind to work on a subject which has exercised it much ever since. I made my first acquaintance with criticism. A dear friend of mine, to whom the book had been sent, as have all my books, wrote me word to Ireland that he had been dining at some club with a man high in authority among the Gods of the *Times* newspaper, and that this special god had almost promised that the O'Kellys should be noticed in that most influential of 'organs'. This information moved me very much; but it set me thinking whether the notice, should it ever appear, would not have been more valuable, at any rate more honest, if it had been produced by other means; – if, for instance, the writer of the notice had been instigated by the merits, or demerits, of the book instead of the friendship of a friend. And I made up my mind then that, should I continue this trade of authorship, I would have no dealings with any critic on my own behalf. I would neither ask for, nor deplore, criticism, nor would I ever thank a critic for praise, or quarrel with him, even in my own heart, for censure. To this rule I have adhered with absolute strictness, and this rule I would recommend to all young authors. What can be got by touting among the critics is never worth the ignominy. The same may of course be said[l] of all things acquired by ignominious means. But in this matter it is so easy to fall into the dirt. *Facilis descensus Averni*.[17] There seems to be but little fault in suggesting to a friend that a few words in this or that journal would be of service. But any praise so obtained must be an injustice to the public, for whose instruction and not for the sustentation of the author such notices are intended. And from such mild suggestion the descent to crawling at the critic's feet, to the sending of presents, and at last to a mutual understanding between critic and criticised is only too easy. Other evils follow for the denouncing of which this is hardly the place – though I trust I may find such place before my work is finished. I took no notice of my friend's letter, but I was not the less careful in watching the *Times*. At last the review came, – a real review in the *Times*. I learned it by heart and can now give, if not the words, the exact purport. 'Of *The Kellys and the O'Kellys* we may say, what the master said to his footman when the man complained of the constant supply of legs of mutton on the kitchen table. "Well, John, – legs of mutton are good substantial food." And we may say also what John replied. "Substantial, Sir; – yes, Sir; – they are substantial, but a little coarse".'[18] That was the review, and even that did not sell the book![m]

From Mr Colburn I did receive an account showing that 375 copies of the book had been printed, that 140 had been sold, – to those I presume who liked substantial food even though[n] it was coarse, – and that he had incurred a loss of £63 10s. 1½d. The truth of the account I never for a moment doubted; – nor did I doubt the wisdom of the advice given to me in the following letter, though I never thought of obeying it.

GREAT MARLBOROUGH STREET,
November 11, 1848.

My dear Sir,

I am sorry to say that absence from town and other circumstances have prevented me from earlier enquiring into the results of the sale of *The Kellys and the O'Kellys*, with which the greatest efforts have been used, but in vain. The sale has been, I regret to say, so small that the loss upon the publication is very considerable; and it appears clear to me that although in consequence of the great number of novels that are published the sale of each, with some few exceptions, must be small, yet it is evident that readers do not like novels on Irish subjects as well as on others. Thus you will perceive it is impossible for me to give any encouragement to you to proceed in novel-writing.

As, however, I understand you have nearly finished the novel *La Vendée*,° perhaps you will favour me with a sight of it when convenient.

I remain, &c &c H. Colburn.

This, though not strictly logical, was a rational letter, telling a plain truth plainly. I did not like the assurance that the 'greatest efforts had been used,' thinking that any efforts which might be made for the popularity of a book ought to have come from the author; – but I took in good part Mr Colburn's assurance that he could not encourage me in the career I had commenced. I would have bet[p] twenty to one against my own success. But, by continuing, I could lose only pen and paper, and if the one chance in twenty did turn up in my favour, then how much might I win!

CHAPTER 5

My First Success.
1849–1855.

I had at once gone to work on a third novel, – and had nearly completed it, when I was informed of the absolute failure of the former. I find however that the agreement for its publication was not made till 1850, – by which time I imagine that Mr Colburn must have forgotten the disastrous result of *The O'Kellys* as he thereby agrees to give me[a] £20 down for my 'new historical novel, to be called *La Vendée*.' He agreed also to pay me £30 more when he had sold 350 copies, and £50 more should he sell 450 within six months. I got my £20, and then heard no more of *La Vendée*, not even receiving any account. Perhaps the historical title had appeared more alluring to him than an Irish subject; – though it was not long afterwards that I received a warning from the very same house of business against historical novels, – as I will tell at length when the proper time comes.

I have no doubt that the result of the sale of this story was no better than that of the two that had gone before. I asked no questions, however, and to this day have received no information. The story is certainly inferior to those which had gone before, – chiefly because I knew accurately the life of the people in Ireland and knew in truth nothing of life in the *La Vendée* country, – and also because the facts of the present time came more within the limits of my powers of story-telling than those of past years. But I read the book the other day, and am not ashamed of it. The conception as to the feeling of the people is I think true, the characters are distinct, and the tale is not dull. As far as I can remember this morsel of criticism is the only one that was ever written on the book.[b]

I had, however, received £20. Alas, alas, years were to roll by before I should earn by my pen another shilling. And indeed I was well aware that I had not earned that, but that the money had been 'talked out of' the worthy publisher by the earnestness of my brother who made the bargain for me. I have known very much of publishers and have been surprised by much in their mode of business, – by the apparent lavishness and by the apparent hardness to all authors in the same men; – but by nothing so much as by the ease with which they can occasionally be persuaded to throw away small sums of money. If you will only make the payment future instead of present you may generally twist a few pounds in your own or your client's favour. 'You might as well promise her twenty pounds. This day six months will do very well.' The publisher, though he knows that the money will never come back to him, thinks it worth his while to rid himself of your importunity at so cheap a price.

But while I was writing *La Vendée* I made a literary attempt in another direction. In 1847 and 1848 there had come upon Ireland the desolation and destruction, first of the famine, and then of the pestilence which followed[c] the famine. It was my duty at that time to be travelling constantly in those parts of Ireland in which the misery and troubles thence arising were, perhaps, at their worst. The western parts of Cork, Kerry, and Clare were preeminently unfortunate. The efforts, – I may say the successful efforts, – made by Government[d] to stay the hand[e] of death will still be in the remembrance of many; – how Sir Robert Peel was instigated to repeal the Corn Laws and how, subsequently, Lord John Russell took measures for employing the people and supplying the country with Indian corn.[2] The expediency of these latter measures was questioned by many. The people themselves wished of course to be fed without working, and the gentry who were mainly responsible for the rates were disposed to think that the management of affairs was taken too much out of their own hands. My mind at the time was busy with the matter, and thinking that the Government was right, I was inclined to defend them as far as my small powers went. S.G.O. (Lord Sydney Godolphin Osborne) was at that time denouncing the Irish scheme of the Administration in the *Times*,[3] using very strong language, – as those who remember his style will know. I fancied then, – as I still think, – that I understood the country much better than he did, and I was anxious to show that the steps taken for mitigating the terrible evil of the times were the best which the Minister of the day could have adopted. In 1848 I was in London, and, full of my purpose, I presented myself to Mr John Forster, – who has since been an intimate and valued friend, – but who was at that time the Editor of the *Examiner*. I think that that portion of the literary world which understands the fabrication of newspapers will admit that neither before his time nor since has there been a more capable Editor of a weekly newspaper. As a literary man he was not without his faults. That which the cabman is reported to have said of him before the magistrate is quite true. He was always 'an arbitrary cove.'[4] As a critic he has belonged[f] to the school of Bentley and Gifford,[5] – who would always bray in a literary mortar all critics who disagreed from them, as though such disagreement were a personal offence, requiring personal castigation. But that very eagerness[g] made him a good Editor. Into whatever he did he put his very heart and soul. During his time the *Examiner* was almost all that a liberal weekly newspaper[h] should be. So to John Forster I went, and was shown into that room on Lincoln's Inn Fields in which, some three or four years earlier, Dickens had given that reading of which there is an illustration with portraits in the second volume of his life.[6]

57

At this time I knew no literary men. A few I had met when living with my mother, but that had been now so long ago that all such acquaintance had died out. I knew who they were, as far as a man could get such knowledge from the papers of the day, and felt myself as in part belonging to the Guild, through my mother, and in some degree by my own unsuccessful efforts. But it was not probable that any one would admit my claim; – nor on this occasion did I make any claim. I stated my name and official position, and the fact that opportunities had been given me of seeing the poor houses in Ireland and of making myself acquainted with the circumstances of the time. Would a series of letters on the subject be accepted by the *Examiner?* The great man, who loomed very large to me, was pleased to say that if the letters should recommend themselves by their style and matter, if they were not too long, and if, – every reader will know how on such occasions an Editor will guard himself, – if this and if that, they should be favourably entertained. They were favourably entertained, – if printing and publication be favourable entertainment. But I heard no more of them. The world in Ireland did not declare that the Government had at[i] last been adequately defended, nor did the Treasurer of the *Examiner* send me a cheque in return.

Whether there ought to have been a cheque I do not even yet know. A man who writes a single letter to a newspaper of course is not paid for it, – nor for any number of letters on some point personal to himself. I have since written sets of letters to newspapers, and have been paid for them, – but then I have bargained for a price. On this occasion I had hopes; – but they never ran high and I was not much disappointed. I have no copy now of those letters, and could not refer to them without much trouble; nor do I remember what I said; but I know that I did my best in writing them.[7]

When my historical novel failed as completely as had its[j] predecessors, the two Irish novels I began to ask myself whether, after all, that was my proper line. I had never thought of questioning the justice of the verdict expressed against me. The idea that I was the unfortunate owner of unappreciated genius never troubled me. I did not look at the books after they were published, feeling sure that they had been, as it were, damned with good reason. But still I was clear in my mind that

I would not lay down my pen. Then and therefore I determined to chance my hand and to attempt a play. I did attempt the play, and in 1850 I wrote a comedy, partly in blank verse and partly in prose, called *The Noble Jilt*. The plot I afterwards used in a novel called *Can You Forgive Her?* I believe that I did give the best of my intellect to the play, and I must own that when it was completed it pleased me much. I copied it and re-copied it, touching it here and touching it there, and then sent it to my[k] very old friend, George Bartley, the actor, who had when I was in London been stage manager of one of the great theatres,[8] and who would, I thought, for my own sake and for my mother's, give me the full benefit of his professional experience.

I have now before me a letter which he wrote to me, – a letter which I have read a score of times. It was altogether condemnatory. 'When I commenced,' he said, 'I had great hopes of your production. I did not think it opened dramatically, but that might have been remedied.' I knew then that it was all over. But as my old friend warmed to the subject the criticism became stronger and stronger, – till my ears tingled. At last came the fatal blow. 'As to the character of your heroine I felt at a loss how to describe it, but you have done it for me in the last speech of Madame Brudo.' Madame Brudo was the heroine's aunt. ' "Margaret, my child, never play the jilt again; 'tis a most unbecoming character. Play it with what skill you will it meets but little sympathy!" And this, be assured, would be its effect upon an audience. So that, I must reluctantly add, that had I been still a manager *The Noble Jilt* is not a play I could have recommended for production.' This was a blow that I did feel. The neglect of a book is a disagreeable fact which grows upon an author by degrees. There is no special moment of agony, – no stunning violence of condemnation. But a piece of criticism such as this, from a friend, and from a man undoubtedly capable of forming an opinion was a blow in the face! But I accepted the judgement loyally, and said not a word on the subject to any one. I merely showed the letter to my wife declaring my conviction, that it must be taken as gospel. And as critical gospel it has since been accepted. In later days I have more than once read the play, and I know that he was right. The dialogue however I think to be good, and I doubt whether some of the scenes be not the brightest and best work I ever did.

Just[l] at this time another literary project loomed before my eyes, and for six or eight months had considerable size. I was introduced to Mr John Murray and proposed to him to write a handbook for Ireland.[9] I explained to him that I knew the country better than most other people, perhaps better than any other person, and could do it well. He asked me to make a trial of my skill and to send him a certain number of pages, undertaking to give me an answer within a fortnight after he should have received my work. I came back to Ireland and for some weeks I laboured very hard. I 'did' the city of Dublin, and the County of Kerry in which lies the lake scenery of Killarney; and I 'did' the route from Dublin to Killarney altogether completing nearly a quarter of the proposed volume. The roll of manuscript was sent to Albemarle Street – but was never opened. At the expiration of nine months from the date on which it reached that time-honoured spot it was returned without a word, in answer to a very angry letter from myself. I insisted on having back my property, – and got it. I need hardly say that my property has never been of the slightest use to me. In all honesty I think that had he been less dilatory John Murray would have got a very good Irish guide at a cheap rate.

Early in 1851, I was sent upon a special job of official[m] work which for two years so completely absorbed my time that I was able to write nothing. A plan was formed for extending the rural delivery of letters and for adjusting the work which up to that time had been done in a very irregular manner. A country Letter Carrier would be sent in one direction in which there were but few letters to be delivered, the arrangement having originated probably at the request of some influential person, while in another direction there was no Letter Carrier because no influential person had exerted himself. It was intended to set this right throughout England, Ireland, and Scotland, and I quickly did the work in the Irish district to which I was attached. I was then invited to do the same in a portion of England, and I spent two of the happiest years of my life at the task. I began in Devonshire and visited I think I may say every nook in that county, in Cornwall, Somersetshire, the greater part of Dorsetshire, the Channel Islands, part of Oxfordshire, Wiltshire, Gloucestershire, Worcestershire, Herefordshire, Monmouthshire, and the six southern Welsh counties. In this way I had an opportunity of seeing a considerable portion of Great Britain with a minuteness which few have enjoyed. And I did my business after a fashion in which no other official man has worked at least for many years. I went almost every where on horseback. I had two hunters of my own, and here and there, where I could, I hired a third horse. I had an Irish groom with me, an old man, who has now been in my service for thirty five years,[10] and in this manner I saw almost every house – I think I may say every house of importance, – in this large district. The object was to create a postal net-work which should catch all recipients of letters. In France it was, and I suppose still is, the practice to deliver every letter. Wherever the man may live to whom a letter is addressed it is the duty of some Letter Carrier to take that letter to his house, – sooner or later. But this of course must be done slowly. With us a delivery much delayed was thought to be worse than none at all. In some places we did establish posts three times a week, and perhaps occasionally twice a week; but such halting arrangements were considered to be objectionable, and we were bound down by a salutary law as to expense which came from our masters at the Treasury. We were not allowed to establish any messenger's walk on which a sufficient number of letters would not be delivered to pay the man's wages counted at a halfpenny a letter. But then the counting was in our own hands, and an enterprising official might be sanguine in his figures. I think I was sanguine. I did not prepare false accounts; but I fear that the Postmasters and clerks who absolutely had the country to do became aware that I was anxious for good results. It is amusing to watch how a passion will grow upon a man. During those two years it was the ambition of my life to cover the country with rural Letter Carriers. I do not remember that in any case a rural post proposed by me was negatived by the authorities, but I fear that some of them broke down afterwards as being too poor, or because in my anxiety to include this house and that I had sent the men too far afield. Our law was that a man should not be required to walk more than sixteen miles a day. Had the work to be done been all on a measured road, there would have been no need for doubt as to the distances. But my Letter Carriers went here and there across the fields. It was my special delight to take them by all short cuts; – and as I measured on horseback the short cuts which they would have to make on foot, perhaps I was sometimes a little unjust to them.

All this I did on horseback, riding on an average forty miles a day. I was paid 6d a mile for the distance travelled and it was necessary that I should at any rate travel enough to pay for my equipage. This I did, and got my hunting out of it also. I have often surprised some small country Postmaster, who had never seen or heard of me before, by coming down upon him at nine in the morning with a red coat and boots and breeches, and interrogating him as to the disposal of every letter which came into his office. And in the same guise I would ride up to farm houses, or parsonages, or other lone residences about the country, and ask the people how they got their letters, at what hour, and especially whether they were delivered free or at a certain charge. For a damnable habit[n] had crept into use, which came to be, in my eyes, at that time, the one sin for which there was no pardon, in accordance with which these rural Letter Carriers used to charge a penny a letter, alleging that the house was out of their beat, and that they must be paid for their extra work. I think that I did stamp out that evil. In all these visits I was in truth a beneficent angel to the public, – bringing everywhere with me an earlier, cheaper, and much more regular delivery of letters. But not unfrequently the angelic nature of my mission was imperfectly understood. I was perhaps a little in a hurry to get on, and did not allow as much time as was necessary to explain to the wondering mistress of the house, or to an open-mouthed farmer, why it was that a man arrayed for hunting, asked so many questions, which might be considered impertinent as applying to his or her private affairs. 'Good morning, Sir. I have just called to ask a few questions. I am a Surveyor of the Post Office. How do you get your letters? As I am a little in a hurry perhaps you can explain at once.' Then I would take out my pencil and note book, and wait for information. And in fact there was no other way in which the truth could be ascertained. Unless I came down suddenly as a summer's storm upon them, the very people who were robbed by our messengers would not confess the robbery, fearing the ill will of the men. It was necessary to startle them into the revelations which I required them to make for their own good. And I did startle them. I became thoroughly used to it, and soon lost my native bashfulness; – but sometimes my visits astonished the retiring inhabitants of country houses. I did, however do my work, and I can look back upon what I did with thorough satisfaction. I was altogether in earnest, and I believe that many a farmer now has his letters brought daily to his house free of charge, who but for me would still have had to send to the post town for them twice a week, or° have paid a man for bringing them irregularly to his door.

This work took up my time so completely, and entailed upon me so great an amount of writing that I was in fact unable to do any literary work. From day to day I thought of it, still purporting to make another effort, and often turning over in my head some fragment of a plot which had occurred to me. But the day did not come in which I could sit down with pen and paper and begin another novel. For, after all, what could it be but a novel? The play had failed more absolutely than the novels, for the novels had attained the honour of print. The cause of this pressure of official work lay, not in the demands of the General Post Office, which more than once expressed itself as astonished by my celerity, but in the necessity which was incumbent on me to travel miles enough to pay for my horses, and upon the amount of correspondence, returns, figures, and reports which such an amount of daily travelling brought with it. I may boast that the work was done very quickly and very thoroughly, – with no fault but an overeagerness to extend postal arrangements far and wide.

✦ In the course of this° job I visited Salisbury and whilst wandering there on a° midsummer evening round the purlieus of the Cathedral I conceived the story of *The Warden*, – from whence came that series of novels of which Barchester with its bishops, deans, and archdeacon was the central site. I may as well declare at once that no one at the commencement could have had less reason than myself to presume himself to be able to write about clergymen. I have been often asked in what period of my early life I had lived so long in a Cathedral city as to have become intimate with the ways of a Close. I never lived in any Cathedral city, – except London, never knew anything of any Close, and at that time had enjoyed no peculiar intimacy with any clergyman.ᶦᶦᶦ My Archdeacon, who has been said to be life-like, and for whom I confess that I have all a parent's fond affection, was, I think, the simple result of an effort of my moral consciousness. It was such as that in my opinion that an archdeacon should be, – or at any rate would be with such advantages as an archdeacon might have; and lo, an Archdeacon was produced who has been declared by competent authorities to be a real archdeacon down to the very ground. And yet, as far as I can remember, I had not then even spoken to an archdeacon. I have felt the compliment to be very great. The Archdeacon came whole from my brain after this fashion, – but in writing about clergymen generally I had to pick up as I went whatever I might know or pretend to know about them. But my first idea had no reference to clergymen in general. I had been struck by two opposite evils, – or what seemed to me to be evils, – and with an absence of all art-judgement in such matters, I thought that I might be able to expose them, or rather to describe them, both in one and the same tale. The first evil was the possession by the Church of certain funds and endowments which had been intended for charitable purposes but which had been allowed to become incomes for idle Church dignitaries. There had been more than one such case brought to public notice at the time, in which there seemed to have been an egregious malversation of charitable purposes. The second evil was its very opposite. Though I had been much struck by the injustice above described, I had also often been angered by the undeserved severity of the newspapers towards the recipients of such incomes, who could hardly be considered to be the chief sinners in the matter. When a man is appointed to a place it is natural that he should accept the income allotted to that place without much enquiry. It is seldom that he will be the first to find out that his services are overpaid. Though he be called upon only to look beautiful and to be dignified upon State occasions he will think £2000 a year little enough for such beauty and dignity as he brings to the task. I felt that there had been some tearing to pieces which might have been spared. But I was altogether wrong in supposing that the two things could be combined. Any writer in advocating a cause must do so after the fashion of an advocate, – or his writing will be ineffective. He should take up one side and cling to that; – and then he may be powerful. There should be no scruples of conscience. Such scruples make a man impotent for such work. It was open to me to have described a bloated parson, with a red nose and all other iniquities, openly neglecting every duty required from him, and living riotously on funds purloined from the poor, – defying as he did so the moderate remonstrances of a virtuous press. Or I might have painted a man as good, as sweet, and as mild as my Warden, who should also have been a hard-working, ill-paid minister of God's word, and might have subjected him to the rancorous venom of some daily Jupiter, who without a leg to stand on, without any true case, might have been induced by personal spite to tear to rags the poor clergyman with poisonous, anonymous, and ferocious leading articles. But neither of these programmes recommended itself to my honesty. Satire, though it may exaggerate the vice it lashes, is not justified in creating it in order that it may be lashed. Caricature may too easily become a slander and satire a libel. I believed in the existence neither of the red-nosed clerical cormorant, nor in that of the venomous assassin of the journals. I did believe that through want of care and the natural tendency of every class to take care of itself money had slipped into the pockets of certain clergymen which should have gone elsewhere; and I believed also, that through the equally natural propensity of men to be as strong as they know how to be, certain writers of the press had allowed themselves to use language which was cruel, though it was in a good cause. But the two objects should not have been combined; – and I now know myself well enough to be aware that I was not the man to have carried out either of them.

Nevertheless I thought much about it, and on the 29th July 1853, – having been then two years without having made any literary effort, – I began *The Warden* at Tenbury in Worcestershire. It was then more than twelve months since I had stood for an hour on the bridge in Salisbury and had made out to my own satisfaction the spot on which Hiram's hospital should stand. Certainly no other work[s] that I ever did took up so much of my thoughts. On this occasion I did no more than write the first chapter, even if so much. I had determined that my official work should be moderated, so as to allow me some time for writing; but then, just at this time, I was sent to take the postal charge of the northern counties in Ireland, – of Ulster and the Counties Meath and Louth. Hitherto in official language I had been a Surveyor's clerk, – now I was to be a Surveyor. The difference consisted mainly in an encrease of income from about £450 to about £800; – for at that time the sum netted still depended on the number of miles travelled. Of course that English work to which I had become so warmly wedded, had to be abandoned. Other parts of England were being done by other men, and I had nearly finished the area which had been entrusted to me. I should have liked to ride over the whole country and to have sent a rural-post Letter Carrier to every' parish, every village, every hamlet, and every grange in England.

We were at this time very much unsettled as regards any residence. While we were living at Clonmel two sons had been born, who certainly were important enough to have been mentioned sooner. At Clonmel we had lived in lodgings, and from there had moved to Mallow, a town in the County Cork, where we had taken a house. Mallow was in the centre of a hunting country and had been very pleasant to me. But our house there had been given up when it was known that I should be detained in England; and then we had wandered about in the Western Counties, moving our head quarters from one town to another. During this time we had lived at Exeter, at Bristol, at Carmarthen, at Cheltenham, and at Worcester. Now we again moved and settled ourselves for eighteen months at Belfast. After that we took a house at Donnybrook, the well-known suburb of Dublin.

The work of taking up a new district, which requires not only that the man doing it should know the nature of the postal arrangements, but also the characters and the peculiarities of the Postmasters and their clerks, was too heavy to allow of my going on with my book at once. It was not till the end of 1852 that I recommenced it, and it was in the autumn of 1853 that I finished the work. It was only one small volume, and in later days would have been completed in six weeks, – or in two months at the longest if other work had pressed. On looking at the title page, I find that it was not published till 1855. I had made acquaintance through my friend John Merivale with William Longman the publisher, and had received from him an assurance that the manuscript should be 'looked at'. It was 'looked at', and Messrs Longman made me an offer to publish it at half profits. I had no reason to love 'half profits,' but I was very anxious to have my book published and I acceded. It was now more than ten years since I had commenced writing *The Macdermots*, and I thought that if any success was to be achieved the time surely had come. I had not been impatient, but, if there was to be a time, surely it had come.

The novel reading world did not go mad about *The Warden*, but I soon felt that it had not failed as the others had failed. There were notices of it in the press, and I could discover that people around me knew that I had written a book. Mr Longman was complimentary and after a while informed me that there would be profits to divide. At the end of 1855 I received a cheque for £9 8s. 8d., which was the first money I had ever earned by literary work – that £20 which poor Mr Colburn had been made to pay certainly never having been earned at all. At the end of 1856 I received another sum of £10 15s. 1d. The pecuniary success was not great. Indeed as regarded remuneration for the time stone breaking would have done better. A thousand copies were printed, of which after a lapse of five or six years about 300 had to be converted into another form and sold as belonging to a cheap edition. In its original form *The Warden* never reached the essential honour of a second edition.

I have already said of the work that it failed altogether in the purport for which it was intended. But it has a merit of its own, – a merit, by my own perception of which I was enabled to see wherein lay whatever strength I did possess. The characters of the Bishop, of the Archdeacon, of the Archdeacon's wife, and especially of the Warden are all well and clearly drawn. I had realised to myself a series of portraits and had been able so to put them on the canvas that my readers should see that which I meant them to see. There is no gift which an author can have more useful to him than this. And the style of the English was good, though from most unpardonable carelessness the grammar was not unfrequently faulty. With such results I had no doubt but that I would at once begin another novel.[u]

I will here say one word as a long-deferred answer to an item of criticism which appeared in the *Times* newspaper as to *The Warden*. In an article – if I remember rightly on *The Warden* and *Barchester Towers* combined; – which I would call good-natured but that I take it for granted that the critics of the *Times* are actuated by higher motives than good nature, that little book and its sequel are spoken of in terms which were very pleasant to the author. But there was added to this a gentle word of rebuke at the morbid condition of the author's mind which had prompted him to indulge in personalities, – the personalities in question having reference to some Editor or Manager of the *Times* newspaper. For I had introduced one Tom Towers as being potent among the contributors to the 'Jupiter', under which name I certainly did allude to the *Times*. But at that time, living away in Ireland, I had not even heard the name of any gentleman connected with the *Times* newspaper, and could not have intended to represent any individual by Tom Towers. As I had created an archdeacon, so had I created a journalist, and the one creation was no more personal or indicative of morbid tendencies than the other. If Tom Towers was at all like any gentleman then connected with the *Times* my moral consciousness must again have been very powerful.[12]

CHAPTER 6

'Barchester Towers' and the 'Three Clerks'.
1855–1858.

It was, I think, before I started on my English tours among the rural posts that I made my first attempt at writing for a magazine. I had read soon after they came out the two first volumes of Charles Merivale's *History of the Romans under the Empire*[1] and had got into some correspondence with the author's brother as to the author's views about Caesar. Hence arose in my mind a tendency to investigate the character of probably the greatest man who ever lived, which tendency in after years produced a little book[2] of which I shall have to speak when its time comes, – and also a taste generally for latin literature which has been one of the chief delights of my later life. And I may say that I became at this time as anxious about Caesar and as desirous of reaching the truth as to his character as we all have been in regard to Bismarck[3] in these latter days. I lived in Caesar, and debated with myself constantly whether he crossed the Rubicon[4] as a tyrant, or a patriot. In order that I might review Mr Merivale's book without feeling that I was dealing unwarrantably with a subject beyond me I studied the *Commentaries* thoroughly and went through a mass of other reading which the object of a magazine article hardly justified, – but which has thoroughly justified itself in the subsequent pursuits of my life. I did write two articles, the first mainly on Julius Caesar and the second on Augustus, which appeared in the *Dublin University Magazine.*[5] They were the result of very much labour, but there came from them no pecuniary product. I had been very modest when I sent them to the Editor, as I had been when I called on John Forster, not venturing to suggest the subject of money. After a while I did call upon the proprietor of the magazine in Dublin and was told by him that such articles were generally written to oblige friends, and that articles written to oblige friends were not usually paid for. The Dean of Ely, as the author of the work in question now is, was my friend; but I think I was wronged as I certainly had no intention of obliging him by my criticism. Afterwards when I returned to Ireland I wrote other articles for the same magazine, one of which, intended to be very savage in its denunciation, was on an official blue book just then brought out preparatory to the introduction of competitive examinations for the Civil Service. For that and some other article,[6] I now forget what, I was paid. Up to the end of 1857 I had received £55 for the hard work of ten years.

It was while I was engaged on *Barchester Towers* that I adopted a system of writing which for some years afterwards I found to be very serviceable to me. My time was greatly occupied in travelling, and the nature of my travelling was now changed. I could not any longer do it on horseback. Railroads afforded me my means of conveyance, and I found that I passed in railway carriages very many hours of my existence. Like others I used to read, – though Carlyle has since told me that a man when travelling should not read but 'sit still and label his thoughts.'[7] But if I intended to make a profitable business out of my writing, and at the same time to do my best for the Post Office, I must turn these hours to more account than I could do even by reading. I made for myself therefore a tablet and found after a few days' exercise that I could write as quickly in a railway carriage as I could at my desk. I worked with a pencil and what I wrote my wife copied afterwards. In this way was composed the greater part of *Barchester Towers* and of the novel which succeeded it, and much also of others subsequent to them. My only objection to the practice came from the appearance of literary ostentation to which I felt myself to be subject when going to work before four or five fellow passengers. But I got used to it as I had done to the amazement of the West Country farmers' wives when asking them after their letters.

In the writing of *Barchester Towers* I took great delight. The Bishop and Mrs Proudie were very real to me, as were also the troubles of the Archdeacon and the loves of Mr Slope. When it was done Mr W. Longman required that it should be subjected to his reader, and he returned the manuscript to me with a most laborious and voluminous criticism,[8] – coming from whom I never knew. This was accompanied by an offer to print the novel on the half profit system, with a payment of £100 in advance out of my half profits, – on condition that I would comply with the suggestions made by his critic. One of these suggestions required that I should cut the novel down to two volumes. In my reply I went through the criticisms, rejecting one and accepting another, almost alternately, but declaring at last that no consideration should induce me to put out a third of my work. I am at a loss to know how such a task could be performed. I could burn the manuscript, no doubt, and write another book on the same story; but how two words out of every six are to be withdrawn from a written novel I cannot conceive. I believe such tasks have been attempted, – perhaps performed; but I refused to make even the attempt. Mr Longman was too gracious to insist on his critic's terms, and the book was published, certainly none the worse, and I do not think much the better, for the care that had been taken with it.

The work succeeded just as *The Warden* had succeeded. It achieved no great reputation but it was one of the novels which novel readers were called upon to read. Perhaps I may be assuming more to myself[a] than I have a right to do in saying, now, that *Barchester Towers* has become one of those novels which do not die quite at once, – which live and are read for perhaps a quarter of a century; but if that be so, its life has been so far prolonged by the vitality of some of its younger brothers. *Barchester Towers* would hardly be so well known as it is, had there been no *Framley Parsonage* and no *Last Chronicle of Barset*.

I received my £100, in advance, with profound delight. It was a positive and most welcome encrease to my income, and might probably be regarded as a first real step in the road[b] to substantial success. I am well aware that there are many who think that an author in his authorship should not regard money, – nor a painter or sculptor or composer in his art. I do not know that this unnatural self-sacrifice is supposed to extend itself further. A barrister, a clergyman, a doctor, an engineer, and even actors and architects, may without disgrace follow the bent of human nature and endeavour to fill their bellies and clothe their backs, and also those of their wives and children, as comfortably as they can by the exercise of their abilities and crafts. They may be as rationally realistic, as may the butchers and the bakers; – but the artist and the author forget the high glories of their callings if they condescend to make a money return a first object. They who preach this doctrine will be much offended by my theory and by this book of mine, if my theory and my book come beneath their notice. They require the practice of a so-called virtue which is contrary to nature and which, in my eyes, would be no virtue if it were practised. They are like clergymen who preach sermons against the love of money, but who know that the love of money is so distinctive a characteristic of humanity that such sermons are mere platitudes, called for by customary but unintelligent piety. All material progress has come from man's desire to do the best he can for himself and those about him, and civilisation, and Christianity itself, have been made possible by such progress. Though we do not all of us argue this matter out within our breasts we do all feel it; and we know that the more a man earns the more useful he is to his fellow men. The most useful lawyers as a rule have been those who have made the greatest incomes, – and it is the same with the doctors. It would be the same in the Church if they who have the choosing of bishops always chose the best man. And it has in truth been so too in art and authorship. Did Titian or Rubens disregard their pecuniary rewards? As far as we know Shakespeare worked always for money, giving the best of his intellect to support his trade as an actor. In our own century what literary names stand higher than those of Byron, Tennyson, Scott, Dickens, Macaulay and Carlyle? And I think I may say that none of those great men neglected the pecuniary result of their labours. Now and then a man may arise among us who in any calling, whether it be in law, in physic, in religious teaching, in art, or literature,^{c} may, in his professional enthusiasm, utterly disregard money. All will honour his enthusiasm, and if he be wifeless and childless, his disregard of the great object of men's work will be blameless. But it is a mistake to suppose that a man is a better man because he despises money. Few do so, and those few, in doing so suffer a defeat. Who does not desire to be hospitable to his friends, generous to the poor, liberal to all, munificent to his children, and to be himself free from the carking fears which poverty creates? The subject will not stand an argument, – and yet authors are told that they should disregard payment for their work, and be content to devote their unbought brains to the welfare of the public. Brains that are unbought will never serve the public much. Take away from English authors their copyrights, and you would very soon take away also from England her authors.

I say this here, because it is my purpose as I go on to state what to me has been the result of my profession in the ordinary way in which professions are regarded, so that by my example may be seen what prospect there is that a man devoting himself to literature with industry, perseverance, certain necessary aptitudes, and fair average talents, may succeed in gaining a livelihood, as another man does in another profession. The result with me has been comfortable but not splendid, as I think was to have been expected from the combination of such gifts.

I have certainly always had also before my eyes the charms of reputation. Over and above the money view of the question I wished from the beginning to be something more than a clerk in the Post Office. To be known as somebody, – to be Anthony Trollope if it be no more, – is to me much. The feeling is a very general one, and I think beneficent. It is that which has been called the 'last infirmity of noble minds.'^{9} The infirmity is so human that the man who lacks it is either above or below humanity. I own to the infirmity. But I confess that my first object in taking to literature as a profession was that which is common to the barrister when he goes to the bar, and to the baker when he sets up his oven. I wished to make an income on which I and those belonging to me might live in comfort.

If indeed a man writes his books badly or paints his pictures badly because he can make his money faster, in that fashion, than by doing them well and at the same time proclaims them to be the best he can do, – if, in fact, he sells shoddy for broad-cloth, – he is dishonest as is any other fraudulent dealer. So may be the barrister who takes money that he does not earn, or the clergyman who is contented[d] to live on a sinecure. No doubt the author or the artist may have a difficulty which will not occur to the seller of cloth in settling within himself what is good work and what is bad, – when labour enough has been given, and when the task has been scamped. It is a danger as to which he is bound to be severe with himself, – in which he should feel that his conscience should be set fairly in the balance against the natural bias of his interest. If he do not do so, sooner or later his dishonesty will be discovered, and he will be estimated accordingly. But in this he is to be bound[e] only by the plain rules of honesty which should govern us all. Having said so much, I shall not scruple as I go on to attribute to the pecuniary result of my labours all the importance which I felt them to have at the time.

Barchester Towers, for which I had received £100 in advance sold well enough to bring me further payments, – moderate payments from the publishers. From that day up to this very time in which I am writing, that book and *The Warden* together have given me almost every year some small income. I get the accounts very regularly and I find that I have received £727 11s. 3d. for the two. It is more than I got for the three or four works that came afterwards, but the payments have been spread over twenty years.

When I went to Mr Longman with my next novel, *The Three Clerks*, in my hand I could not induce him to understand that a lump sum down was more pleasant than a deferred annuity. I wished him to buy it from me at a price which he might think to be a fair value, and I argued with him that as soon as an author has put himself into a position which ensures a sufficient sale of his works to give a profit, the publisher is not entitled to expect the half of such proceeds. While there is a pecuniary risk the whole of which must be borne by the publisher, such division is fair enough; but such a demand on the part of the publisher is monstrous as soon as the article produced is known to be a marketable commodity. I thought that I had now reached that point, but Mr Longman did not agree with me. And he endeavoured to convince me that I might lose more than I gained even though I should get more money by going elsewhere. 'It is for you,' said he, 'to think whether our names on your title page are not worth more to you than the encreased payment.' This seemed to me to savour of that high-flown doctrine of the contempt of money which I have never admired. I did think much of Messrs Longman's name, but I liked it best at the bottom of a cheque.

I was also scared from the august columns of Paternoster Row[10] by a remark made to myself by one of the firm which seemed to imply that they did not much care for works of fiction. Speaking of a fertile writer of tales who was not then dead he declared that — (naming the author in question), had spawned upon them (the publishers) three novels a year! Such language is perhaps justifiable, in regard to a man who shows so much of the fecundity of the herring; but I did not know how fruitful might be my own muse, and I thought that I had better go elsewhere.

I had then written *The Three Clerks* which, when I could not sell it to Messrs Longmans, I took in the first instance to Messrs Hurst & Blackett who had become successors to Mr Colburn. I had made an appointment with one of the firm, which however that gentleman was unable to keep. I was on my way from Ireland to Italy and had but one day in London in which to dispose of my manuscript. I sat for an hour in Great Marlborough Street expecting the return of the peccant publisher who had broken his tryst, and I was about to depart with my bundle under my arm when the foreman of the house came to me. He seemed to think it a pity that I should go and wished me to leave my work with him. This, however, I would not do unless he would undertake to buy it then and there. Perhaps he lacked authority. Perhaps his judgement was against such purchase. But while we debated the matter he gave me some advice. 'I hope it's not historical, Mr Trollope,' he said. 'Whatever you do, don't be historical. Your historical novel is not worth a damn.' Thence I took *The Three Clerks* to Mr Bentley and on the same afternoon succeeded in selling it to him for £250. His son still possesses it, and the firm have I believe done very well with the purchase. It was certainly the best novel I had as yet written. The plot is not so good as that of the *Macdermots*, nor are there any characters in the book equal to those of Mrs Proudie and the Warden; – but the work has a more continued interest, and contains the first well-described love-scene that I ever wrote. The passage in which Kate Woodward, thinking that she will die, tries to take leave of the lad she loves, still brings tears to my eyes when I read it. I had not the heart to kill her. I never could do that. And I do not doubt but that they are living happily together to this day.

The lawyer Chaffanbrass made his first appearance in this novel and I do not think that I have cause to be ashamed of him. But this novel now is chiefly noticeable to me from the fact that in it I introduced a character under the name of Sir Gregory Hardlines by which I intended to lean very heavily on that much loathed scheme of competitive examination of which at that time Sir Charles Trevelyan was the great apostle.[11] Sir Gregory Hardlines was intended for Sir Charles Trevelyan, – as any one at the time would know who had taken an interest in the Civil Service. 'We always call him Sir Gregory,' Lady Trevelyan said to me afterwards when I came to know her and her husband. I never learned to love competitive examination, but I became and am, very fond of Sir Charles Trevelyan. Sir Stafford Northcote, who is now Chancellor of the Exchequer,[12] was then leagued with his friend Sir Charles, and he too appears in *The Three Clerks* under the feebly facetious name of Sir Warwick West End.

But for all that *The Three Clerks* was a good novel.[f]

When that sale was made I was on my way to Italy with my wife, paying a third visit there to my mother and brother. This was in 1857, and she had then given up her pen. It was the first year in which she had not written, and she expressed to me her delight that her labours should be at an end and that mine should be beginning in the same field. In truth they had already been continued for a dozen years, but a man's career will generally be held to date itself from the commencement of his success. On those foreign tours I always encountered adventures which as I look back upon them now tempt me almost to write a little book of my long past continental travels. On this occasion as we made our way slowly through Switzerland and over the Alps we encountered again and again a poor forlorn Englishman, who had no friend and no aptitude for travelling. He was always losing his way and finding himself with no seat in the coaches and no bed at the inns. On one occasion I found him at Coire[13] seated at 5 a.m. in the *coupé* of a diligence[14] which was intended to start at noon for the Engadine, while it was his purpose to go over the Alps in another which was to leave at 5.30, and which was already crowded with passengers. 'Ah,' he said 'I am in time now, and nobody shall turn me out of this seat,' alluding to former little misfortunes of which I had been a witness. When I explained to him his position, he was as one to whom life was too bitter to be borne. But he made his way into Italy and encountered me again at the Pitti palace in Florence. 'Can you tell me something,' he said to me in a whisper, having touched my shoulder. 'The people are so ill-natured I don't like to ask them. Where is it they keep The Medical Venus?' I sent him to the Uffizzi, but I fear he was disappointed.[15]

We ourselves, however, on entering Milan had been in quite as much distress as any that he suffered. We had not written for beds, and on driving up to a hotel at ten in the evening found it full. Thence we went from one hotel to another finding them all full. The misery is one well known to travellers, but I never heard of another case in which a man and his wife were told at midnight to get out of the conveyance into the middle of the street because the horse could not be made to go any further. Such was our condition. I induced the driver, however, to go again to the hotel which was nearest to him, and which was kept by a German. Then I bribed the porter to get the master to come down to me; and, though my French is ordinarily very defective, I spoke with such eloquence to that German innkeeper that he, throwing his arms round my neck in a transport of compassion, swore that he would never leave me nor my wife till he had put us to bed. And he did so; but, ah, there were so many in those beds! It is such an experience as this which teaches a travelling foreigner how different on the continent is the accommodation provided for him, and that which is supplied for the inhabitants of the country.

It was on a previous visit to Milan, when the telegraph wires were only just opened to the public by the Austrian authorities,[16] that we had decided one day at dinner that we would go to Verona that night. There was a train at six reaching Verona at midnight, and we asked some servant of the hotel to telegraph for us, ordering supper and beds. The demand seemed to create some surprise; but we persisted, and were only mildly grieved when we found ourselves charged twenty zwanzigers[17] for the message. Telegraphy was new at Milan and the prices were intended to be almost prohibitory. We paid our twenty zwanzigers and went on, consoling ourselves with the thought of our ready supper and our assured beds. When we reached Verona there arose a great cry along the platform for Signor Trollope. I put out my head and declared my identity, when I was waited upon by a glorious personage, dressed like a beau for a ball, with half a dozen others almost as glorious behind him, who informed me with his hat in his hand that he was the landlord of the 'Due Torre.' It was a heating moment, but it became more hot when he asked me after my people, – 'mes gens.' I could only turn round, and point to my wife and brother-in-law. I had no other 'people.' There were three carriages provided for us, each with a pair of grey horses. When we reached the house it was all lit up. We were not allowed to move without an attendant with a lighted candle. It was only gradually that the mistake came to be understood. On us there was still the horror of the bill, the extent of which could not be known till the hour of departure had come. The landlord, however, had acknowledged to himself that his inductions had been ill-founded, and he treated us with clemency. He had never before received a telegram.

I apologise for these tales which are certainly outside my purpose, and will endeavour to tell no more that shall not have a closer relation to my story. I had finished *The Three Clerks*[18] just before I left England, and when in Florence was cudgelling my brain for a new plot. Being then with my brother I asked him to sketch me a plot, and he drew out that of my next novel, called *Doctor Thorne*.[g19] I mention this particularly because it was the only occasion in which I have had recourse to other[h] source than my own brains for the thread of a story. How far I may unconsciously have adopted incidents from what I have read, –

either from history or from works of imagination, – I do not know. It is beyond question that a man employed as I have been must do so. But when doing it I have not been aware that I have done it. I have never taken on another man's work and deliberately framed my work upon it. I am far from censuring this practice in others. Our greatest masters in works of imagination have obtained such aid for themselves. Shakespeare dug out of such quarries wherever he could find them. Ben Jonson, with heavier hand, built up his structures on his studies of the classics, not thinking it beneath him, to give, without direct acknowledgment, whole pieces translated both from poets and historians. But in those days no such acknowledgment was usual. Plagiary[i] existed and was very common; – but was not known as a sin. It is different now; – and I think that an author when he uses either the words or the plot of another, should own as much, demanding to be credited with no more of the work than he has himself produced. I may say also that I have never printed as my own a word that has been written by others.* It might probably have been better for my readers had I done so, as I am informed that *Doctor Thorne* the novel of which I am now speaking has a larger sale than any other book of mine.

Early in 1858, while I was writing *Doctor Thorne*, I was asked by the great men at the General Post Office to go to Egypt to make a treaty with the Pasha[21] for the conveyance of our mails through that country by railway. There was a treaty in existence, but that had reference to the carriage of bags and boxes by camels from Alexandria to Suez. Since its date the railway had grown and was now nearly completed, and a new treaty was wanted. So I came over from Dublin to London, on my road, and again went to work among the publishers. The other novel was not finished, but I thought that I had now progressed far enough to arrange a sale while the work was still on the stocks. I went to Mr Bentley and demanded £400, – for the copyright. He acceded, but came to me the next morning at the General Post Office to say that it could not be. He had gone to work at his figures after I had left him

---

* I must make one exception to this declaration. The legal opinion as to heirlooms in *The Eustace Diamonds* was written for me by Charles Merewether[20] the present member for Northampton. I am told that it has become the ruling authority on the subject.

and found that £300 would be the outside value of the novel. I was in-
tent upon the larger sum and, in furious haste, – for I had but an hour
at my disposal, – I rushed to Chapman & Hall in Piccadilly, and said
what I had to say to Mr Edward Chapman[22] in a quick torrent of words.
They were the first of a great many words which have since been
spoken by me in that back shop. Looking at me as he might have done
at a highway robber who had stopped him on Hounslow Heath he said
that he supposed that he might as well do as I desired. I considered this
to be a sale, – and it was a sale. I remember that he held the poker in
his hand all the time that I was with him; – but in truth, even though
he had declined to buy the book, there would have been no danger.

CHAPTER 7

*'Doctor Thorne' – 'The Bertrams' – 'The West Indies'
and the 'Spanish Main'.*

As I journeyed across France to Marseilles and made thence a terribly
rough voyage to Alexandria I wrote my allotted number of pages
every day. On this occasion more than once I left my paper on the
cabin table, rushing away to be sick in the privacy of my state room. It
was February and the weather was miserable, but still I did my work.
Labor omnia vincit improbus.[a1] I do not say that to all men has been given
physical strength sufficient for such exertion as this, but I do believe
that real exertion will enable most men to work at almost any season. I
had, previously to this, arranged a system of task work for myself
which I would strongly recommend to those who feel, as I have felt,
that labour, when not made absolutely obligatory by the circumstances
of the hour, should never be allowed to become spasmodic. There was
no day on which it was my positive duty to write for the publishers, as
it was my duty to write reports for the Post Office. I was free to be idle
if I pleased. But as I had made up my mind to undertake this second
profession I found it to be expedient to bind myself by certain self-
imposed laws. When I have commenced a new book, I have always

prepared a diary,[2] divided into weeks, and carried it on for the period which I have allowed myself for the completion of the work. In this I have entered, day by day, the number of pages I have written, so that if, at any time, I have slipped into idleness for a day or two, the record of that idleness has been there, staring me in the face and demanding of me encreased labour so that the deficiency might be supplied. According to the circumstances of the time, – whether my other business might be then heavy or light, or whether the book which I was writing was or was not wanted with speed, – I have allotted myself so many pages a week. The average number has been about forty. It has been placed as low as twenty and has risen to 112. And as page is an ambiguous term, my page has been made to contain 250 words; and as words, if not watched, will have a tendency to straggle, I have had every word counted as I went. In the bargains I have made with publishers I have, – not of course with their knowledge, but in my own mind, – undertaken always to supply them with so many words, and I have never put a book out of hand short of the number by a single word. I may also say that the excess has been very small. I have prided myself on completing my work exactly within the proposed dimensions. But I have prided myself especially on completing it within the proposed time, – and I have always done so. There has ever been the record before me and a week passed with an insufficient number of pages has been a blister to my eye, and a month, so disgraced, would have been a sorrow to my heart.

I have been told that such appliances are beneath the notice of a man of genius. I have never fancied myself to be a man of genius, but had I been so I think I might well have subjected myself to these trammels. Nothing surely is so potent as a law that may not be disobeyed. It has the force of the water-drop that hollows the stone.[3] A small daily task, if it be really daily, will beat the labours of a spasmodic Hercules. It is the tortoise which always catches the hare. The hare has no chance. He loses more time in glorifying himself for a quick spurt than suffices for the tortoise to make half his journey.

I have known authors whose lives have always been troublesome and painful because their tasks have never been done in time. They have ever been as boys struggling to learn their lesson as they entered the school gates. Publishers have distrusted them, and they have failed to write their best because they have seldom written at ease. I have done double their work, – though burdened with another profession, – and have done it almost without an effort. I have not once, through all my literary career, felt myself in danger of being late with my task. I have known no anxiety as to 'copy'. The needed pages, far ahead, – very far ahead, – have almost always been in the drawer beside me. And that little diary, with its dates and ruled spaces, its record that must be seen, its daily, weekly demand upon my industry, has done all that for me.

There are those who would be ashamed to subject themselves to such a task master and who think that the man who works with his imagination should allow himself to wait till – inspiration moves him. When I have heard such doctrine preached I have hardly been able to repress my scorn. To me it would not be more absurd if the shoe-maker[4] were to wait for inspiration, or the tallow-chandler for the divine moment of melting. If the man whose business it is to write has eaten too many good things, or has drunk[b] too much, or smoked too many cigars, – as men who write sometimes will do, – then his condition may be unfavourable for work; but so will be the condition of a shoemaker who has[c] been similarly imprudent. I have sometimes thought that the inspiration wanted has been the remedy which time will give to the evil results of such imprudence. *Mens sana in corpore sano*[5] The author wants that, as does every other workman, – that and a habit of industry. I was once told that the surest aid to the writing of a book was a piece of cobbler's wax on my chair. I certainly believe in the cobbler's wax much more than the inspiration.

It will be said, perhaps, that a man whose work has risen to no higher pitch than mine has attained has no right to speak of the strains and impulses to which real genius is exposed. I am ready to admit the great variations in brain power which are exhibited by the products of different men, and am not disposed to rank my own very high; but my experience[d] tells me that a man can always do the work for which his brain is fitted, if he will give himself the habit of regarding his work as the normal condition of his life. I therefore venture to advise young men who look forward to authorship as the business of their lives, even when they propose that the authorship should be of the highest class known, to avoid enthusiastic rushes with their pens and to seat themselves at their desks day by day, as though they were lawyers' clerks; – and so let them sit until the allotted task shall be accomplished.

While I was in Egypt I finished *Doctor Thorne*, and on the following day began *The Bertrams*. I was moved now by a determination to excel, if not in quality, at any rate in quantity. An ignoble ambition for an author, my readers will, no doubt, say. But not, I think, altogether ignoble if an author can bring himself to look at his work as does any other workman. This had become my task, this was the furrow in which my plough was set, this was the thing the doing of which had fallen into my hands, and I was minded to work at it with a will. It is not on my conscience that I have ever scamped my work. My novels, whether good or bad, have been as good as I could make them. Had I taken three months of idleness between each they would have been no better. Feeling convinced of this[e] I finished *Doctor Thorne* on one day, and began the *Bertrams* on the next.

I had then been nearly two months in Egypt and had at last succeeded in settling the terms of a postal treaty. Nearly twenty years have passed since that time, and other years may yet run on before these pages are printed. I trust I may commit no official sin by describing here the nature of the difficulty which met me. I found on my arrival that I was to communicate with an officer of the Pasha who was then called Nubar Bey.[6] I presume him to have been the gentleman who has lately dealt with our Government as to the Suez canal shares and who is now well known to the political world as Nubar Pasha. I found him a most courteous gentleman, an Armenian. I never went to his office nor do I know that he had an office. Every other day he would come to me at my hotel and bring with him servants and pipes and coffee. I enjoyed his coming greatly, but there was one point on which we could not agree. As to money and other details it seemed as though he could hardly accede fast enough to the wishes of the Postmaster General, but on one point he was firmly opposed to me. I was desirous that the mails should be carried through Egypt in twenty four hours, and he thought that forty eight hours should be allowed. I was obstinate and he was obstinate, and for a long time we could come to no agreement. At last his oriental tranquillity seemed to desert him, and he took upon himself to assure me with almost more than British energy that, if I insisted on the quick transit a terrible responsibility would rest on my own head.[f] I made this mistake, he said – that I supposed that a rate of travelling which would be easy and secure in England could be attained with safety in Egypt. 'The Pasha, his master, would,' he said, 'no doubt accede to any terms demanded by the British Post Office, so great was his reverence for everything British. In that case he, Nubar, would at once resign his position and retire into obscurity. He would be ruined; but the loss of life and bloodshed which would certainly follow so rash an attempt should not be on his head.' I smoked my pipe, or rather his, and drank his coffee, with oriental quiescence, but British firmness. Every now and again, through three or four visits, I renewed the expression of my opinion that the transit could easily be made in twenty four hours. At last he gave way, – and astonished me by the cordiality of his greeting. There was no longer any question of bloodshed or of resignation of office, as[g] he assured me with energetic complaisance that it should be his care to see that the time was punctually kept. It was punctually kept and I believe is so still. I must confess, however, that my persistency was not the result of any courage specially personal to myself. While the matter was being debated it had been whispered to me that the Peninsular and Oriental Steam Ship Company had conceived that forty eight hours would suit the purposes of their traffic better than twenty four, and that as they were the great paymasters on the railway the Minister of the Egyptian State who managed the railway might probably wish to accommodate them. I often wondered who originated that frightful picture of blood and desolation. That it came from an English heart and an English hand I was always sure.

From Egypt I visited the Holy Land, and on my way inspected the Post Offices in Malta and Gibraltar. I could fill a volume with true tales of my adventures. The *Tales of All Countries* have, most of them, some foundation in such occurrences. There is one called 'John Bull on the Guadalquivir', the chief incident in which occurred to me and a friend of mine on our way up that river to Seville. We both of us handled the gold ornaments of a man whom we believed to be a bull-fighter, but who turned out to be a Duke; – and a Duke too who could speak English! How gracious he was to us and yet how thoroughly he covered us with ridicule!

On my return home I received £400 from Messrs Chapman & Hall for *Doctor Thorne*, and agreed to sell them *The Bertrams* for the same sum. This latter novel was written under very vagrant circumstances, – at Alexandria, Malta, Gibraltar, Glasgow, – then at sea, and at last finished in Jamaica. Of my journey to the West Indies I will say a few words presently, but I may as well speak of these two novels here. *Doctor Thorne* has, I believe, been the most popular book that I have written, – if I may take the sale as proof of comparative popularity. *The Bertrams* has had quite an opposite fortune. I do not know that I have ever heard it well spoken of even by my friends, and I cannot remember that there is any character in it that has dwelt in the minds of novel readers. I myself think that they are of about equal merit, but that neither of them is good. They fall away very much from *The Three Clerks* both in pathos and humour. There is no personage in either of them comparable to Chaffanbrass the lawyer. The plot of *Doctor Thorne* is good, and I am led therefore to suppose that a good plot, – which to my own feeling is the most insignificant part of a tale, – is that which will most raise it or most condemn it in the public judgement. The plots of *Tom Jones* and of *Ivanhoe* are almost perfect, and they are probably the most popular novels of the schools of the last and of this century; but to me the delicacy of Amelia and the rugged strength of Burley and Meg Merrilies[7] say more for the power of those great novelists than[h] the gift of construction shown in the two works I have named. A novel should give a picture of common life enlivened by humour, and sweetened by pathos. To make that picture worthy of attention the canvas should be crowded with real portraits, – not of individuals known to the world or to the author, – but of created personages impregnated with traits of character which are known. To my thinking the plot is but the vehicle for all this; and when you have the vehicle without the passengers, a story of mystery in which the agents never spring to life, you have but a wooden show. There must however be a story. You must provide a vehicle of some sort. That of *The Bertrams* was more than ordinarily bad, and as the book was redeemed[i] by no special character it failed. Its failure never surprised me; – but I have been surprised by the success of *Doctor Thorne*.

At this time there was nothing in the success of the one or the failure of the other to affect me very greatly. The immediate sale, and the notices elicited from the critics, and the feeling which had now come to me of a confident standing with the publishers, all made me know that I had achieved my object. If I wrote a novel I could certainly sell it. And if I could publish three in two years, – confining myself to half the fecundity of that terrible author of whom the publisher in Paternoster Row had complained to me, – I might add £600 a year to my official income. I was still living in Ireland and could keep a good house over my head, insure my life, educate my two boys, and hunt perhaps twice a week very comfortably on[j] £1400 a year. If more should come, it would be well; – but £600 a year I was prepared to reckon as success. It had been slow in coming but was very pleasant when it came.

On my return from Egypt I was sent down to Scotland to revise the Glasgow Post Office. I almost forget now what it was that I had to do there, but I know that I walked all over the city with the Letter Carriers, going up to the top flats of the houses, as the men would have declared me incompetent to judge the extent of their labours, had I not trudged every step with them. It was midsummer and wearier work I never performed. The men would grumble, and then I would think how it would be with them if they had to go home afterwards and write a love scene. But the love scenes written in Glasgow, – all belonging to *The Bertrams*, – are not good.

Then in the autumn of that year, – 1858 – I was asked to go to the West Indies and cleanse the Augean stables[8] of our Post Office system there. Up to that time, and at that time, our colonial post offices generally were managed from home and were subject to the British Postmaster General. Gentlemen were sent out from England to be Postmasters, Surveyors, and what not; and as our West Indian islands have never been regarded as being of themselves happily situated for residence, the gentlemen so sent were sometimes more conspicuous for want of income than for official zeal and ability. Hence the stables had become Augean. I was also instructed to carry out in some of the islands a plan for giving up this postal authority to the island Governor, and in others to propose some such plan. I was then to go on to Cuba, to make a postal treaty with the Spanish authorities, and to Panama for the same purpose with the government of New Grenada. All this work I performed to my satisfaction, and I hope to that of my masters in St Martin's-le-Grand.

But the trip is at the present moment of importance to my subject as having enabled me to write that which on the whole I regard as the best book that has come from my pen. It is short, and, I think I may venture to say, amusing, useful, and true. As soon as I had learned from the Secretary at the General Post Office that this journey would be required, I proposed the book to Messrs Chapman & Hall, demanding £250 for a single volume. The contract was made without any difficulty, and, when I returned home, the work was complete in my desk. I began it on board the ship in which I left Kingston, Jamaica, for Cuba, and from week to week I carried it on as I went. From Cuba I made my way to St Thomas and through the island down to Demerara, then back to St Thomas, – which is the starting point for all places in that part of the globe, – to Santa Martha, Carthagena, Aspinwall, over the Isthmus to Panama, up the Pacific to a little harbour on the coast of Costa Rica thence across Central America, through Costa Rica, and down the Nicaragua river to the Mosquito Coast, and, after that, home by Bermuda and New York. Should any one want further details of the voyage, are they not written in my book? The fact memorable to me now is that I never made a single note while writing or preparing it. Preparation indeed there was none. The descriptions and opinions came hot on to the paper from their causes. I will not say that this is the best way of writing a book intended to give accurate information. But it is the best way of producing to the eye of the reader and to his ear, that which the eye of the writer has seen and his ear heard. There are two kinds of confidence which a reader may have in his author, – which two kinds the reader who wishes to use his reading well should carefully discriminate. There is a confidence in facts, and a confidence in vision. The one man tells you accurately what has been. The other suggests to you what may, – or perhaps what must have been or what ought to have been. The former requires simple faith. The latter calls upon you to judge for yourself and form your own conclusions. The former does not pretend to be prescient, nor the latter accurate. Research is the weapon used by the former; observation by the latter. Either may be false, – wilfully false; as also may either be steadfastly true. As to that the reader must judge for himself. But the man who writes *currente calamo*,[9] – who works with a rapidity which will not admit of accuracy, may be as true, and in one sense as trustworthy as he who bases every word upon a rock of facts. I have written very much as I have travelled about, and, though I have been very inaccurate, I have always written the exact truth as I saw it; and I have, I think, drawn my pictures correctly.

The view I took of the relative position in the West Indies of black men and white men was the view of the *Times* newspaper at that period and there appeared three articles in that journal, one closely after another, which made the fortune of the book. Had it been very bad I suppose its fortune could not have been made for it, even by the *Times* newspaper. I afterwards became acquainted with the writer of those articles, – the contributor himself informing me that he had written them.[10] I told him that he had done me a greater service than can often be done by one man to another, but that I was under no obligation to him. I do not think that he saw the matter quite in the same light.

I am aware that by that criticism I was much raised in my position as an author. Whether such lifting up by such means is good or bad for literature is a question which I hope to discuss in a future chapter. But the result was immediate for me for I at once went to Chapman & Hall and successfully demanded £600 for my next novel.

CHAPTER 8

The Cornhill Magazine and 'Framley Parsonage'.

Soon after my return from the West Indies I was enabled to change my district in Ireland for one in England. For some time past my official work had been chiefly of a special nature, taking me out of my own district, but, through all that, Dublin had been my home, and there my wife and children had lived. I had often sighed to return to England, – with a silly longing. My life in England for twenty six years from the time of my birth to the day on which I left it, had been wretched. I had been poor, friendless, and joyless. In Ireland it had been constantly happy. I had achieved the respect of all with whom I was concerned, I had made for myself a comfortable home, and I had enjoyed many pleasures. Hunting itself was a great delight to me; and now, as I contemplated a move to England and a house in the neighbourhood of London, I felt that hunting must be abandoned.* Nevertheless I thought that a man who could write books ought not to live in Ireland, – ought to live within the reach of the publishers, the clubs, and the dinner-parties of the metropolis. So I made my request at head quarters, and with some little difficulty got myself appointed to the Eastern District of England, – which comprised Essex, Suffolk, Norfolk, Cambridgeshire, Huntingdonshire and the greater part of Hertfordshire.

At this time I did not stand very well with the dominant interest at the General Post Office. My old friend Colonel Maberly had been, some time since, squeezed out,[a] and his place was filled by Mr Rowland Hill the originator of the Penny Post.[1] With him I never had any sympathy nor he with me. In figures and facts he was most accurate, but I never came across any one who so little understood the ways of men, – unless it was his brother Frederic. To the two brothers the servants of the Post Office, – men numerous enough to have formed a large army in old days, – were so many machines who could be count-

* It was not abandoned till sixteen more years had passed away.

ed on for their exact work without deviation as wheels may be counted on which are kept going always at the same pace and always by the same power. Rowland Hill was an industrious public servant, anxious for the good of his country, but he was a hard taskmaster and one who would, I think, have put the great department with which he was concerned altogether out of gear by his hardness, had he not been at last controlled. He was the Chief Secretary, my brother in law who afterwards succeeded him came next to him, and Mr Hill's[b] brother was the Junior Secretary. In the natural course of things, I had not, from my position, anything to do with the management of affairs; – but from time to time I found myself more or less mixed up in it. I was known to be a thoroughly efficient public servant – I am sure I may say so much of myself without fear of contradiction from any one who has known the Post Office; – I was very fond of the department, and when matters came to be considered, I generally had an opinion of my own. I have no doubt that I often made myself very disagreeable. I know that I sometimes tried to do so. But I could hold my own because I knew my business and was useful. I had given official offence by the publication of *The Three Clerks*. I afterwards gave greater offence by a lecture on the Civil Service[2] which I delivered in one of the large rooms at the General Post Office to the clerks there. On this occasion the Postmaster General,[3] with whom personally I enjoyed friendly terms, sent for me and told me that Mr Hill had told him that I ought to be dismissed. When I asked his Lordship whether he was prepared to dismiss me, he only laughed. The threat was no threat to me, as I knew myself to be too good to be treated in that fashion. The lecture had been permitted, and I had disobeyed no order. In the lecture which I delivered there was nothing to bring me to shame, – but it advocated the doctrine that a Civil Servant is only a servant so far as his contract goes; and that he is, beyond that, entitled to be as free a man in politics, as free in his general pursuits, and as free in opinion as those who are in open professions and open trades. All this is very nearly admitted now, but it certainly was not admitted then. At that time no one in the Post Office could even vote for a member of Parliament.

Through my whole official life I did my best to improve the style of official writing. I have written I should think some thousands of reports, – many of them necessarily very long; some of them dealing with subjects so absurd as to allow a touch of burlesque; some few in which a spark of indignation or a slight glow of pathos might find an entrance. I have taken infinite pains with these reports, habituating myself always to write them in the form in which they should be sent, – without a copy. It is by writing thus that a man can throw on to his paper the exact feeling with which his mind is impressed at the moment. A rough copy, or that which is called a draught,^{c} is written in order that it may be touched and altered and put upon stilts. The waste of time, moreover, in such an operation is terrible. If a man knows his craft with his pen he will have learned to write without the necessity of changing his words or the form of his sentences. I had learned so to write my reports that they who read them should know what it was that I meant them to understand. But I do not think that they were regarded with favour. I have heard horror expressed because the old forms were disregarded and language used which had no savour of red tape. During the whole of this work in the Post Office it was my principle always to obey authority in everything instantly but never to allow my mouth to be closed as to the expression of opinion. They who had the ordering of me very often did not know the work as I knew it – could not tell as I could what would be the effect of this or that change. When carrying out instructions which I knew should not have been given I never scrupled to point out the fatuity of the improper order in the strongest language that I could decently employ. I have revelled in these official correspondences, and look back to some of them as the greatest delights of my life. But I am not sure that they were so delightful to others.

I succeeded, however, in getting the English district, – which could hardly have been refused to me, – and prepared to change our residence towards the end of 1859. At the time I was writing *Castle Richmond*, the novel which I had sold to Messrs Chapman & Hall for £600. But there arose at this time a certain literary project which probably had a great effect upon my career. Whilst travelling on postal service abroad, or riding over the rural districts in England, or arranging the mails in Ireland, – and such for the last eighteen years had now been my life, – I had no opportunity of becoming acquainted with literary life in London. It was probably some feeling of this which had made me anxious to move my Penates[4] back to England. But even in Ireland, where I was still living in October 1859, I had heard of the *Cornhill Magazine* which was to come out on the 1st of January 1860 under the editorship of Thackeray.[5]

I had at this time written from time to time certain short stories which had been published in different periodicals, and which in due time were republished under the name of *Tales of All Countries*. On 23d of October 1859 I wrote to Thackeray, whom I had, I think, never then seen, offering to send to him for the magazine certain of these stories. In reply to this I received two letters, one from Messrs Smith & Elder the proprietors of the *Cornhill* dated 26 of October, and the other from the Editor, written two days later. That from Mr Thackeray was as follows.

36 ONSLOW SQUARE, S.W.,
October 28.

My Dear Mr Trollope

Smith & Elder have sent you their proposals; and the business part done, let me come to the pleasure and say how very glad indeed I shall be to have you as a cooperator in our new magazine. And looking over the annexed programme, you will see whether you can't help us in many other ways besides tale-telling. Whatever a man knows about life and its doings that let us hear about. You must have tossed a good deal about the world, and have countless sketches in your memory and your portfolio. Please to think if you can furbish up any of these besides a novel. When events occur and you have a good lively tale bear us in mind. One of our chief objects in this magazine is the getting out of novel spinning, and back into the world. Don't understand me to disparage our craft, especially *your* wares. I often say I am like the pastry cook, and don't care for tarts, but prefer bread and cheese; but the public love the tarts (luckily for us) and we must bake and sell them. There was quite an excitement in my family one evening when Paterfamilias (who goes to sleep on a novel almost always when he tries it after dinner) came up stairs into the Drawing Room wide awake and calling for the second volume of the Three

Clerks. I hope the *Cornhill Magazine* will have as pleasant a story. And the Chapmans if they are the honest men I take them to be I've no doubt have told you with what sincere liking your works have been read by

yours very faithfully,

W. M. THACKERAY.

This was very pleasant, and so was the letter from Smith & Elder offering me £1000 for the copyright of a three volume novel, to come out in the new magazine, – on condition that the first portion of it should be in their hands by December 12th. There was much in all this that astonished me; – in the first place the price, which was more than double what I had yet received, and nearly double that which I was about to receive from Messrs Chapman & Hall. Then there was the suddenness of the call. It was already the end of October, and a portion of the work was required to be in the printer's hands within six weeks! *Castle Richmond* was indeed half written, but that was sold to Chapman. And it had already been a principle with me in my art that no part of a novel should be published till the entire story was completed.[6] I knew, from what I read from month to month, that this hurried publication of uncompleted work was frequently, I might perhaps say, always adopted by the leading novelists of the day. That such has been the case is proved by the fact that Dickens, Thackeray, and Mrs Gaskell died with unfinished novels of which portions had been already published.[7] I had not yet entered upon the system of publishing novels in parts, and therefore had never been tempted. But I was aware that an artist should keep in his hand the power of fitting the beginning of his work to the end. No doubt it is his first duty[d] to fit the end to the beginning, and he will endeavour to do so. But he should still keep in his hand the power of remedying any defect in this respect.

Servetur ad imum
Qualis ab incepto processerit,[8]

should be kept in view as to every character and every string of action. Your Achilles should, all through, from beginning to end, be 'impatient, fiery, ruthless, keen.'[9] Your Achilles, such as he is, will probably keep up his character. But your Davus also should be always Davus,[10] and that is more difficult. The rustic driving his pigs to market cannot always make them travel by the exact path which he has intended for them. When some young lady at the end of a story cannot be made to be quite perfect in her conduct that vivid description of angelic purity with which you laid the first lines of her portrait should be slightly toned down. I had felt that the rushing mode of publication, to which the system of serial stories had given rise, and by which small parts as they were written were sent, hot to the press, was injurious to the work done. If I now complied with the proposition made to me, I must act against my own principle. But such a principle becomes a tyrant if it cannot be superseded on just occasion. If the reason be 'tanti', the principle should for the occasion be put in abeyance. I sat as judge and decreed that the present reason was 'tanti'. On this, my first attempt at a serial story, I thought it fit to break my own rule. I can say, however, that I have never broken it since.[11]

But what astonished me most was the fact that at so late a day this new *Cornhill Magazine* should be in want of a novel! Perhaps some of my future readers will be able to remember the great expectations which were raised as to this periodical. Thackeray's was a good name with which to conjure. The Proprietors, Messrs Smith & Elder, were most liberal in their manner of initiating the work, and were able to make an expectant world of readers believe that something was to be given them for a shilling very much in excess of anything they had ever received for that or double the money. Whether these hopes were or were not fulfilled, it is not for me to say as, for the first few years of the magazine's existence, I wrote more for it than any other one person. But such was certainly the prospect; – and how had it come to pass that, with such promises made, the Editor and the proprietors were, at the end of October, without anything fixed as to what must be regarded as the chief dish in the banquet to be provided?

I fear that the answer to this question must be found in the habits of procrastination which had at that time grown upon the Editor. He had, I imagine, undertaken the work himself, and had postponed its commencement till there was left to him no time for commencing. There was still, it may be said, as much time for him as for me. I think there was – for though he had his magazine to look after, I had the Post Office. But he thought, when unable to trust his own energy, that he might rely upon that of a new recruit. He was but four years my senior in life, but he was at the top of the tree while I was still at the bottom.

Having made up my mind to break my principle, I started at once from Dublin to London. I arrived there on the morning of Thursday, 3rd of November, and left it on the evening of Friday. In the mean time I had made my agreement with Messrs Smith & Elder, and had arranged my plot. But, when in London, I first went to Edward Chapman at 193 Piccadilly. If the novel I was then writing for him would suit the *Cornhill*, might I consider my arrangement with him to be at an end? Yes; I might. But if that story would not suit the *Cornhill*, was I to consider my arrangement with him as still standing, – that agreement requiring that my manuscript should be in his hands in the following March? As to that I might do as I pleased. In our dealings together Mr Edward Chapman always acceded to every suggestion made to him. He never refused a book, and never haggled at a price. Then I hurried into the city and had my first interview with Mr George Smith. When he heard that *Castle Richmond* was an Irish story, he begged that I would endeavour to frame some other for his magazine. He was sure that an Irish story would not do for a commencement; – and he suggested the Church, as though it were my peculiar subject. I told him that *Castle Richmond* would have to 'come out', while any other novel that I might write for him would be running through the magazine; – but to that he expressed himself altogether indifferent. He wanted an English tale, on English life, with a clerical flavour. On these orders I went to work and framed what I suppose I must call the plot of *Framley Parsonage*.

On my journey back to Ireland, in the railway carriage, I wrote the first few pages of that story. I had got into my head an idea of what I meant to write, – a morsel of the biography of an English clergyman who should not be a bad man but one led into temptation by his own youth and by the unclerical accidents of the life around him. The love of his sister for the young lord was an adjunct necessary because there must be love in a novel. And then by placing Framley parsonage near Barchester I was able to fall back upon my old friends Mrs Proudie and the Archdeacon. Out of these slight elements I fabricated a hodge-podge in which the real plot consisted at last simply of a girl refusing to marry the man she loved till the man's friends agreed to accept her lovingly. Nothing could be less efficient or artistic. But the characters were so well handled that the work from the first to the last was popular, – and was received as it went on with still encreasing favour by both Editor and proprietor of the magazine. The story was thoroughly English. There was a little fox-hunting, and a little tuft-hunting; some Christian virtue, and some Christian cant. There was no heroism, and no villainy. There was much Church, but more love-making. And it was downright honest love, – in which there was no pretence on the part of the lady that she was too ethereal to be fond of a man, – no half-and-half inclination on the part of the man to pay a certain price and no more for a pretty toy. Each of them longed for the other, and they were not ashamed to say so. Consequently they in England who were living, or had lived, the same sort of life, liked *Framley Parsonage*. I think myself that Lucy Robarts is perhaps the most natural English girl that I ever drew, – the most natural at any rate of those who have been good girls. She was not as dear to me as Kate Woodward in *The Three Clerks*; – but I think she is more like real human life. Indeed I doubt whether such a character could be made more life-like than Lucy Robarts.

And I will say also that in this novel there is no very weak part, – no long succession of dull pages. The production of novels in serial form forces upon the author the conviction that he should not allow himself to be tedious in any single part. I hope no reader will misunderstand me. In spite of that conviction the writer of stories in parts will often be tedious. That I have been so myself is a fault that will lie heavy on my tomb stone. But the writer when he embarks in such a business should feel that he cannot afford to have many pages skipped out of the few which are to meet the reader's eye at the same time. Who can imagine the first half of the first volume of *Waverley* coming out in shilling numbers? I had realized this when I was writing *Framley Parsonage*;

and working on the conviction which had thus come home to me, I fell into no bathos of dullness.

I subsequently came across a piece of criticism which was written on me as a novelist by a brother novelist very much greater than myself, and whose brilliant intellect and warm imagination led him to a kind of work the very opposite of mine. This was Nathaniel Hawthorne, the American, whom I did not then know, but whose works I knew. Though it praises myself highly I will insert it here, because it certainly is true in its nature: 'It is odd enough,' he says, 'that my own individual taste is for quite another class of works than those which I myself am able to write. If I were to meet with such books as mine by another writer I don't believe I should be able to get through them. Have you ever read the novels of Anthony Trollope? They precisely suit my taste, – solid and substantial, written on strength of beef and through the inspiration of ale, and just as real as if some giant had hewn a great lump out of the earth and put it under a glass case, with all its inhabitants going about their daily business, and not suspecting that they were made a show of. And these books are just as English as a beefsteak. Have they ever been tried in America? It needs an English residence to make them thoroughly comprehensible, but still I should think that Human Nature would give them success anywhere.'[12]

This was dated early in 1860, and could have had no reference to *Framley Parsonage*; – but it was as true of that work as of any that I have written. And the criticism, whether just or unjust, describes with wonderful accuracy the purport that I have ever had in view in my writing. I have always desired to 'hew out some lump of the earth', and to make men and women walk upon it just as they do walk here among us, – with not more of excellence, nor with exaggerated baseness, – so that my readers might recognise human beings like to themselves, and not feel themselves to be carried away among gods or demons. If I could do this, then, I thought, I might succeed in impregnating the mind of the novel reader with a feeling that honesty is the best policy, that truth prevails while falsehood fails; that a girl will be loved as she is pure and sweet and unselfish; – that a man will be honoured as he is true and honest and brave of heart; that things meanly done are ugly and odious, and things nobly done beautiful and gracious. I do not say that lessons such as these may not be more grandly taught by higher flights than mine. Such lessons come to us from our greatest poets. But there are so many who will read novels and understand them, who either do not read the works of our great poets, or reading them miss the lesson! And, even in prose fiction, the character whom the fervid imagination of the writer has lifted somewhat into the clouds will hardly give so plain an example to the hasty normal reader as the humbler personage whom that reader unconsciously feels to resemble himself, – or herself. I do think that a girl would more probably dress her own mind after Lucy Robarts than after Flora MacDonald.[13]

There are many who would laugh at the idea of a novelist teaching either virtue or nobility, – those, for instance, who regard the reading of novels as a sin, and those also who think it to be simply an idle pastime. They look upon the tellers of stories as among the tribe of those who pander to the wicked pleasures of a wicked world. I have regarded my art from so different a point of view, that I have ever thought of myself as a preacher of sermons, and my pulpit as one which I could make both salutary and agreeable to my audience. I do believe that no girl has risen from the reading of my pages less modest than she was before, and that some may have learned from them that modesty is a charm well worth preserving. I think that no youth has been taught that in falseness and flashness is to be found the road to manliness; but some may perhaps have learned from me that it is to be found in truth and a high but gentle spirit. Such are the lessons I have striven to teach, and I have thought that it might best be done by representing to my readers characters like themselves, – or to which they might liken themselves.

Framley Parsonage – or rather my connexion with the *Cornhill*, – was the means of introducing me very quickly to that literary world from which I had hitherto been severed by the fact of my residence in Ireland. In December 1859, while I was still very hard at work on my novel, I came over to take charge of the Eastern District, and settled myself at a residence about twelve miles from London, in Hertfordshire, but on the borders both of Essex and Middlesex, – which was somewhat too grandly called Waltham House. This I took on lease, and subsequently bought after I had spent about £1000 on improvements. From hence I was able to make myself frequent both in Cornhill and Piccadilly, and to live, when the opportunity came, among men of my own pursuit.

I think it was in March[e] 1860 that Mr George Smith – to whose enterprise we owe not only the *Cornhill Magazine* but the *Pall Mall Gazette*,[14] – gave a sumptuous dinner to his contributors. It was a memorable banquet in many ways, but chiefly so to me because on that occasion I first met many men who afterwards became my most intimate associates. It can rarely happen that one such occasion can be the first starting point of so many friendships! It was at that table and on that day that I first saw Thackeray, Charles Taylor (Sir) – than whom in latter life I have loved no man better, – Robert Bell, G. H. Lewes, Russell of the *Times*[f] and John Everett Millais.[15] With all these men I afterwards lived on affectionate terms; – but I will here speak specially of the last, because from that time he was joined with me in so much of the work that I did.

Mr Millais was engaged to illustrate *Framley Parsonage*, but this was not the first work he did for the magazine. In the second number there is a picture of his accompanying Monckton Milnes' 'unspoken dialogue'.[16] The first drawing he did for *Framley Parsonage* did not appear till after the dinner of which I have spoken, and I do not think that I knew at the time that he was engaged on my novel. When I did know it, it made me very proud. He afterwards illustrated *Orley Farm*, *The Small House at Allington*,[g] *Rachel Ray*, and *Phineas Finn*. Altogether he drew from my tales eighty seven drawings, and I do not think that more conscientious work was ever done by man. Writers of novels know well, – and so ought readers of novels to have learned, – that there are two modes of illustrating, either of which may be adopted equally by a bad and by a good artist. To which class Mr Millais belongs I need not say; but, as a good artist, it was open to him simply to make a pretty picture, or to study the work of the author from whose writing he was bound to take his subject. I have too often found that the former alternative has been thought to be the better as it certainly is the easier method. An artist will frequently dislike to subordinate his ideas to those of an author, and will sometimes be too idle to find out what those ideas are. But this artist was neither proud nor idle. In every figure that he drew it was his object to promote the views of the writer whose work he had undertaken to illustrate, and he never spared himself any pains in studying that work so as to enable himself to do so. I have carried on some of those characters from book to book, and have had my own early ideas impressed indelibly on my memory by the excellence of his delineations. Those illustrations were commenced fifteen years ago, and from that time up to this day my affection for the man of whom I am speaking has encreased. To see him has always been a pleasure. His voice has been a sweet sound in my ears. Behind his back I have never heard him praised without joining the eulogist; I have never heard a word spoken against him without opposing the censurer. These words, should he ever see them, will come to him from the grave, and will tell him of my regard, – as one living man never tells another.

Sir Charles Taylor, who carried me home in his brougham that evening and thus commenced an intimacy which has since been very close, was born to wealth and was therefore not compelled by the necessities of a profession to enter the lists as an author. But he lived much with those who did so, – and could have done it himself had want or ambition stirred him. He was our king at the Garrick Club, to which however I did not yet belong. He gave the best dinners of my time, and was, – happily I may say is,* – the best giver of dinners. A man rough of tongue, brusque in his manners, odious to those who dislike him, somewhat inclined to tyranny, he is the prince of friends, honest as the sun, and as openhanded as Charity itself.

Robert Bell has now been dead nearly ten years. As I look back over the interval and remember how intimate we were it seems odd to me that we should have known each other for no more than six years. He was a man who had lived by his pen from his very youth; – and was so far successful that I do not think that want ever came near him. But he never made that mark which his industry and talents would have seemed to ensure. He was a man well known to literary men, but not known to readers. As a journalist he was useful and conscientious; but

* Alas, within a year of the writing of this he went from us.

his plays and novels never made themselves popular. He wrote a life of Canning[17] and he brought out an annotated edition of the British poets, – but he achieved no great success. I have known no man better read in English literature. Hence his conversation had a peculiar charm, but he was not equally happy with his pen. He will be long re-membered at the Literary Fund Committees,[18] of which he was a staunch and most trusted supporter. I think it was he who first intro-duced me to that Board. It has often been said that literary men are peculiarly apt to think that they are slighted and unappreciated. Robert Bell certainly never achieved the position in literature which he once aspired to fill, and which he was justified in thinking that he could earn for himself. I have frequently discussed these subjects with him, but I never heard from his mouth a word of complaint as to his own literary fate. He liked to hear the chimes go at midnight, and he loved to have ginger hot in his mouth.[19] On such occasions no sound ever came out of a man's lips sweeter than that of his[h] wit and gentle revelry.

George Lewes, – with his wife whom all the world knows as George Eliot,[i] – has also been and still is one of my dearest friends. He is I think the acutest critic I know, – and the severest. His severity, how-ever, is a fault. His intention to be honest, even when honesty may give pain, has caused him to give pain when honesty has not required it. He is essentially a doubter, and has encouraged himself to doubt till the faculty of trusting has almost left him. I am not speaking of the per-sonal trust which one man feels in another, but of that confidence in literary excellence which is I think necessary for the full enjoyment of literature. In one modern writer he does[j] believe thoroughly. Nothing can be more charming than the unstinted admiration which he has accorded to everything that comes from the pen of the wonderful woman to whom his lot has been united. To her name I shall recur again when speaking of the novelists of the present day.

Of 'Billy Russell' as we always used to call him I may say that I never knew but one man equal to him in the quickness and continu-ance of witty speech. That one man was Charles Lever,[20] also an Irishman, – whom I had known from an earlier date and also with close intimacy. Of the two I think that Lever was perhaps the more astounding producer of good things. His manner was perhaps a little the happier, and his turns more sharp and unexpected. But 'Billy' also was marvellous. Whether abroad, as special correspondent, or at home amidst the flurry of his newspaper work he was a charming companion – but hardly a staff to be trusted in a literary enterprise. He once promised to write for me an article on the American telegraph wires. Much after the time named the first half came; – long after the whole should have been in print came the last quarter with an intimation that the missing bit should reach me by the next post. The missing bit never reached me, and the unconnected fragments were joined together at the last moment by the printer's type. I did not hear that any one ever found out the difference. It was useless on such occasions either to argue with him or accuse him.[k] His ready wit always gave him the last word. He has fallen away latterly among Princes,[21] and his old friends do not see much of him.[l]

Of Thackeray I will speak again when I record his death.[m]

There were many others whom I met for the first time at George Smith's table. Albert Smith, – for the first and indeed the last time, as he died soon after; Higgins, whom the world knew as Jacob Omnium, a man I greatly regarded; Dallas, who for a time was literary critic to the *Times* and who certainly in that capacity did better work than has appeared since in the same department; George Augustus Sala, who had he given himself fair play would have risen to higher eminence than that of being the best writer in his day of sensational leading articles; and Fitzjames Stephen,[22] a man of very different calibre, who has not yet culminated, but who no doubt will culminate among our judges. There were many others; – but I cannot now recall their various names as identified with those banquets.

Of *Framley Parsonage* I need only further say that as I wrote it I became more closely than ever acquainted with the new shire which I had added to the English counties. I had it all in my mind, its roads and railroads, its towns and parishes, its members of Parliament, and the different hunts which rode over it. I knew all the great lords and their castles, the squires and their parks, the rectors and their churches. This was the fourth novel of which I had placed the scene in Barsetshire, and as I wrote it I made a map of the dear county.

Throughout these stories there has been no name given to a fictitious site, which does not represent to me a spot of which I know all the accessories, as though I had lived and wandered there.[n]

CHAPTER 9

'Castle Richmond'; 'Brown, Jones, and Robinson'; 'North America'; 'Orley Farm'.

When I had half finished *Framley Parsonage*, I went back to my other story, *Castle Richmond*, which I was writing for Messrs Chapman & Hall, and completed that. I think that this was the only occasion on which I have had two different novels in my mind at the same time. This, however, did not create either difficulty or confusion. Many of us live in different circles, and when we go from our friends in town to our friends in the country, we do not usually fail to remember the little details of the one life or the other. The parson at Rusticum with his wife and his wife's mother and all his belongings, and our old friend the Squire with his family history, and Farmer Mudge who has been cross with us because we rode so unnecessarily over his barley, and that rascally poacher, once a gamekeeper, who now traps all the foxes, and pretty Mary Cann whose marriage with the wheelwright we did something to expedite; though we are alive to them all, do not drive out of our brain the club gossip, nor the memories of last season's dinners, nor any incident of our London intimacies. In our lives we are always weaving novels, and we manage to keep the different tales distinct. A man does, in truth, remember that which it interests him to remember; and when we hear that memory has gone as age has come on we should understand that the capacity for interest in the matter concerned has perished. A man will be generally very old and feeble before he forgets how much money he has in the funds. There is a good deal to be learned by any one who wishes to write a novel well; – but when the art has been acquired I do not see why two or three should not be well written at the same time. I have never found myself thinking much about the work that I had to do till I was doing it. I have indeed for many years almost abandoned the effort to think, trusting myself, with the narrowest thread of a plot, to work the matter out when the pen is in my hand. But my mind is constantly employing itself on the work I have done. Had I left either *Framley Parsonage* or *Castle Richmond* half finished fifteen years ago, I think I could complete the tales now with very little trouble. I have not looked at *Castle Richmond* since it was published, and, poor as the work is, I remember all the incidents.

Castle Richmond certainly was not a success, – though the plot is a fairly good plot, and is much more of a plot than I have generally been able to find. The scene is laid in Ireland, during the famine, and I am well aware now that English readers no longer like Irish stories. I cannot understand why it should be so, as the Irish character is peculiarly well fitted for romance. But Irish subjects generally have become distasteful. This novel, however, is of itself a weak production. The characters do not excite sympathy. The heroine has two lovers of whom one is a scamp and the other a prig. As regards the scamp the girl's mother is her own rival. Rivalry of the same nature has been admirably depicted by Thackeray in his *Esmond*, but there the mother's love seems to be justified by the girl's indifference. In *Castle Richmond* the mother strives to rob her daughter of the man's love. The girl herself has no character, and the mother, who is strong enough, is almost revolting. The dialogue is often lively, and some of the incidents are well told; – but the story as a whole was a failure. I cannot remember, however, that it was roughly handled by the critics when it came out, and I much doubt whether anything so hard was said of it then as that which I have said here.[1]

I was now settled at Waltham Cross in a house in which I could entertain a few friends modestly, where we grew our own cabbages and strawberries, made our own butter, and killed our own pigs. I occupied it for twelve years and they were years to me of great prosperity. In 1861 I became a member of the Garrick Club, with which institution I have since been much identified. I had belonged to it about two years, when, on Thackeray's death, I was invited to fill his place on the Committee, and I have been one of that august body ever since. Having up to that time lived very little among men, having known hitherto nothing of clubs, having even as a boy been banished from social gatherings, I enjoyed infinitely at first the gaiety of the Garrick. It was a festival to me to dine there, – which I did indeed but seldom, and a great delight to play a rubber in the little room upstairs of an afternoon. I am speaking now of the old club in King Street. This playing of whist before dinner has since that become a habit with me, – so that unless there be something else special to do, unless there be hunting, or I am wanted to ride in the park by the young tyrant of my household,[2] it is 'my custom always in the afternoon.'[3] I have sometimes felt sore with myself for this persistency, feeling that I was making myself a slave to an amusement which has not after all very much to recommend it. I have often thought that I would break myself away from it, and 'swear off', as Rip Van Winkle says.[4] But my swearing off has been like that of Rip Van Winkle. And now, as I think of it coolly, I do not know but that I have been right to cling to it. As a man grows old he wants amusement, more even than when he is young, and then it becomes so difficult to find amusement. Reading should no doubt be the delight of one's[a] leisure hours. Had I to choose between books and cards I should no doubt take the books. But I find that I can seldom read with pleasure for above an hour and a half at a time, or more than three hours a day. As I write this I am aware that hunting must soon be abandoned. After sixty it is given but to few men to ride straight across country, and I cannot bring myself to adopt any other mode of riding. I think that without cards I should now be much at a loss. When I began to play at the Garrick I did so simply because I liked the society of the men who played.

I think that I became popular among those with whom I associated. I have long been aware of a certain weakness in my own character which I may call a craving for love. I have ever had a wish to be liked by those around me, – a wish that during the first half of my life was never gratified. In my school days no small part of my misery came from the envy with which I regarded the popularity of popular boys. They seemed to me to live in a social Paradise while the desolation of my Pandemonium was complete. And afterwards, when I was in London as a young man, I had but few friends. Among the clerks in the

Post Office I held my own fairly after[b] the first two or three years, but even then I regarded myself as something of a Pariah. My Irish life had been much better. I had had my wife and children, and had been sustained by a feeling of general respect. But even in Ireland I had in truth lived but little in society. Our means had been sufficient for our wants, but insufficient for entertaining others. It was not till we had settled ourselves at Waltham that I really began to live much with others. The Garrick Club was the first assemblage of men at which I felt myself to be popular.

I soon became a member of other clubs. There was the Arts Club in Hanover Square of which I saw the opening but from which after three or four years I withdrew my name, having found that during these three or four years I had not once entered the building. Then I was one of the originators of the Civil Service Club, – not from judgement but instigated to do so by others. That also I left for the same reason. In 1864 I received the honour of being elected by the Committee at the Athenaeum. For this I was indebted to the kindness of Lord Stanhope,[5] and I never was more surprised than when I was informed of the fact. About the same time I became a member of the Cosmopolitan, – a little club that meets twice a week in Charles Street, Berkeley Square, and supplies to all its members and its members' friends tea and brandy and water without charge! The gatherings there I used to think very delightful. One met Jacob Omnium, Monckton Milnes, Tom Hughes, William Stirling, Henry Reeve, Arthur Russell, Tom Taylor,[6] and such like; – and generally a strong political element, thoroughly well-mixed, gave a certain spirit to the place. Lord Ripon, Lord Stanley, William Forster, Lord Enfield, Lord Kimberley, George Bentinck, Vernon Harcourt, Davenport Bromley,[c] Knatchbull Hugessen,[d7] with many others, used to whisper the secrets of Parliament with free tongues. Afterwards I became a member of 'The Turf', which I found to be serviceable, – or the reverse, – only for the playing of whist at high points.

In August 1861 I wrote another tale for the *Cornhill Magazine*. It was a short story, about one volume in length, and was called *The Struggles of Brown, Jones, and Robinson*. In this I attempted a style for which I certainly was not qualified, and to which I never had again recourse. It was meant to be funny, was full of slang, and was intended as a satire on the ways of trade. Still I think that there is some good fun in it, but I have heard no one else express such an opinion. I do not know that I ever heard any opinion expressed on it, – except by the publisher who kindly remarked that he did not think it was equal to my usual work. Though he had purchased the copyright, he did not republish the story, in a book form, till 1870, – and then it passed into the world of letters *sub silentio*.[8] I do not know that it was ever criticised or ever read.[9] I received £600 for it. From that time to this I have been paid at about that rate for my work, – £600 for the quantity contained in an ordinary novel-volume, – or £3000 for a long tale, published in twenty parts which is equal in length to five such volumes. I have occasionally received something more than this, – never I think less for any tale except when I have published my work anonymously.* Having said so much I need not further specify the prices as I mention the books as they were written. I will however, when I am completing this memoir, give a list of all the sums I have received for my literary labours. I think that *Brown, Jones, and Robinson* was the hardest bargain I ever sold to a publisher.

In 1861 the War of Secession had broken out in America, and from the first I interested myself much in the question. My mother had thirty years previously written a very popular, but, as I had thought, a somewhat unjust book about our cousins over the water. She had seen what was distasteful in the manners of a young people, but had hardly recognised their energy. I had entertained for many years an ambition to follow her footsteps there, and to write another book. I had already paid a short visit to New York city and State on my way home from the West Indies but had not seen enough then to justify me in the expression of any opinion. The breaking out of the war did not make me think that the time was peculiarly fit for such enquiry as I wished to make, but it did represent itself as an occasion on which a book might be popular. I consequently consulted the two great powers with whom I was concerned. Messrs Chapman & Hall the publishers were one power, and I had no difficulty in arranging my affairs with them. They

---

* Since the date at which this was written I have encountered a diminution in price.

agreed to publish the book on my terms and bade me God speed on my journey. The other power was the Postmaster General and Mr R. Hill the Secretary of the Post Office. I wanted leave of absence for the unusual period of nine months, and fearing that I should not get it by the ordinary process of asking the Secretary, I went direct to his Lordship. 'Is it on the plea of ill health?'[e] he asked, looking into my face, which was then that of a very robust man. His Lordship knew the Civil Service as well as any one living and must have seen much of falseness and fraudulent pretence or he could not have asked that question. I told him that I was very well, but that I wanted to write a book. 'Had I any special ground to go upon in asking for such indulgence?' I had, I said, done my duty well by the Service. There was a good deal of demurring, but I got my leave for nine months, – and I knew that I had earned it. Mr Hill attached to the minute granting me the leave an intimation that it was to be considered as a full equivalent for the special services rendered by me to the department. I declined, however, to accept the grace with such a stipulation, and it was withdrawn by the directions of the Postmaster General.*

I started for the States in August and returned in the following May. The war was raging during the time that I was there, and the country was full of soldiers. A part of the time I spent in Virginia, Kentucky, and Missouri among the troops, along the line of attack. I visited all the States (excepting California) which had not then seceded, – failing to make my way into the seceding States unless I was prepared to visit them with an amount of discomfort I did not choose to endure. I worked very hard at the task I had assigned to myself, and did I think see much of the manners and institutions of the people. Nothing struck me more than their persistence in the ordinary pursuits of life in spite of the war which was around them. Neither industry nor[f] amusement seemed to meet with any check. Schools, hospitals and institutes were by no means neglected because new regiments were

---

* During the period of my service in the Post Office I did very much special work for which I never asked any remuneration, – and never received any, though payments for special services were common in the department at that time. But if there was to be a question of such remuneration, I did not choose that my work should be valued at the price put upon it by Mr Hill.

daily required. The truth, I take it, is that we, all of us, soon adapt ourselves to the circumstances around us. Though three parts of London were in flames, I should no doubt expect to have my dinner served to me, if I lived in the quarter which was free from fire.

The book I wrote was very much longer than that on the West Indies but was also written almost without a note. It contained much information, and, with many inaccuracies, was a true book. But it was not well done. It is tedious and confused, and will hardly, I think, be of future value to those who wish to make themselves acquainted with the United States. It was published about the middle of the war, – just at the time in which the hopes of those who loved the South were most buoyant and the fears of those who stood by the North were the strongest. But it expressed an assured confidence, – which never quavered in a page or in a line, – that the North would win. This assurance was based on the merits of the Northern cause, on the superior strength of the Northern party, and on a conviction that England would never recognise the South and that France would be guided in her policy by England. I was right in my prophecies, and right, I think on the grounds on which they were made. The Southern cause was bad. The South had provoked the quarrel because its political supremacy was checked by the election of Mr Lincoln to the Presidency. It had to fight as a little man against a big man and fought gallantly. That gallantry, – and a feeling based on a misconception as to American character that the Southerners are better gentlemen than their Northern brethren – did create great sympathy here; but I believed[g] that the country was too just to be led into political action by a spirit of romance, and I was warranted in that belief. There was a moment in which the Northern cause was in danger, and the danger lay certainly in the prospect of British interference. Messrs Slidell and Mason, – two men insignificant in themselves, – had been sent to Europe by the Southern party, and had managed to get on board the British Mail Steamer called 'The Trent' at The Havannah. A most undue importance was attached to this mission by Mr Lincoln's government, and efforts were made to stop them. A certain Commodore Wilkes, doing duty as policeman on the seas, did stop 'The Trent' and took the men out. They were carried, one to Boston and one to New York, and were incarcerated amidst the triumph of the nation. Commodore Wilkes, who had done nothing in which a brave man could take glory, was made a hero and received a prize sword. England of course demanded her passengers back, and the States for a while refused to surrender them. But Mr Seward was at that time the Secretary of State, and Mr Seward, with many political faults, was a wise man. I was at Washington at the time and it was known there that the contest among the leading Northerners was very sharp on the matter. Mr Sumner and Mr Seward were, under Mr Lincoln, the two chiefs of the party. It was understood that Mr Sumner was opposed to the rendition of the men, and Mr Seward in favour of it. Mr Seward's counsels at last prevailed with the President, and England's declaration of war was prevented. I dined with Mr Seward on the day of the decision, meeting Mr Sumner at his house, and was told as I left the dining room what the decision had been. During the afternoon I and others had received intimation through the embassy that we might probably have to leave Washington at an hour's notice. This I think was the severest danger that the Northern cause encountered throughout[h] the war.[10]

But my book, though it was right in its views on this subject, – and wrong in none other as far as I know, – was not a good book. I can recommend no one to read it now, in order that he may be either instructed or amused, – as I can do that on the West Indies. It served its purpose at the time and was well received by the public and by the critics.

Before starting to America I had completed *Orley Farm*, a novel which appeared in shilling numbers, – after the manner in which *Pickwick*, *Nicholas Nickleby*, and many others had been published. Most of those among my friends who talk to me now about my novels, and are competent to form an opinion on the subject, say that this is the best I have written. In this opinion I do not coincide. I think that the highest merit which a novel can have consists in perfect delineation of character rather than in plot, or humour, or pathos, and I shall before long mention a subsequent work in which I think the main character of the story is so well developed as to justify me in asserting its claim above the others. The plot of *Orley Farm* is probably the best I have ever made, – but it has the fault of declaring itself and thus coming to an end too early in the book. When Lady Mason tells her ancient lover that she did forge the will, the plot of *Orley Farm* has unravelled itself; – and this she does in the middle of the tale. Independently, however, of this the novel is good. Sir Peregrine Orme, his grandson, Madeline Staveley, Mr Furnival, Mr Chaffanbrass, and the 'commercial gentlemen' are all good. The hunting is good. The lawyers' talk is good. Mr Moulder carves his turkey admirably, and Mr Kantwise sells his tables and chairs with spirit. I do not know that there is a dull page in the book. I am fond of *Orley Farm*, – and am especially fond of its illustrations, by Millais, which are the best I have seen in any novel in any language.

I now felt that I had gained my object. In 1862 I had achieved that which I contemplated when I went to London in 1834, and towards which I made my first attempt when I began *The Macdermots* in 1843. I had created for myself a position among literary men, and had secured to myself an income on which I might live in ease and comfort, – which ease and comfort have been made to include many luxuries. From this time for a period of twelve years my income averaged £4500 a year. Of this I spent about two thirds, and put by one. I ought perhaps to have done better, – to have spent one third and put by two; – but I have ever been too well inclined to spend freely that which has come easily.

This, however, has been so exactly the life which my thoughts and aspirations had marked out, – thoughts and aspirations which used to cause me to blush with shame because I was so slow in forcing myself to the work which they demanded – that I have felt some pride in having attained it. I have before said how entirely I fail to reach the altitude of those who think that a man devoted to letters should be indifferent to the pecuniary results for which work is generally done. An easy income has always been regarded by me as a great blessing. Not to have to think of sixpences, or very much of shillings, not to be unhappy because the coals have been burned too quickly and the house linen wants renewing, not to be debarred by the rigour of necessity from opening one's hands, perhaps foolishly, to one's friends, – all this to me has been essential to the comfort of life. I have enjoyed the comfort, for I may almost say, the last twenty years, though no man in his youth had less prospect of doing so or would have been less likely at twenty five to have had such luxuries foretold to him by his friends.

But though the money has been sweet, the respect, the friendships, and the mode of life which has been achieved have been much sweeter. In my boyhood, when I would be crawling up to school with dirty boots and trousers through the muddy lanes, I was always telling myself that the misery of the hour was not the worst of it, but that the mud, and solitude, and poverty of the time would ensure me mud and solitude and poverty through my life. Those lads about me would go into Parliament, or become rectors and deans, or squires of parishes, or advocates thundering at the bar. They would not live with me now – but neither should I be able to live with them in after years. Nevertheless I have lived with them. When, at the age in which others go to the Universities, I became a clerk in the Post Office I felt that my old visions were being realised. I did not think it a high calling. I did not know then how very much good work may be done by a member of the Civil Service who will show himself capable of doing it. The Post Office at last grew upon me and forced itself into my affections. I became intensely anxious that people should have their letters delivered to them punctually. But my hope to rise had always been built on the writing of novels, and, at last, by writing novels I had risen.

I do not think that I ever toadied any one, or that I have acquired the character of a tuft hunter. But here I do not scruple to say that I prefer the society of distinguished people, and that even the distinction of wealth confers many advantages. The best education is to be had at a price as well as the best broad-cloth. The son of a peer is more likely to rub his shoulders against well-informed men than the son of a tradesman. The graces come easier to the wife of him who has had great-grandfathers than they do to her whose husband has been less, – or more fortunate, as he may think it. The discerning man will recognise the information and the graces when they are achieved without such assistance and will honour the owners of them the more because of the difficulties they have overcome; – but the fact remains that the society of the well-born and of the wealthy will as a rule be worth seeking. I say this now because these are the rules by which I have lived, and these are the causes which have instigated me to work.

I have heard the question argued, – on what terms should a man of inferior rank live with those who are manifestly superior to him?[i] If a Marquis or an Earl honour me, who have no rank, with his intimacy, am I in my intercourse with him to remember our close acquaintance or his high rank? I have always said that where the difference in position is quite marked, – as in such a case it would be, – the overtures[j] to intimacy should always come from the higher rank; but if the intimacy be ever fixed, then that rank should be held of no account. It seems to me that intimate friendship admits of no standing but that of equality. I cannot be the Sovereign's friend, nor probably the friend of many very much beneath the Sovereign, because such equality is impossible.

When I first came to Waltham Cross in the winter of 1895–1860, I had almost made up my mind that my hunting was over. I could not then count upon an income which would enable me to carry on an amusement which I should doubtless find much more expensive in England than in Ireland. I brought with me out of Ireland one mare, but she was too light for me to ride in the hunting field. As, however, the money came in I very quickly fell back into my old habits. First one horse was bought, then another, and then a third, till it became established as a fixed rule that I should not have less than four hunters in the stable. Sometimes when my boys have been at home I have had as many as six. Essex was the chief scene of my sport, and gradually I became known there almost as well as though I had been an Essex Squire, to the manner born. Few have investigated more closely than I have done the depth, and breadth, and water-holding capacities of an Essex ditch. It will, I think, be accorded to me by Essex men generally that I have ridden hard. The cause of my delight in the amusement I have never been able to analyse to my own satisfaction. In the first place, even now, I know very little about hunting, – though I know very much of the accessories of the field. I am too blind to see hounds turning, and cannot therefore tell whether the fox has gone this way or that. Indeed all the notice I take of hounds is not to ride over them. My eyes are so constituted that I can never see the nature of a fence. I either follow some one, or ride at it with the full conviction that I may be going into a horse pond or a gravel pit. I have jumped into both one and the other. I am very heavy, and have never ridden expensive horses. I am also now old for such work, being so stiff that I cannot get on to my horse without the aid of a block or a bank. But I ride still after the same fashion, with a boy's energy, determined to get ahead if it may possibly be done, hating the roads, despising young men who ride them, and with a feeling that life cannot, with all her riches, have given me anything better, than when I have gone through a long run to the finish, keeping a place, not of glory, but of credit among my juniors.[k]

CHAPTER 10

'The Small House at Allington', 'Can You Forgive Her?' 'Rachel Ray', and the 'Fortnightly Review'.

During the early months of 1862 *Orley Farm* was still being brought out in numbers and at the same time *Brown, Jones, and Robinson* was appearing in the *Cornhill Magazine*. In September 1862 the *Small House at Allington* began its career in the same periodical. The work on North America had also come out in 1862. In August 1863 the first number of *Can You Forgive Her?* was published as a separate serial and was continued through 1864. In 1863 a short novel was produced in the ordinary volume form, called *Rachel Ray*. In addition to these I published during the time two volumes of stories called *The Tales of all Countries*. In the early spring of 1865 *Miss Mackenzie* was issued in the same form as *Rachel Ray*, and in May of the same year *The Belton Estate* was commenced with the commencement of the *Fortnightly Review*, – of which periodical I will say a few words in this chapter.

I quite admit that I crowded my wares into the market too quickly, – because the reading world could not want such a quantity of matter from the hands of one author in so short a space of time. I had not been quite so fertile as the unfortunate gentleman who disgusted the publisher in Paternoster Row, – in the story of whose productiveness I have always thought there was a touch of romance, – but I had probably done enough to make both publishers and readers think that I was coming too often beneath their notice. Of publishers, however, I must speak collectively, as my sins were, I think, chiefly due to the encouragement which I received from them individually. What I wrote for the *Cornhill Magazine* I always wrote at the instigation of Mr Smith. My other works were published by Messrs Chapman & Hall in compliance with contracts made by me with them and always made with their good will. Could I have been two separate persons at one and the same time, of whom one might have been devoted to Cornhill and the other to the interests of the firm in Piccadilly, it might have been very well; – but as I preserved my identity in both places, I myself became aware that my name was too frequent on title pages.

Critics, if they ever trouble themselves with these pages, will of course say that in what I have now said I have ignored altogether the one great evil of rapid production, – namely that of inferior work. And, of course, if the work was inferior because of the too great rapidity of production the critics would be right. Giving to the subject the best of my critical abilities, and judging of my own work as nearly as possible as I would that of another, I believe that the work which has been done quickest has been done the best. I have composed better stories, – that is, have created better plots – than those of *The Small House at Allington* and *Can You Forgive Her?*, and I have portrayed two or three better characters than are to be found in the pages of either of them; but, taking these books all through, I do not think that I have ever done better work. Nor would these have been improved by any effort in the art of story-telling, had each of these been the isolated labour of a couple of years. How short is the time devoted to the manipulation of a plot can be known only to those who have written plays and novels; – I may say also how very little time the brain is able to devote to such wearing work. There are usually some hours of agonizing doubt, almost of despair, – so at least it has been with me; – or perhaps some days. And then, with nothing settled in my brain as to the final development of events, with no capability of settling any thing, but with a most distinct conception of some character or characters, I have rushed at the work, as a rider rushes at a fence which he does not see. Sometimes I have encountered what, in hunting language, we call a cropper. I had such a fall in two novels of which I have already spoken – *The Bertrams* and *Castle Richmond.* I shall have to speak of other such troubles. But these failures have not arisen from over-hurried work. When my work has been quicker done, – and it has sometimes been done very quickly, – the rapidity has been achieved by hot pressure not in the conception, but in the telling of the story. Instead of writing eight pages a day, I have written sixteen; – instead of working five days a week I have worked seven. I have trebled my usual average, and have done so in circumstances which have enabled me to give up all my thoughts for the time to the book I have been writing. This has generally been done at some quiet spot among the mountains, – where there has been no society, no hunting, no whist, no ordinary household duties. And I am sure that the work so done has had in it the best truth and the highest spirit that I have been able to produce. At such times I have been able to imbue myself thoroughly with the characters I have had in hand. I have wandered alone among the rocks and woods crying at their grief, laughing at their absurdities, and thoroughly enjoying their joy. I have been impregnated with my own creations till it has been my only excitement to sit with the pen in my hand and drive my team before me at as quick a pace as I could make them travel.

The critics will again say that all this may be very well as to the rough work of the author's own brain, but it will be very far from well in reference to the style in which that work is given to the public. After all the vehicle which a writer uses for conveying his thoughts to the public should not be less important to him than the thoughts themselves. An author can hardly hope to be popular unless he can use popular language. That is quite true, but then comes the question of achieving a popular – in other words I may say a good and lucid style. How may an author best acquire a mode of writing which shall be agreeable and easily intelligible to the reader? He must be correct, because without correctness he can be neither agreeable nor intelligible. Readers will expect him to obey those rules which they, consciously or unconsciously, have been taught to regard as binding on language, – and unless he does obey them he will disgust. Without much labour no writer will achieve such a style. He has very much to learn, and when he has learned that much, he has to acquire the habit of using what he has learned with ease. But all this must be learned and acquired, – not while he is writing that which shall please, – but long before. His language must come from him as music comes from the rapid touch of the great performer's fingers, as words come from the mouth of the indignant orator, as letters fly from the fingers of the trained compositor, as the syllables tinkled out by little bells form themselves to the ear of the telegraphist. A man who thinks much of his words as he writes them will generally leave behind him work that smells of oil. I speak here, of course, of prose; for in poetry we know what care is necessary and we form our taste accordingly.

Rapid writing no doubt will give rise to inaccuracy, – chiefly because the ear, quick and true as may generally be[a] its operation, will occasionally break down under pressure, and, before a sentence be closed, will forget the nature of the composition with which it was commenced. A singular nominative will be disgraced by a plural verb because other pluralities have intervened and have tempted the ear into plural tendencies. Tautologies will occur because the ear, in demanding fresh emphasis, has forgotten that the desired force has been already expressed. I need not multiply these causes of error which must have been stumbling-blocks indeed when men wrote in the long sentences of Gibbon, but which Macaulay with his multiplicity of divisions has done so much to enable us to avoid. A rapid writer will hardly avoid these errors altogether. Speaking of myself I am ready to declare that with much training I have been unable to avoid them. But the writer for the press is rarely called upon – a writer of books should never be called upon, – to send his manuscript hot from his hand to the printer. It has been my practice to read everything four times at least, – thrice in manuscript and once in print. Very much of my work I have read twice in print. In spite of this I know that inaccuracies have crept through, – not single spies but in battalions.[1] From this I gather that the supervision has been insufficient, – not that the work itself has been done too fast. I am quite sure that those passages which have been written with the greatest stress of labour and consequently with the greatest haste, have been the most effective and by no means the most inaccurate.[b]

The Small House at Allington redeemed my reputation with the spirited proprietor of the *Cornhill*, which must I should think have been damaged by *Brown, Jones, and Robinson*. In it appeared Lily Dale, one of the characters which readers of my novels have liked the best. In the love with which she has been greeted, I have hardly joined with much enthusiasm, feeling that she is somewhat of a female° prig. She became first engaged to a snob who jilted her, and then, though in truth she loved another man who was hardly good enough, she could not extricate herself sufficiently from the collapse of her first great misfortune to be able to make up her mind to be the wife of one whom, though she loved him, she did not altogether reverence. Prig as she was, she made her way into the hearts of many readers, – both young and old, – so that, from that time to this, I have been continually honoured with letters the purport of which has always been to beg me to marry Lily Dale to Johnny Eames. Had I done so however, Lily would never have so endeared herself to these people as to induce them to write letters to the author concerning her fate. It was because she could not get over her troubles that they loved her. Outside Lily Dale and the chief interest of the novel, *The Small House at Allington* is, I think, good. The De Courcy family are alive, as is also Sir Raffle Buffle who is a hero of the Civil Service. Sir Raffle was intended to represent a type, not a man; – but the man for the picture was soon chosen, and I was often assured that the portrait was very like. I have never seen the gentleman with whom I am supposed to have taken the liberty. There is also an old squire down at Allington whose life as a country gentleman, with rather straitened means, is I think well described.

Of *Can you Forgive Her?* I cannot speak with too great affection, though I do not know that of itself it did very much to encrease my reputation. As regards the story it was formed chiefly on that of the play which my friend Mr Bartley had rejected long since, the circumstances of which the reader may perhaps remember. The play had been called *The Noble Jilt;* – but I was afraid of the name for a novel, – lest the critics might throw a doubt on the nobility. There was more of tentative humility in that which I at last adopted. The character of the girl is carried through with considerable strength, but is not attractive. The humorous characters, which are also taken from the play, – a buxom widow who, with her eyes open chooses the most scampish of two selfish suitors because he is the better looking, – are well done. Mrs Greenow between Captain Bellfield and Mr Cheeseacre is very good fun, – as the fun of novels is. But that which endears the book to me is the first presentation which I made in it of Plantagenet Palliser with his wife Lady Glencora.

By no amount of description or asseveration could I succeed in making any reader understand how much these characters with their belongings have been to me in my latter life, or how frequently I have used them for the expression of my political and social convictions. They have been as real to me as free trade was to Mr Cobden, or the dominion of a party to Mr Disraeli; and, as I have not been able to speak from the benches of the House of Commons, or to thunder from platforms, or to be efficacious as a lecturer, they have served me as safety valves by which to deliver my soul. Mr Plantagenet Palliser had appeared in *The Small House at Allington*, but his birth had not been accompanied by many hopes. In the last pages of that novel he is made to seek a remedy for a foolish false step in life by marrying the grand heiress of the day; – but the personage of the great heiress does not appear till she comes on the scene as a married woman in *Can You Forgive Her?* He is the nephew and heir to a Duke – the Duke of Omnium, – who was first introduced in *Doctor Thorne* and afterwards in *Framley Parsonage*, and who is one of the belongings of whom I have spoken. In these personages and their friends, political and social, I have endeavoured to depict the faults and frailties and vices, – as also the virtues, the graces and the strength of our highest classes, and if I have not made the strength and virtues predominate[d] over the faults and vices I have not painted the picture as I intended. Plantagenet Palliser I think to be a very noble gentleman, – such a one as justifies to the nation the seeming anomaly of an hereditary peerage and of primogeniture. His wife is in all respects inferior to him; but she too has, or has been intended to have, beneath the thin stratum of her follies, a basis of good principle, which enabled her to live down the conviction of the original wrong which was done to her, and taught her to endeavour to do her duty in the position to which she was called.[2] She had received a great wrong, – having been made when little more than a child, to marry a man for whom she cared nothing, – when, however, though she was little more than a child, her love had been given else-where. She had very heavy troubles, but they did not overcome her.

As to the heaviest of these troubles I will say a word in vindica-tion of myself and of the way I handled it in my work. In the pages of *Can You Forgive Her?* the girl's first lover is introduced, beautiful, well-born and utterly worthless. To save a girl from wasting herself, and an heiress from wasting her property on such a scamp was cer-tainly the duty of the girl's friends. But it must ever be wrong to force a girl into a marriage with a man she does not love, – and certainly the more so when there is another whom she does love. In my endeavour to teach this lesson I subjected the young wife to the terrible danger of overtures from the man to whom her heart had been given. I was walking no doubt on ticklish ground, leaving for a while a doubt on the question whether the lover might or might not succeed. Then there came to me a letter from a distinguished dignit-ary of our Church,³ a man whom all men honoured, treating me with severity for what I was doing. It had been one of the innocent joys of his life, said the clergyman, to have my novels read to him by his daughters. But now I was writing a book which caused him to bid them close it! Must I, also, turn away to vicious sensation such as this? Did I think that a wife contemplating adultery was a character fit for my pages? I asked him in return whether from his pulpit, or at any rate from his communion table, he did not de-nounce adultery to his audience; and, if so, why it shouldᵉ not be open to me to preach the same doctrine to mine. I made known nothing which the purest girl could not but have learned and ought not to have learned elsewhere, and I certainly lent no attraction to the sin which I indicated. His rejoinder was full of grace, and en-abled him to avoid the annoyance of argumentation without aban-doning his cause. He said that the subject was so much too long for letters that he hoped I would go and stay a week with him in the country, – so that we might have it out. That opportunity, however, has never yet arrived.

Lady Glencora overcomes that trouble, and is brought, partly by her own sense of right and wrong and partly by the genuine nobility of her husband's conduct, to attach herself to him after a certain fashion.

The romance of her life is gone, but there remains a rich reality of which she is fully able to taste the flavour. She loves her rank and becomes ambitious, first of social, and then of political ascendancy. He is thoroughly true to her, after his thorough nature, and she, after her less perfect nature, is imperfectly true to him.

In conducting these characters from one story to another I realised the necessity not only of consistency, – which, had it been maintained by a hard exactitude would have been untrue to nature, – but also of those changes which time always produces. There are perhaps but few of us who after the lapse of ten years will be found to have changed our chief characteristics. The selfish man will still be selfish, and the false man false. But our manner of showing or of hiding these characteristics will be changed, – as also our power of adding to or diminishing their intensity. It was my study that these people as they grew in years should encounter the changes which come upon us all; and I think that I have succeeded. The Duchess of Omnium when she is playing the part of Prime Minister's wife, is the same woman as that Lady Glencora who almost longs to go off with Burgo Fitzgerald, but yet knows that she will never do so; and the Prime Minister Duke, with his wounded pride and sore spirit is he who for his wife's sake left power and place when they were first offered to him; – but they have undergone the changes which a life so stirring as theirs would naturally produce. To do all this thoroughly was in my heart from first to last, but I do not know that the game has been worth the candle. To carry out my scheme I have had to spread my picture over so wide a canvas that I cannot expect that any lover of such art should trouble himself to look at it as a whole. Who will read *Can You Forgive Her?*, *Phineas Finn*, *Phineas Redux*, and *The Prime Minister* consecutively in order that they may understand the characters of the Duke of Omnium, Plantagenet Palliser, and Lady Glencora? Who will even know that they should be so read? But in the performance of the work I had much gratification, and was enabled from time to time to have in this way that fling at the political doings of the day, which every man likes to take, if not in one fashion then in another. I look upon this string of characters, – carried sometimes into other novels than those just named, – as the best work of my life. Taking him altogether I think that Plantagenet Palliser stands more firmly on the ground than any other personage I have created.

On Christmas day 1863 we were startled by the news of Thackeray's death. He had then for many months given up the editorship of the *Cornhill Magazine*, – a position for which he was hardly fitted either by his habits or temperament, – but was still employed in writing for its pages. I had known him only for four years, but had grown into much intimacy with him and his family. I regard him as one of the most tender-hearted human beings I ever knew, who, with an exaggerated contempt for the foibles of the world at large, would entertain an almost equally exaggerated sympathy with the joys and troubles of individuals around him. He had been unfortunate in early life, – unfortunate in regard to money, unfortunate with an afflicted wife, unfortunate in having his home broken up before his children were fit to be his companions. This threw him too much upon clubs, and taught him to dislike general society. But it never affected his heart, or clouded his imagination. He could still revel in the pangs and joys of fictitious life, and could still feel, – as he did to the very last, – the duty of showing to his readers the evil consequences of evil conduct. It was, perhaps, his chief fault as a writer that he could never abstain from that dash of satire which he felt to be demanded by the weak-ness[f] which he saw around him. The satirist who writes nothing but satire should write but little, – or it will seem that his satire springs rather from his own caustic nature than from the sins of the world in which he lives. I myself regard *Esmond* as the greatest novel in the English language, basing that judgement on the excellence of its language, on the clear individuality of the characters, on the truth of its delineations in regard to the time selected, and on its great pathos. There are also in it a few scenes so told that even Scott has never equalled the telling. Let any one who doubts this read the passage in which Lady Castlewood induces the Duke of Hamilton to think that his nuptials with Beatrice will be honoured if Colonel Esmond will give away the bride. When he went from us he left behind living novelists with great names, but I think that they who best understood the matter felt that the greatest master of fiction of this age had gone.

Rachel Ray underwent a fate which no other novel of mine has encountered. Some years before this a periodical called *Good Words* had been established under the editorship of my friend Dr Norman Macleod, a well-known Presbyterian pastor in Glasgow. In 1863 he asked me to write a novel for his magazine, explaining to me that his principles did not teach him to confine his matter to religious subjects, and paying me the compliment of saying that he would feel himself quite safe in my hands. In reply I told him I thought he was wrong in his choice; – that though he might wish to give a novel to the readers of *Good Words*, a novel from me would hardly be what he wanted, and that I could not undertake to write either with any specially religious tendency, or in any fashion different from that which was usual to me. As worldly and, – if any one thought me wicked, – as wicked as I had heretofore been, I must still be, should I write for *Good Words*. He persisted in his request, and I came to terms as to a story for the periodical. I wrote it, and sent it to him, and shortly afterwards received it back, – a considerable portion having been printed, – with an intimation that it would not do. A letter more full of wailing and repentance no man ever wrote. It was he said all his own fault. He should have taken my advice. He should have known better. But the story, such as it was, he could not give to his readers in the pages of *Good Words*. Would I forgive him? Any pecuniary loss to which his decision might subject me, the owner of the publication would willingly make good. Of course I informed him that I felt no anger. There was some loss, – or would have been, – and that money I exacted, – feeling that the fault had in truth been with the Editor. There is the tale now to speak for itself. It is not brilliant, nor in any way very excellent, – but it certainly is not very wicked. There is some dancing in one of the early chapters, described, no doubt, with that approval of the amusement which I have always entertained; and it was this to which my friend demurred. It is more true of novels than perhaps of any thing else that one man's food is another man's poison.[4]

Miss Mackenzie was written with a desire to prove that a novel may be produced without any love; – but even in this attempt it breaks down before the conclusion. In order that I might be strong in my purpose I took for my heroine a very unattractive old maid who was overwhelmed by[g] money troubles; but even she was in love before the end of the book and made a romantic marriage with an old man. There is in this story an attack upon charitable bazaars made with a violence which will I think convince any reader that such attempts at raising money were at the time very odious to me. I beg to say that since that I have had no occasion to alter my opinion. *Miss Mackenzie* was published in the early spring of 1865.

At the same time I was engaged with others in establishing a periodical review in which some of us trusted much, and from which we expected great things. There was, however, in truth so little combination of idea among us that we were not justified in our trust or our expectations. And yet we were honest in our purpose, and have, I think, done some good by our honesty. The matter on which we were all agreed was freedom of speech combined with personal responsibility. We would be neither conservative nor liberal, neither religious nor freethinking, neither popular nor exclusive; – but we would let any man who had a thing to say and knew how to say it speak freely. But he should always speak with the responsibility of his name attached. In the very beginning I militated against this impossible negation of principles, – and did so most irrationally, seeing that I had agreed to the negation of principles, – by declaring that nothing should appear denying or questioning the divinity of Christ. It was a most preposterous claim to make for such a publication as we proposed, and it at once drove from us one or two who had proposed to join us. But we went on, and our company, – limited, – was formed. We subscribed I think £1250 each. I at least subscribed that amount, and, – having agreed to bring out our publication every fortnight after the manner of the well-known French publication,[5] – we called it *The Fortnightly*. We secured the services of G. H. Lewes as our Editor. We agreed to manage our finances by a Board which was to meet once a fortnight and of which I was the Chairman. And we determined that the payments for our literature should be made on a liberal and strictly ready money system. We carried out our principles till our money was all gone, and then we sold the copyright to Messrs Chapman & Hall for a trifle. But before we parted with our property we found that a fortnightly issue was not popular with the trade through whose hands the work must reach the public; and, as our periodical had not become sufficiently popular itself to bear down such opposition, we succumbed, and brought it out once a month. Still it was *The Fortnightly*, and still it is *The Fortnightly*. Of all the serial publications of the day it is probably the most serious, the most earnest, the least devoted to amusement, the least flippant, the least jocose – and yet it has the face to show itself month after month to the world with so absurd a misnomer! It is, as all who know the laws of modern literature are aware, a very serious thing to change the name of a periodical. By doing so you begin an altogether new enterprise. Therefore should the name be well chosen; – whereas this was very ill chosen, a fault for which I alone was responsible.

That theory of eclecticism was altogether impracticable. It was as though a gentleman should go into the House of Commons determined to support no party but to serve his country by individual utterances. Such gentlemen have gone into the House of Commons, but they have not served their country much. Of course the project broke down. Liberalism, free-thinking, and open enquiry will never object to appear in company with their opposites, because they have the conceit to think that they can quell those opposites; but the opposites will not appear in conjunction with liberalism, free-thinking and open enquiry. As a natural consequence our new publication became an organ of liberalism, free-thinking and open enquiry. The result has been good; and though there is much in the now established principles of the *Fortnightly* with which I do not myself agree, I may safely say that the publication has assumed an individuality and asserted for itself a position in our periodical literature which is well understood and highly respected.

As to myself, and my own hopes in the matter, – I was craving after some encrease in literary honesty, which I think is still desirable, but which is hardly to be attained by the means which then recommended themselves to me. In one of the early numbers I wrote a paper advocating the signature of the authors to periodical writing,[6] – admitting that the system should not be extended to journalistic articles on political subjects. I think that I made the best of my case; but further consideration has caused me to doubt whether the reasons which induced me to make an exception in favour of political writing, do not extend themselves also to writing on other subjects. Much of the literary criticism which we now have is very bad indeed; – so bad as to be open to the charge both of dishonesty and incapacity. Books are criticised without being read, – are criticised by favour, – and are trusted by Editors to the criticism of the incompetent. If the names of the critics were demanded Editors would be more careful. But I fear the effect would be that we should get but little criticism, and that the public would put but little trust in that little. An ordinary reader would not care to have his books recommended to him by Jones; – but the recommendation of the great unknown comes to him with all the weight of the *Times*, the *Spectator*, or the *Saturday*.

Though I admit so much I am not a recreant from the doctrine I then preached. I think that the name of the author does tend to honesty, and that the knowledge that it will be inserted adds much to the author's industry and care. It debars him also from illegitimate license and dishonest assertions. A man should never be ashamed to acknowledge that which he is not ashamed to publish. In the *Fortnightly* everything has been signed, and in this way good has, I think, been done. Signatures to articles in other periodicals have become much more common since the *Fortnightly* was commenced.

After a time Mr Lewes retired from the editorship, feeling that the work pressed too severely on his moderate strength. Our loss in him was very great, and there was considerable difficulty in finding a successor. I must say that the present proprietor has been fortunate in the choice which he did make. Mr John Morley has done the work with admirable patience, zeal, and capacity. Of course he has got around him a set of contributors whose modes of thought are, what we may call, much advanced – he being 'much advanced' himself could not work with other aids. The periodical has a peculiar tone of its own. But it holds its own with ability, and though there are many who perhaps hate it, there are none who despise it. When the Company sold it having spent about £9000 on it, it was worth little or nothing. Now I believe it to be a good property.

My own last personal concern with it was on a matter of fox-hunting.* There came out in it an article, from the pen of Mr Freeman the historian, condemning the amusement, which I love, on the grounds of cruelty and general brutality. Was it possible, asked Mr Freeman, quoting from Cicero,[7] that any educated man should find delight in so coarse a pursuit? Always bearing in mind my own connexion with the *Fortnightly*, I regarded this almost as the rising of a child against the father. I felt at any rate bound to answer Mr Freeman in the same columns, and I obtained Mr Morley's permission to do so. I wrote my defence of fox-hunting, and there it is. In regard to the charge of cruelty Mr Freeman seems to assert that nothing unpleasant should be done to any of God's creatures except for a useful purpose. The protection of a lady's shoulders from the cold is a useful purpose, and therefore a dozen fur-bearing animals may be snared in the snow and left to starve to death in the wires in order that the lady may have the tippet, – though a tippet of wool would serve the purpose as well as a tippet of fur. But the congregation and healthful amusement of one or two hundred persons, on whose behalf a single fox may or may not be killed, is not a useful purpose. I think that Mr Freeman has failed to perceive that amusement is as needful and almost as necessary as food and raiment. The absurdity of the further charge as to the general brutality of the pursuit and its consequent unfitness for an educated man is to be attributed to Mr Freeman's ignorance of what is really done and said in the hunting field, – perhaps to his misunderstanding of Cicero's words.

There was a rejoinder to my answer, – and I asked for space for further remarks. I could have it, the Editor said, if I much wished it, but he preferred that the subject should be closed. Of course I was silent. His sympathies were all with Mr Freeman, – and against the foxes who, but for fox-hunting, would cease to exist in England. And I felt that the *Fortnightly* was hardly the place for the defence of the sport. Afterwards Mr Freeman kindly suggested to me that he would be glad to publish my article in a little book to be put out by him condemnatory of fox-hunting generally. He was to have the last word and the first word, and that power of picking to pieces which he is known to use in

* I have written various articles for it since, especially two on Cicero,[8] to which I devoted great labour.[h]

so masterly a manner, without any reply from me! This I was obliged to decline. If he would give me the last word, – as he would have the first, then, I told him, I should be proud to join him in the book. This offer did not, however, meet his views.[i]

It had been decided by the Board of Management, somewhat in opposition to my own ideas on the subject, that the *Fortnightly Review* should always contain a novel. It was of course natural that I should write the first novel, and I wrote *The Belton Estate*. It is similar in its attributes to *Rachel Ray* and to *Miss Mackenzie*. It is readable and contains scenes which are true to life, but it has no peculiar merits and will add nothing to my reputation as a novelist. I have not looked at it since it was published, and now turning back to it in my memory, I seem to remember almost less of it than of any book that I have written.

CHAPTER II

'The Claverings', the 'Pall Mall Gazette',
'Nina Balatka', and 'Linda Tressel'.

The Claverings which came out in 1866 and 1867 was the last novel which I wrote for the *Cornhill*; and it was this for which I received the highest rate of pay that was ever accorded to me. It was the same length as *Framley Parsonage*, and the price was £2800. Whether much or little, it was offered by the Proprietor of the magazine, and was paid in a single cheque. In *The Claverings* I did not follow the habit which had now become very common to me of introducing personages whose names were already known to the readers of novels and whose characters were familiar to myself. If I remember rightly no one appears here who had appeared before or has been allowed to appear since. I consider the story as a whole to be good, though I am not aware that the public has ever corroborated that verdict. The chief character is that of a young woman who has married manifestly for money and rank, – so manifestly that she does not herself pretend, even while she is making the marriage, that she has any other reason. The man is old, disreputable, and a worn out debauchee. Then comes the punishment natural to the offence. When she is free the man whom she had loved and who had loved her is engaged to another woman. He vacillates and is weak, – in which weakness is the fault of the book as he plays the part of hero. But she is strong, – strong in her purpose, strong in her desires, and strong in her consciousness that the punishment which comes upon her has been deserved.

But the chief merit of *The Claverings* is in the genuine fun of some of the scenes. Humour has not been my forte, but I am inclined to think that the characters of Captain Boodle, Archie Clavering, and Sophie Gordeloup are humorous. Count Pateroff the brother of Sophie is also good, and disposes of the young hero's interference in a somewhat masterly manner. In *The Claverings*, too, there is a wife, whose husband is a brute to her, who loses an only child, – his heir, – and who is re-buked by her lord because the boy dies. Her sorrow is I think pathetic. From beginning to end the story is well told. But I doubt now whether any one reads *The Claverings*. When I remember how many novels I have written I know that I have[a] no right to expect that above a few of them shall endure even to the second year beyond publication. This story closed my connexion with the *Cornhill Magazine;* – but not with its owner, Mr George Smith, who subsequently brought out a further novel of mine in a separate form,[1] and who about this time established the *Pall Mall Gazette* to which paper I was for some years a contributor.

It was in 1865 that the *Pall Mall Gazette* was commenced, the name having been taken from a fictitious periodical which was the offspring of Thackeray's brain.[2] It was set on foot by the unassisted energy and resources of George Smith who had succeeded by means of his maga-zine and his publishing connexion in getting around him a society of literary men who sufficed as far as literary ability went to float the paper at once under favourable auspices. His two strongest staffs, probably were Jacob Omnium, whom I regard as the most forcible newspaper writer of my days, and Fitzjames[b] Stephen, the most con-scientious and industrious. To them the *Pall Mall Gazette* owed very much of its early success, – and to the untiring energy and general ability of its proprietor. Among its other contributors were George Lewes, Hannay – who I think, came up from Edinburgh for employment on its columns, Lord Houghton, Lord Strangford, Charles Merivale, Greenwood the present Editor, Greg,[3] myself, and very many others; – so many others that I have met at a *Pall Mall* dinner a crowd of guests who would have filled the House of Commons more respectably than I have seen it filled even on important occasions. There are many who now remember, – and no doubt when this is published there will still be[c] left some to remember, – the great stroke of business which was done by the revelations of a visitor to one of the casual wards in London.[4] A person had to be selected who would undergo the misery of a night among the usual occupants of a casual ward in a London poorhouse and who should all the same[d] be able to record what he felt and saw. The choice fell upon Mr Greenwood's brother, who certainly possessed the courage and the powers of endurance. The description which was very well given, was I think chiefly written by the brother of the Casual himself. It had a great effect, which was encreased by secrecy as to the person who encountered all the horrors of that night. I was more than once assured that Lord Houghton was the man. I heard it asserted also that I myself had been the hero. At last the unknown one could endure no longer that his honours should be hidden and revealed the truth, – in opposition I fear to promises to the contrary and instigated by a conviction that if known he could turn his honours to account. In the mean time, however, that record of a night passed in a workhouse had done more to establish the sale of the journal than all the legal lore of Stephen, or the polemical power of Higgins, or the critical acumen of Lewes.

My work was very various. I wrote much on the subject of the American War,[5] on which my feelings were at the time very keen, – subscribing, if I remember right, my name to all that I wrote. I contributed also some sets of sketches, of which those concerning hunting found favour with the public. They were republished afterwards and had a considerable sale, and may I think be still recommended to those who are fond of hunting as being accurate in their description of the different classes of people who are to be met in the hunting field. There was also a set of clerical sketches which was considered to be of sufficient importance to bring down on my head the critical wrath of a great Dean of that period. The most ill-natured review that was ever written upon any work of mine appeared in the *Contemporary* with reference to these *Clerical Sketches*. The critic told me that I did not understand Greek. That charge has been made not unfrequently by those who have felt themselves strong in that pride-producing language. It is much to read Greek with ease, but it is not disgraceful to be unable to do so. To pretend to be able to read[e] it without being able, – that is disgraceful. The critic, however, had been driven to wrath by my saying that Deans of the Church of England loved to revisit the glimpses of the Metropolitan Moon.'

I also did some critical work for the *Pall Mall* – as I did also for the *Fortnightly*. It was not to my taste, but was done in conformity with strict conscientious scruples. I read what I took in hand, and said what I believed to be true, – always giving to the matter time altogether incommensurate with the pecuniary result to myself. In doing this for the *Pall Mall* I fell into great sorrow. A gentleman, whose wife was dear to me as if she were my own sister, was in some trouble as to his conduct in the public service.[7] He had been blamed, as he thought unjustly, and vindicated himself in a pamphlet. This he handed to me one day asking me to read it, and express my opinion about it if I found that I had an opinion. I thought the request injudicious and I did not read the pamphlet. He met me again, and handing me a second pamphlet pressed me very hard. I promised him that I would read it, and that if I found myself able would express myself; – but that I must say, not what I wished to think, but what I did think. To this of course he assented. I then went very much out of my way to study the subject, – which was one requiring study. I found, or thought that I found, that the conduct of the gentleman in his office had been indiscreet; but that charges made against himself affecting his honour were baseless. This I said, emphasising much more strongly than was necessary the opinion which I had formed of his indiscretion, – as will so often be the case when a man has a pen in his hand. It is like a club or a sledge-hammer, – in using which either for defence or attack a man can hardly measure the strength of the blows which he gives. Of course there was offence, – and a breaking off of intercourse between loving friends, – and a sense of wrong received, and, I must own, too, of wrong done. It certainly was not open to me to whitewash with honesty him whom I did not find to be white; but there was no duty incumbent on me to declare what was his colour in my eyes, – no duty even to ascertain. But I had been ruffled by the persistency of the gentleman's request, – which should not have been made, and I punished him for his wrong-doing by doing a wrong myself. I must add that before he died his wife succeeded in bringing us together.

In the early days of the paper the proprietor, who at that time acted also as chief Editor, asked me to undertake a duty – of which the agony would, indeed, at no one moment have been so sharp as that endured in the casual ward, but might have been prolonged until human nature sank under it. He suggested to me that I should, during an entire season, attend the May meetings in Exeter Hall [8] and give a graphic, and if possible amusing description of the proceedings. I did attend one, – which lasted three hours, – and wrote a paper which I think was called 'A Zulu in search of a religion'. [9] But when the meeting was over, I went to that spirited proprietor and begged him to impose upon me some task more equal to my strength. Not even on behalf of the *Pall Mall Gazette* which was very dear to me, could I go through a second May meeting, – much less endure a season of such martyrdom.

I have to acknowledge that I found myself unfit for work on a newspaper. I had not taken to it early enough in life to learn its ways and bear its trammels. I was fidgetty when any word was altered in accordance with the judgement of the Editor, – who of course was responsible for what appeared. I wanted to select my own subjects, – not to have them selected for me; to write when I pleased, – and not when it suited others. As a permanent member of a staff I was of no use, and after two or three years I dropped out of the work.

From the commencement of my success as a writer, which I date from the beginning of the *Cornhill Magazine,* I had always felt an injustice in literary affairs which had never afflicted me or even suggested itself to me while I was unsuccessful. It seemed to me that a name once earned carried with it too much favour. I, indeed, had never reached a height to which praise was awarded as a matter of course; but there were others who sat on higher seats to whom the critics brought unmeasured incense and adulation even when they wrote, as they sometimes did write, trash which from a beginner would not have been thought worthy of the slightest notice. I hope no one will think that, in saying this, I am actuated by jealousy of others. Though I never reached that height, still I had so far progressed that that which I wrote was received with too much favour. The injustice which struck me did not consist in that which was withheld from me, but in that which was given to me. I felt that aspirants coming up below me might do work as good as mine, and probably much better work, and yet fail to have it appreciated. In order to test this, I determined to be such an aspirant myself, and to begin a course of novels anonymously in order that I might see whether I could obtain a second identity – whether as I had made one mark by such literary ability as I possessed I might succeed in doing so again. In 1865 I began a short tale called *Nina Balatka,* which in 1866 was published anonymously in *Blackwood's Magazine.* In 1867 this was followed by another of the same length called *Linda Tressel.* I will speak of them together as they are of the same nature and of nearly equal merit. Mr Blackwood who himself read the manuscript of *Nina Balatka* expressed an opinion that it would not from its style be discovered to have been written by me; – but it was discovered by Mr Hutton of the *Spectator* who found the repeated use of some special phrase which had rested upon his ear too frequently when reading for the purpose of criticism other works of mine. He declared in his paper that *Nina Balatka* was by me, showing I think more sagacity than good nature. I ought not, however, to complain of him, as of all the critics of my work, he has been the most observant and generally the most eulogistic.[10] *Nina Balatka* never rose sufficiently high in reputation to make its detection a matter of any importance. Once or twice I heard the story mentioned by readers who did not know me to be the author, and always with praise; but it had no real success. The same may be said of *Linda Tressel.* Blackwood, who of course knew the author, was willing to publish them, trusting that works by an experienced writer would make their way, even without the writer's name, – and he was willing to pay me for them perhaps half what they would have fetched with my name. But he did not find the speculation answer, and declined a third attempt though a third such tale was written for him.[11]

Nevertheless I am sure that the two stories are good. Perhaps the first is somewhat the better, as being the less lachrymose. They were both written very quickly but with a considerable amount of labour, – and both were written immediately after visits to the towns in which the scenes are laid, – Prague, mainly, and Nuremberg. Of course I had endeavoured to change not only my manner of language, but my manner of story-telling also, and in this, *pace* Mr Hutton, I think that I was successful. English life in them there was none. There was more of romance proper than had been usual with me. And I made an attempt at local colouring, at descriptions of scenes and places, which has not been usual with me. In all this I am confident that I was in a measure successful. In the loves and fears and hatreds of both Nina and Linda there is much that is pathetic. Prague is Prague and Nuremberg is Nuremberg. I know that the stories are good but they missed the object with which they had been written. Of course there is not in this any evidence that I might not have succeeded a second time, as I succeeded before, had I gone on with the same dogged perseverance. Mr Blackwood, had I still further reduced my price, would probably have continued the experiment; – no doubt would have done so had I continued it without any price.[f] Another ten years of unpaid unflagging labour might have built up a second reputation. But this at any rate did seem clear to me that with all the encreased advantage which practice in my art must have given me I could not at once induce English readers to read what I gave to them, – unless I gave it with my name.

I do not wish to have it supposed from this that I quarrel with public judgement in affairs of literature. It is a matter of course that in all things the public should trust to established reputation. It is as natural that a novel reader wanting novels should send to a library for those by George Eliot or Wilkie Collins, as that a lady when she wants a pie for a picnic should go to Fortnum and Mason. Fortnum and Mason can only make themselves Fortnum and Mason by dint of time and good pies combined. If Titian were to send us a portrait from the other world, as certain dead poets send their poetry, by means of a medium, it would be some time before the art critic of the *Times* would discover its value. We may sneer at the want of judgement thus displayed; – but such slowness of judgement is human and has always existed. I say all this here because my thoughts on the matter have forced upon me the conviction that very much consideration is due to the bitter feelings of disappointed authors.

We who have succeeded are so apt to tell new aspirants not to aspire because the thing to be done may probably be beyond their reach. 'My dear young lady, had you not better stay at home and darn your stockings?' 'As, Sir, you have asked for my candid opinion I can only counsel you to try some other work of life which may be better suited to your abilities.' What old established successful author has not said such words as these to humble aspirants for critical advice till they have become almost formulas. No doubt there is cruelty in such answers, but the man who makes them has considered the matter within himself and has resolved that such cruelty is the best mercy. No doubt the chances against literary aspirants are very great. It is so easy to aspire – and to begin! A man cannot make a watch or a shoe without a variety of tools and many materials. He must also have learned much. But any young lady can write a book who has a sufficiency of pens and paper. It can be done anywhere, in any clothes – which is a great thing, at any hours – to which happy accident in literature I owe my success. And the success when achieved is so pleasant! The aspirants of course are very many, and the experienced councillor when asked for his candid judgement as to this or that effort, knows that among every hundred efforts there will be ninety nine failures. Then the answer is so ready: 'My dear young lady, do darn your stockings, it will be for the best.' Or perhaps less tenderly to the male aspirant: 'You must earn some money, you say. Don't you think that a stool in a counting house might be better?' The advice will probably be good advice; – probably no doubt, as may be proved by the terrible majority of failures. But who is to be sure that he is not expelling an angel from the heaven to which, if less roughly treated, he would soar, – that he is not dooming some Milton to be mute and inglorious,[12] who, but for such cruel ill-judgement would become vocal to all ages?

The answer to all this seems to be ready enough. The judgement whether cruel or tender should not be ill-judgement. He who consents to sit as judge should have capacity for judging. But in this matter no accuracy of judgement is possible. It may be that the matter subjected to the critic is so bad or so good as to make an assured answer possible. 'You at any rate cannot make this your vocation' or, 'You at any rate can succeed if you will try.' But cases as to which such certainty can be expressed are rare. The critic who wrote the article on the early verses of Lord Byron which produced the *English Bards and Scotch Reviewers*, was justified in his criticism by the merits of the *Hours of Idleness*. The lines had nevertheless been written by that Lord Byron who became our Byron. In a little satire called *The Biliad*, which I think nobody knows, are the following well-expressed lines.

> When Payne Knight's *Taste* was issued to the Town,
> A few Greek verses in the text set down
> Were torn to pieces, mangled into hash,
> Doomed to the flames as execrable trash, -
> In short were butchered rather than dissected,
> And several false quantities detected;
> Till, when the smoke had vanished from the cinders,
> 'Twas just discovered that the lines were Pindar's[13]

There can be no assurance against cases such as these, and yet we are so free with our advice, always bidding the young aspirant to desist!

There is perhaps no career of life so charming as that of a successful man of letters. Those little unthought of advantages which I just now named are in themselves attractive. If you like the town live in the town, and do your work there; if you like the country choose the country. It may be done on the top of a mountain or in the bottom of a pit. It is compatible with the rolling of the sea, and the motion of a railway. The clergyman, the lawyer, the doctor, the member of Parliament, the clerk in a public office, the tradesman, and even his assistant in the shop, must dress in accordance with certain fixed laws; – but the author need sacrifice to no grace, hardly even to Propriety. He is subject to no bonds such as those which bind other men. Who else is free from all shackle as to hours? The judge must sit at ten, and the Attorney-General who is making his £20,000 a year must be there with his bag. The Prime Minister must be in his place on that weary front bench shortly after prayers, and must sit there, either asleep or awake, even though — or — should be addressing the House. During all that Sunday which he maintains should be a day of rest, the active clergyman toils like a galley-slave. The actor when eight o'clock comes is bound to his footlights. The Civil Service clerk must sit there from ten till four, – unless his office be fashionable when from twelve to six is just as heavy on him. The author may do his work at five in the morning when he is fresh from his bed or at three in the morning before he goes there. And the author wants no capital, and encounters no risks. When once he is afloat, the publisher finds all that, – and indeed, unless he be rash, finds it whether he be afloat or not. But it is in the consideration which he enjoys that the successful author finds his richest reward. He is, if not of equal rank, yet of equal standing with the highest, and, if he be open to the amenities of society, may choose his own circles. He without money can enter doors which are closed against almost all but him and the wealthy. I have often heard it said that in this country the man of letters is not recognised. I believe the meaning of this to be that men of letters are not often invited to be Knights and Baronets. I do not think that they wish it; – and if they had it they would, as a body, lose much more than they would gain. I do not at all desire to have letters put after my name or to be called Sir Anthony, but if my friends Tom Hughes and Charles Reade became Sir Thomas and Sir Charles, I do not know how I might feel, – or how my wife might feel, if we were left unbedecked. As it is, the man of letters who would be selected for titular honour, if such bestowal of honours were customary, receives from the general respect of those around him a much more pleasant recognition of his worth.

If this be so, – if it be true that the career of the successful literary man be thus pleasant, – it is not wonderful that many should attempt to win the prize. But how is a man to know whether or not he has within him the qualities necessary for such a career? He makes an attempt and fails; – repeats his attempt, and fails again! So many have succeeded at last who have failed more than once or twice! Who will tell him the truth as to himself? Who has power to find out that truth? The hard man sends him off without a scruple to that office stool. The soft man assures him that there is much merit in his manuscript!

O, my young aspirant, – if ever such a one should read these pages,

– be sure that no one can tell you. To do so it would be necessary not only to know what there is now within you, but also to foresee what time will produce there. This however, I think may be said to you, without any doubt as to the wisdom of the counsel given, that if it be necessary for you to live by your work, do not begin by trusting to literature. Take the stool in the office as recommended to you by the hard man, and then, in such leisure hours as may belong to you, let the praise which has come from the lips of that soft man induce you to persevere in your literary attempts. Should you fail, then your failure will not be fatal, – and what better could you have done with those leisure hours had you not so failed? Such double toil, you will say, is severe. Yes. But if you want this thing you must submit to severe toil.

Some time before this I had become one of the Committee appointed for the distribution of the moneys of the Royal Literary Fund, and in that capacity I heard and saw much of the sufferings of authors. I may in a future chapter speak further of this Institution, which I regard with great affection and in reference to which I should be glad to record certain convictions of my own; but I allude to it now because the experience I have acquired in being active in its cause forbids me to advise any young man or woman to enter boldly on a literary career in search of bread. I know how utterly I should have failed myself had my bread not been earned elsewhere while I was making my efforts. During ten years of work, which I commenced with some aid from the fact that others of my family were in the same profession, I did not earn enough to buy me the pens, ink and paper which I was using. And then, when, with all my experience in my art, I began again as from a new springing point, I should have failed again unless again I could have given years to the task. Of course there have been many who have done better than I, – many whose powers have been infinitely greater. But then too I have seen the failure of many who were greater.

The career, when success has been achieved, is certainly very pleasant; but the agonies which are endured in the search for that success are often terrible. And the author's poverty is I think harder to be borne than any other poverty. The man, whether rightly or wrongly, feels that the world is using him with extreme injustice. The more absolutely he fails, the higher, it is probable, he will reckon his own merits; and the keener will be the sense of injury in that he whose work is of so high a nature cannot get bread, while they whose tasks are mean, are lapped in luxury. 'I, with my well-filled mind, with my clear intellect, with all my gifts, cannot earn a poor crown a day, while that fool who simpers in a little room behind a shop, makes his thousands every year!' The very charity, to which he too often is driven, is bitterer to him than to others. While he takes it he almost spurns the hand that gives it to him, and every fibre of his heart within him is bleeding with a sense of injury.

The career when successful is pleasant enough certainly; – but when unsuccessful it is of all careers the most agonising.

CHAPTER 12

On Novels and the Art of Writing Them.

It is nearly twenty years since I proposed to myself to write a history of English Prose Fiction. I shall never do it now, but the subject is so good a one, that I recommend it heartily to some man of letters who shall at the same time be indefatigable and light-handed. I acknowledge that I broke down in the task, because I could not endure the labour in addition to the other labours of my life. Though the book might be charming the work was very much the reverse. It came to have a terrible aspect to me, as did that proposition that I should sit out all the May meetings of a season. According to my plan of such a history it would be necessary to read an infinity of novels, and not only to read them but so to read them as to be able to point[a] out the excellence of those which are most excellent, and to explain the defects of those which, though defective, had still reached sufficient reputation to make them worthy of notice. I did read many after this fashion, – and here and there I have the criticisms which I wrote. In regard to many they were written on some blank page within the book. I have not however, even a list of the books so criticised. I think that *The*

Arcadia was the first, and *Ivanhoe* the last. My plan, as I settled it at last, had been to begin with *Robinson Crusoe* which is the earliest really popular novel which we have in our language,[1] and to continue the review so as to include the works of all English novelists of reputation excepting[b] those who might still be living when my task should be completed. But when Dickens and Bulwer died[2] my spirit flagged, and that which I had already found to be very difficult had become almost impossible to me at my then period of life.

I began my own studies on the subject with works much earlier than *Robinson Crusoe*, and made my way through a variety of novels which were necessary for my purpose but which, in the reading, gave me no pleasure whatever. I never worked harder than at the *Arcadia*, or read more detestable trash than the stories written by Mrs Aphra Behn;[3] – but these two were necessary to my purpose, which was not only to give an estimate of the novels as I found them, but to describe how it had come to pass that the English novels of the present day have become what they are, to point out the effects which they have produced, and to enquire whether their great popularity has on the whole done good or evil to the people who read them. I still think that the book is one well worthy to be written.

I intended to write that book to vindicate my own profession as a novelist, and also to vindicate that public taste in literature which has created and nourished the profession which I follow. And I was stirred up to make such an attempt by a conviction that there still exists among us Englishmen a prejudice in respect to novels, which might perhaps be lessened by such a work. This prejudice is not against the reading of novels, as is proved by their general acceptance among us. But it exists strongly in reference to the appreciation in which they are professed to be held, and it robs them of much of that high character which they may claim to have earned by their grace, their honesty and good teaching.

No man can work long at any trade without being brought to consider much whether that which he is daily doing tends to evil or to good. I have written many novels, and have known many writers of novels, and I can assert that such thoughts have been strong with them and with myself. But in acknowledging that these writers have received from the public a full measure of credit for such genius, ingenuity, or perseverance as each may have displayed, I feel that there is still wanting to them a just appreciation of the excellence of their calling and a general understanding of the high nature of the work which they perform.

By the common consent of all mankind who have read, poetry takes the highest place in literature. That nobility of expression and all but divine grace of words which she is bound to attain before she can make her footing good, is not compatible with prose. Indeed it is that which turns prose into poetry. When that has been in truth achieved the reader knows that the writer has soared above the earth, and can teach his lessons somewhat as a God might teach. He who sits down to write his tale in prose makes no such attempt, nor does he dream that the poet's honour is within his reach; – but his teaching is of the same nature, and his lessons all tend to the same end. By either, false sentiment may be fostered, false notions of humanity may be engendered; false honour, false love, false worship may be created; by either, vice instead of virtue may be taught. But by each, equally, may true honour, true love, true worship, and true humanity be inculcated; and that will be the greatest teacher who will spread such truth the widest. But at present, much as novels, as novels, are bought and read, there exists still an idea, – a feeling which is very prevalent, – that novels at their best are but innocent. Young men and women, – and old men and women too, – read more of them than they read of poetry because such reading is easier than the reading of poetry; but they read them, – as men eat pastry after dinner,[4] – not without some inward conviction that the taste is vain if not vicious. I take upon myself to say that it is neither vicious nor vain.

But all writers of fiction who have desired to think well of their own work will probably have had doubts on their minds before they have arrived at this conclusion. Thinking much of my own daily labour and of its nature I felt myself at first to be much afflicted and then to be deeply aggrieved by the opinion expressed by wise and thinking men as to the work done by novelists.[c5]

But when, by degrees, I dared to examine and sift the sayings of such men, I found them to be sometimes silly and often arrogant.[d] I began to enquire what had been the nature of English novels since they first became common in our own language, and to be desirous of ascertaining whether they had done harm or good. I could well remember that in my own young days they had not taken that undisputed possession of drawing-rooms which they now hold. Fifty years ago, when George IV was King, they were not indeed treated as Lydia had been forced to treat them in the preceding reign, when, on the approach of elders, *Peregrine Pickle* was hidden beneath the bolster, and *Lord Aimsworth*[6] put away under the sofa. But the families in which an unrestricted permission was given for the reading of novels were very few, and from many they were altogether banished. The high poetic genius and correct morality of Walter Scott had not altogether succeeded in making men and women understand that lessons which were good in poetry could not be bad in prose. I remember that in those days an embargo was laid upon novel-reading as a pursuit, which was to the novelist a much heavier tax than that want of full appreciation of which I now complain.

There is, we all know, no such embargo now. May we not say that young people of an age to read have got too much power into their own hands to endure any very complete embargo? Novels are read right and left, above stairs and below, in town houses and in country parsonages, by young countesses and by farmer's daughters, by old lawyers and by young students. It has not only come to pass that a special provision of them has to be made for the godly but that the provision so made must now include books which a few years since the godly would have thought to be profane. It was this necessity which a few years since induced the Editor of *Good Words* to apply to me for a novel, – which indeed, when supplied, was rejected, but which now probably, owing to further change in the same direction, would have been accepted.[7]

If such be the case, if the extension of novel-reading be so wide as I have described it, then very much good or harm must be done by novels. The amusement of the time can hardly be the only result of any book that is read, and certainly not so with a novel which appeals especially to the imagination and solicits the sympathy of the young. A vast proportion of the teaching of the day, – greater probably than many of us have acknowledged to ourselves, – comes from these books which are in the hands of all readers. It is from them that girls learn what is expected from them, and what they are to expect, when lovers come; and also from them that young men unconsciously learn what are, or should be, or may be, the charms of love, – though I fancy that few young men will think so little of their natural instincts and powers as to believe that I am right in saying so. Many other lessons also are taught. In these times, when the desire to be honest is pressed so hard, is so violently assaulted by the ambition to be great; in which riches are the easiest road to greatness; when the temptations to which men are subjected dull their eyes to the perfected iniquities of others; when it is so hard for a man to decide vigorously that the pitch, which so many are handling, will defile him if it be touched; men's conduct will be actuated much by that which is from day to day depicted to them as leading to glorious or inglorious results.[e] The woman who is described as having obtained all that the world holds to be precious by lavishing her charms and her caresses unworthily and heartlessly will induce other women to do the same with theirs, – as will she who is made interesting by exhibitions of bold passion teach others to be spuriously passionate. The young man who in a novel becomes a hero, perhaps a member of Parliament and almost a Prime Minister by trickery, falsehood and flash cleverness will have many followers whose attempts to rise in the world ought to lie heavily on the conscience of novelists who create fictitious Cagliostros.[8] There are Jack Sheppards other than those who break into houses and out of prisons; – Macheaths[9] who deserve the gallows more than Gay's hero.

Thinking of all this, as a novelist surely must do, – as I certainly have done through my whole career, – it becomes to him a matter of deep conscience how he shall handle those characters by whose words and doings he hopes to interest his readers. It will very frequently be the case that he will be tempted to sacrifice something for effect, to say a word or two here, or to draw a picture there, for which he feels that he has the power and which when spoken or drawn would be alluring. The regions of absolute vice are foul and odious. The savour of them, till custom has hardened the palate and the nose, is disgusting. In these he will hardly tread. But there are outskirts on these regions on which sweet-smelling flowers seem to grow, and grass to be green. It is in these border lands that the danger lies. The novelist may not be dull. If he commit that fault he can do neither harm nor good. He must please, and the flowers and soft grass[f] in these neutral territories sometimes seem to give him so easy an opportunity of pleasing!

The writer of stories must please, or he will be nothing. And he must teach whether he wish to teach or no. How shall he teach lessons of virtue and at the same time make himself a delight to his readers? That sermons are not in themselves often thought to be agreeable we all know. Nor are disquisitions on moral philosophy supposed to be pleasant light reading[g] for our idle hours. But the novelist, if he have a conscience must preach his sermons with the same purpose as the clergyman, and must have his own system of Ethics. If he can do this efficiently, if he can make virtue alluring and vice ugly, while he charms his readers instead of wearying them, then I think Mr Carlyle need not call him distressed, nor talk of that long ear of fiction, nor question whether he be or not the most foolish of existing mortals.[10]

I think that many have done so; – so many that we English novelists may boast as a class that such has been the general result of our work. Looking back to the past generation I may say with certainty that such was the operation of the novels of Miss Edgeworth, Miss Austen, and Walter Scott. Coming down to my own times I find such to have been the teaching of Thackeray, of Dickens, and of George Eliot. Speaking, as I shall speak to any who may read these words with that absence of self-personality which the dead may claim, I will boast that such has been the result of my own writing. Can any one by search through the works of the six great novelists[h] I have named find a scene, a passage, or a word that would teach a girl to be immodest, or a man to be dishonest? When men in their pages have been described as dishonest and women as immodest, have they not ever been punished? It is not for the novelist to say baldly and simply, 'because you lied here, or were heartless there, because you Lydia Bennet forgot the lessons of your honest home, or you Earl Leicester were false through your ambition, or you, Beatrix,[11] loved too well the glitter of the world, therefore you shall be scourged with scourges either in this world or in the next'; but it is for him to show, as he carries on his tale that his Lydia, or his Leicester, or his Beatrix will be dishonoured in the estimation of all readers by his or her vices. Let a woman be drawn clever, beautiful, attractive, – so as to make men love her and women almost envy her, – and let her be made also heartless, unfeminine, and ambitious of evil grandeur, as was Beatrix. What a danger is there not in such a character! To the novelist who shall handle it what peril of doing harm! But if at last it have been so handled that every girl who reads of Beatrix shall say, 'Oh, not like that; – let me not be like that!' and that every youth shall say, 'Let me not have such a one as that to press to my bosom, any thing rather than that!' – then will not the novelist have preached his sermon as perhaps no clergyman can preach it?

Very much of a novelist's work must appertain to the intercourse between young men and young women. It is admitted that a novel can hardly be made interesting or successful without love. Some few might be named but even in those the attempt breaks down, and the softness of love is found to be necessary to complete the story. *Pickwick* has been named as an exception to the rule but even in *Pickwick* there are three or four sets of lovers whose little amatory longings give a softness to the work. I tried it once, with Miss Mackenzie, but I had to make her fall in love at last. In this frequent allusion to the passion which most strongly stirs[i] the imagination of the young, there must be danger. Of that the writer of fiction is probably well aware. Then the question has to be asked whether the danger may not be so averted that good may be the result; – and to be answered.

In one respect the necessity of dealing with love is advantageous, – advantageous from the very circumstance which has made love necessary to all novelists. It is necessary because the passion is one which interests or has interested all. Every one feels it, has felt it, or expects to feel it, – or else rejects it with an eagerness which still perpetuates the interest. If the novelist therefore can so handle the subject as to do good by his handling, as to teach wholesome lessons in regard to love, the good which he does will be very wide. If I can teach politicians that they can do their business better by truth than by falsehood, I do a great service; but it is done to a limited number of persons. But if I can make young men and women believe that truth in love will make them happy, then, if my writings be popular, I shall have a very large class of pupils. No doubt the cause of[1] that fear which did exist as to novels arose from an idea that this[k] matter of love would be treated in an inflammatory and generally unwholesome manner. 'Madam,' says Sir Anthony in the play,[12] 'a circulating library in a town is an evergreen tree of diabolical knowledge. It blossoms through the year; and, depend on it, Mrs Malaprop, that they are who are so fond of handling the leaves, will long for the fruit at last.' Sir Anthony was no doubt right. But he takes it for granted that the longing for the fruit is an evil. The novelist who writes of love thinks differently and believes[l] that the honest love of an honest man is a treasure which a good girl may fairly hope to win, – and that if she can be taught to wish only for that she will have been taught to entertain only wholesome wishes.

I can easily believe that a girl should be taught to wish to love by reading how Laura Bell loved Pendennis.[13] Pendennis was not in truth a very worthy man nor did he make a very good husband; but the girl's love was so beautiful, – and the wife's love when she became a wife, so womanlike and at the same time so sweet, so unselfish, so wifely, so worshipful, – in the sense in which wives are told that they are[m] to worship their husbands, – that I cannot believe that any girl can be injured, or even not benefitted, by reading of Laura's love.

There used[n] to be many who thought, and probably there still are some, even here in England, who think that a girl should hear nothing of love till the time come in which she is to be married. That, no doubt, was the opinion of Sir Anthony Absolute and of Mrs Malaprop. But I am hardly disposed to believe that the old system was more favourable than ours to purity[o] of manners. Lydia Languish, though she was constrained by fear of her aunt to hide the book, yet had *Peregrine Pickle* in her collection. While human nature talks of love so forcibly it can hardly serve our turn to be silent on the subject. '*Naturam expellas furcâ, tamen usque recurret.*'[14] There are countries in which it has been in accordance with the manners of the upper classes that the girl should be brought to marry the man almost out of the nursery – or rather perhaps out of the convent, – without having enjoyed that freedom of thought which the reading of novels and of poetry will certainly produce; but I do not know that the marriages so made have been thought to be happier than our own.

Among English novels of the present day, and among English novelists, a great division is made. There are sensational novels, and anti-sensational; sensational novelists, and anti-sensational; sensational readers, and anti-sensational. The novelists who are considered to be anti-sensational are generally called realistic. I am realistic. My friend Wilkie Collins[15] is generally supposed to be sensational. The readers who prefer the one are supposed to take delight in the elucidation of character. Those who hold by the other are charmed by the construction[p] and gradual development of a plot. All this is I think a mistake, – which mistake arises from the inability of the imperfect artist to be at the same time realistic and sensational. A good novel should be both, – and both in the highest degree. If a novel fail in either, there is a failure in art. Let those readers who believe that they do not like sensational scenes in novels, think of some of those passages from our great novelists which have charmed them most, – of Rebecca in the castle with Ivanhoe, of Burley in the cave with Morton, of the mad lady tearing the veil of the expectant bride in *Jane Eyre*, of Lady Castlewood as, in her indignation, she explains to the Duke of Hamilton Henry Esmond's right to be present at the marriage of his Grace with Beatrix, – may I add of Lady Mason as she makes her confession at the feet of Sir Peregrine Orme?[16] Will any one say that the authors of these passages have sinned in being over-sensational? No doubt a string of horrible incidents bound together without truth in details and told as affecting personages without character, – wooden blocks who cannot make themselves known to the reader as men and women, – does not instruct or amuse or even fill the mind with awe. Horrors heaped upon horrors, and which are horrors only in themselves and not as touching any recognised and known person, are not tragic and soon cease even to horrify. And such would-be tragic elements of a story may be encreased without end and without difficulty. I may tell you of a woman murdered, – murdered in the same street with you, in the next house; that she was a wife, murdered by her husband, – a bride not yet a week a wife. I may add to it for ever. I may say that the murderer roasted her alive. There is no end to it. I may declare that a former wife was treated with equal barbarity, and may assert that as the murderer was led away to execution he declared his only sorrow, his only regret to be that he could not live to treat a third wife after the same fashion. There is nothing so easy as the creation and the cumulation of fearful incidents after this fashion. If such creation and cumulation be the beginning and the end of the novelist's work, – and novels have been written which seem to be without other attractions, – nothing can be more dull or more useless. But not on that account are we averse to tragedy in prose fiction. As in poetry, so in prose, he who can deal adequately with tragic elements is a greater artist and reaches a higher aim than the writer whose efforts never carry him above the mild walks of everyday life. *The Bride of Lammermoor*[17] is a tragedy throughout, in spite of its comic elements. The life of Lady Castlewood of whom I have spoken before, is a tragedy. Rochester's wretched thraldom to his mad wife in *Jane Eyre* is a tragedy. But these stories charm us, not simply because they are tragic, but because we feel that men and women with flesh and blood, creatures with whom we can sympathise, are struggling amidst their woes. It all lies in that. No novel is anything, for purposes[q] either of comedy or tragedy, unless the reader can sympathise with the characters whose names he finds upon the pages. Let an author so tell his tale as to touch his reader's heart and draw his tears, and he has, so far, done his work well. Truth let there be; – truth of description, truth of character, human truth as to men and women. If there be such truth I do not know that a novel can be too sensational.

I did intend when I meditated that history of British fiction to include within its pages some rules for the writing of novels, – or I might perhaps say with more modesty, to offer some advice on the art to such tyros in it as might be willing to take advantage of the experience of an old hand. But the matter I fear would be too long for this episode, and I am not sure that I have as yet got the rules quite settled in my own mind. I will however say a few words on one or two points which my own practice has pointed out to me.

I have from the first felt sure that the writer when he sits down to commence his novel should do so, not because he has to tell a story, but because he has a story to tell. The novelist's first novel will generally have sprung from the right cause. Some series of events, or some development of character will have presented itself to his imagination, – and this he feels so strongly that he thinks he can present his picture in strong and agreeable language to others. He sits down and tells his story, because he has a story to tell; – as you, my friend, when you have heard something which has at once tickled your fancy or moved your pathos will hurry to tell it to the first person you meet. But when that first novel has been received graciously by the public and has made for itself a success, then the writer, naturally feeling that the writing of novels is within his grasp, looks about for something to tell in another. He cudgels his brains, not always successfully, and sits down to write not because he has something which he burns to tell, but because he feels it to be incumbent on him to be telling something. As you, my friend, if you are very successful in the telling of that first story, will become ambitious of further story-telling, and will look out for anec-dotes, – in the narration of which you will not improbably sometimes distress your audience.

So it has been with many novelists, – who after some good work, perhaps after very much good work, – have distressed their audience because they have gone on with their work till their work has become simply a trade with them. Need I make a list of such, seeing that it would contain the names of those who have been greatest in the art of British novel-writing? They have at last become weary of that portion of a novelist's work which is of all the most essential to success. That a man as he grows old should feel the labour of writing to be a fatigue is natural enough. But a man to whom writing well has becume a habit may write well though he be fatigued. But the weary novelist refuses any longer to give his mind to that work of observation and reception from which has come his power, without which work his power cannot be continued, – which work should be going on, not only when he is at his desk, but in all his walks abroad, in all his movements through the world, in all his intercourse with his fellow creatures. He has become a novelist, as another has become a poet, because in those walks abroad he has, unconsciously for the most part, been drawing in matter from all that he has seen and heard. But this has not been done without labour even when the labour has been unconscious. Then there comes a time when he shuts his eyes and shuts his ears. When we talk of memory fading as age comes on it is such shutting of eyes and ears that we mean. The things around cease to interest us and we cannot exercise our minds upon them. To the novelist thus wearied there comes the demand for further novels. He does not know his own defect, and, even if he did, he does not wish to abandon his profession. He still writes, – but he writes because he has to tell a story, not because he has any story to tell. What reader of novels has not felt the 'woodenness' of this mode of telling? The characters do not live and move, but are cut out of blocks and are propped against the wall. The incidents are arranged in certain lines, – the arrangement being as palpable to the reader as it has been to the writer,[s] – but do not follow each other as results naturally demanded by previous action. The reader can never feel, – as he ought to feel, – that only for that flame of the eye, only for that angry word, only for that moment of weakness, all might have been different. The course of the tale is one piece of stiff mechanism in which there is no room for a doubt.

These, it may be said, are reflections which I being an old novelist, might make useful to myself as reasons for discontinuing[t] my work, but can hardly be needed by those tyros of whom I have spoken. That they are applicable to myself I readily admit, – but I also find that they apply to many beginners. Some of us who are old fail at last because we are old. It would be well that each of us should say to himself –

Solve senescentem mature sanus equum, ne
Peccet ad extremum ridendus.[18]

But many young fail also because they endeavour to tell stories when they have none to tell. And this comes from idleness rather than innate incapacity. The mind has not been sufficiently at work when the tale has been commenced, nor is it kept sufficiently at work as the tale is continued. I have never troubled myself much about the construction of plots, and am not now insisting specially on thoroughness in a branch of work in which I myself have not been very thorough. I am not sure that the construction of a perfected plot has been at any period within my power. But the novelist has other aims than the elucidation of his plot. He desires to make his readers so intimately acquainted with his characters that the creations[u] of his brain should be to them speaking, moving, living human creatures. This he can never do unless he know those fictitious personages himself, and he can never know them well unless he can live with them in the full reality of established intimacy. They must be with him as he lies down to sleep and as he wakes from his dreams. He must learn to hate them and to love them. He must argue with them, quarrel with them, forgive them, and even submit to them. He must know of them whether they be cold-blooded or passionate, whether true or false, and how far true and how far false. The depth and the breadth and the narrowness and the shallowness of each should be clear to him. And as, here in our outer world, we know that men and women change, – become worse or better as temptation or conscience may guide them, – so should these creatures[v] of his change, and every change should be noted by him. On the last day of each month recorded every person in his novel should be a month older than on the first. If the would-be novelist have aptitudes that way all this will come to him without much struggling – but if it do not come I think he can only make novels of wood.

It is so that I have lived with my characters, and thence has come whatever success I have obtained. There is a gallery of them and of all in that gallery I may say that I know the tone of the voice, and the colour of the hair, every flame of the eye and the very clothes they wear. Of each man I could assert whether he could[w] have said these or the other words, of every woman whether she would then have smiled or so have frowned. When I shall feel that this intimacy ceases then I shall know that the old horse should be turned out to grass. That I shall feel it when I ought to feel it, I will by no means say. I do not know that I am at all wiser than Gil Blas' Canon.[19] But I do know that the power indicated is one without which the teller of tales cannot tell them to any good effect.

The language in which the novelist is to put forth his story, the colours with which he is to paint his picture, must of course be to him matter of much consideration. Let him have all other possible gifts, imagination, observation, erudition, and industry, they will avail him nothing for his purpose unless he can put forth his work in pleasant words. If he be confused, tedious, harsh, or unharmonious readers will certainly reject him. The reading of a volume of history or on science may represent itself as a duty, and though the duty may by a bad style be made very disagreeable the conscientious reader will perhaps perform it. But the novelist will be assisted by no such feeling. Any reader may reject his work without the burden of a sin. It is the first necessity of his position that he make himself pleasant. To do this much more is necessary than to write correctly. He may, indeed, be pleasant without being correct, – as I think can be proved by the works of more than one distinguished novelist. But he must be intelligible, – intelligible without trouble; and he must be harmonious.

Any writer who has read even a little will know what is meant by the word intelligible. It is not sufficient that there be a meaning which[x] may be hammered out of the sentence, but that the language should be so pellucid that the meaning should be rendered without an effort to the reader, – and not only some proposition of meaning, but the very sense, no more and no less, which the writer has intended to put into his words. What Macaulay says should be remembered by all writers: 'How little the all-important art of making meaning pellucid is studied now! Hardly any popular author except myself thinks of it.'[20] The language used should be as ready and as efficient a conductor of the mind of the writer to the mind of the reader as is the electric spark which passes from one battery to another battery.[y] In all written matter the spark should carry everything, but in matters recondite the recipient will search to see that he misses nothing and that he takes nothing away too much. The novelist cannot expect that any such search will be made. A young writer, who may[z] acknowledge the truth of what I am saying will often feel himself tempted by the difficulties of language to tell himself that some one little doubtful passage, some single collocation of words which is not quite what it ought to be, will not matter. I know well what a stumbling block such a passage may be. But he should leave none such behind him as he goes on. The habit of writing clearly soon comes to the writer who is a severe critic to himself.

As to that harmonious expression which I think is required I shall find it more difficult to express my meaning. It will be granted I think by readers that a style may be rough, and yet both forcible and intelligible; but it will seldom come to pass that a novel written in a rough style will be popular, – and less often that a novelist who habitually uses such a style will become so. The harmony which is required must come from the practice of the ear. There are few ears naturally so dull that they cannot, if time be allowed to them, decide whether a sentence, when read, be or be not harmonious. And the sense of such harmony grows on the ear when the intelligence has once informed itself as to what is and what is not harmonious. The boy, for instance, who learns with accuracy the prosody of a Sapphic stanza, and has received through his intelligence a knowledge of its parts, will soon tell by his ear whether a Sapphic stanza be or be not correct. Take a girl, endowed with gifts of music, well instructed in her art, with perfect ear, and read to her such a stanza with two words transposed; – as for instance;

> *Mercuri, nam te docilis magistro*
> *Movit Amphion canendo lapides,*
> *Tuque, testudo, resonare septem*
> *Callida nervis –*

and she will find no halt in the rhythm. But a schoolboy with none of her musical acquirements or capacities, who has however become familiar with the metres of the poet, will at once discover the fault.[21] And so will the writer become familiar with what is harmonious in prose. But, in order that that familiarity[aa] may serve him in his business, he must so train his ear that he shall be able to weigh the rhythm of every word as it falls from his pen. This, when it has been done for a time, even for a short time, will become so habitual to him, that he will have appreciated the metrical duration of every syllable before it shall have dared to show itself upon paper. The art of the orator is the same, who knows[ab] beforehand how each sound which he is about to utter will affect the force of his climax. If a writer will do so he will charm his readers, though his readers will probably not know how they have been charmed.

In writing a novel the author soon becomes aware that a burden of many pages is before him. Circumstances require that he should cover a certain, and generally not a very confined space. Short novels are not popular with readers generally. Critics often complain of the ordinary length of novels, – of the three volumes to which they are subjected; –

but few novels which have attained great success in England have been told in fewer pages. The novel-writer who sticks to novel-writing as his profession will certainly find that this burden of length is incumbent on him. How shall he carry his burden to the end? How shall he cover his space? Many great artists have by their practice opposed the doctrine which I now propose to preach; – but they have succeeded I think, in spite of their fault, and by dint of their greatness. There should be no episodes in a novel.[22] Every sentence, every word through all those pages, should tend to the telling of the story. Such episodes distract the attention of the reader and always do so disagreeably. Who has not felt this to be the case even with 'The Curious Impertinent,' and with the history of 'The Man of the Hill.'[23] And if it be so with Cervantes and Fielding, who can hope to succeed? Though the novel which you have to write must be long, let it be all one. And this exclusion of episodes should be carried down into the smallest details. Every sentence, and every word used should tend to the telling of the story. 'But,' the young novelist will say, 'with so many pages before me to be filled, how shall I succeed if I thus confine myself; – how am I to know beforehand what space this story of mine will require? There must be the three volumes, or the certain number of magazine pages which I have contracted to supply. If I may not be discursive should occasion require, how shall I complete my task? The painter suits the size of his canvas to his subject; – and must I, in my art, stretch my subject to my canvas?' This undoubtedly must be done by the novelist, and if he will learn his business may be done without injury to his effect. He may not paint different pictures on the same canvas, – which he will do if he allow himself to wander away to matters outside his own story; but by studying proportion in his work he may teach himself so to tell his story that it shall naturally fall into the required length. Though his story should be all one, yet it may have many parts. Though the plot itself may require but few characters, it may be so enlarged as to find its full development in many. There may be subsidiary plots which shall all tend to the elucidation of the main story and which will take their places as part of one and the same work, – as there may be many figures on a canvas which shall not to the spectator seem to form themselves into separate pictures.

There is no portion of a novelist's work in which this fault of episodes is so common as in the dialogue. It is so easy to make any two persons talk on any casual subject with which the writer presumes himself to be conversant! Literature, philosophy, politics, or sport may thus be handled in a loosely discursive style; and the writer, while indulging himself and filling his pages, is apt to think that he is pleasing his reader. I think he can make no greater mistake. The dialogue is generally the most agreeable part of a novel, but it is only so as long as it tends in some way to the telling of the main story. It need not seem to be confined to that, but it should always have a tendency in that direction. The unconscious critical acumen of a reader[ac] is both just and severe. When a long dialogue on extraneous matter reaches his mind, he at once feels that he is being cheated into taking something which he did not bargain to accept when he took up that novel. He does not at that moment require politics or philosophy, but he wants his story. He will not perhaps be able to say in so many words that at some certain point the dialogue has deviated from the story; – but when it does do so[ad] he will feel it, and the feeling will be unpleasant. Let the intending novel-writer, if he doubt this, read one of Bulwer's novels, – in which there is very much to charm, – and then ask himself whether he has not been offended by devious conversations.

And this dialogue, on which the modern novelist in consulting the taste of his probable readers must depend most, has to be constrained also by other rules. The writer may tell much of his story in conversations, but he may only do so by putting such words into the mouths of his personages as persons so situated would probably use. He is not allowed, for the sake of his tale, to make his characters give utterance to long speeches such as are not customarily heard from men and women. The ordinary talk of ordinary people is carried on in short sharp expressive sentences which very frequently are never completed, – the language of which even among educated people is often incorrect. The novel-writer in constructing his dialogue must so steer between absolute accuracy of language, – which would give to his conversation an air of pedantry, – and the slovenly inaccuracy of ordinary talkers, – which if closely followed would offend by an appearance of grimace, – as to produce upon the ear of his reader a sense of reality.

If he be quite real, he will seem to attempt to be funny. If he be quite correct, he will seem to be unreal. And above all let the speeches be short. No character should utter much above a dozen words at a breath, – unless the writer can justify to himself a longer flood of speech by the speciality of the occasion.

In all this human nature must be the novel-writer's guide. No doubt effective novels have been written in which human nature has been set at defiance. I might name *Caleb Williams* as one and *Adam Blair*[24] as another. But the exceptions are not more than enough to prove the rule. But in following human nature he must remember that he does so with a pen in his hand, and that the reader, who will appreciate human nature, will also demand artistic ability and literary aptitude.

The young novelist will probably ask, or more probably bethink himself, how he is to acquire that knowledge of human nature which will tell him with accuracy what men or what women[ae] would say in this or that position. He must acquire it as the compositor who is to print his words has learned the art of distributing his type,[25] by constant and intelligent practice. Unless it be given to him to listen and to observe, so to carry away as it were the manners of people in his memory as to be able to say to himself with assurance that these words might have been said in a given position and that those other words could not have been said, I do not think that in these days he can succeed as a novelist.

And then let him beware of creating tedium! Who has not felt the charm of a spoken story up to a certain point, and then suddenly become aware that it has become too long and is the reverse of charming? It is not only that the entire book may have this fault, but that this fault may occur in chapters, in passages, in pages, in paragraphs. I know no guard against this so likely to be effective as the feeling of the writer himself. When once the sense that the thing is becoming long has grown upon him, he may be sure that it will grow upon the reader.[af] I see the smile of some who will declare to themselves that the words of a writer will never be tedious to himself. Of the writer of whom this may be truly said it may be said with equal truth that he will always be tedious to his readers.

CHAPTER 13

On English Novelists of the Present Day.

In this chapter I will venture to name a few successful novelists of my own time, with whose works I am acquainted, and will endeavour to point whence their success has come, – and why they have failed, when there has been failure.

I do not hesitate to name Thackeray the first. His knowledge of human nature was supreme, and his characters stand out as human beings with a force and a truth which has not, I think, been within the reach of any other English novelist in any period. I know no character in fiction, unless it be Don Quixote, with whom a[a] reader becomes so intimately acquainted as with Colonel Newcome.[b1] How great a thing it is to be a gentleman at all parts! How we admire the man of whom we feel sure that so[c] much may be said with truth! Is there any one of whom we feel more sure in this respect than we do of[d] Colonel Newcome? It is not because Colonel Newcome is a perfect gentleman that we think Thackeray's work to have been so excellent, but because he has had the power to describe him as such and to force us to love him, a weak and silly old man, on account of this grace of character.

It is evident from all Thackeray's best work that he lived with the characters he was creating. He had always a story to tell till[e] quite late in life; and he shows us that this was so, not by the interest which he had in his own plots, – for I doubt whether his plots did occupy much of his mind, – but by convincing us that his characters were alive to himself. With Becky Sharp,[f] with Lady Castlewood and her daughter and with Esmond, with Warrington, Pendennis and the Major, with Colonel Newcome, and with Barry Lyndon[2] he must have lived in perpetual intercourse. Therefore he has made these personages real to us.

Among all our novelists his style is the purest, as to my ear it is also the most harmonious. Sometimes it is disfigured by a slight touch of affectation, by little conceits which smell of the oil; – but the language is always lucid. The reader without labour knows what he means and knows all that he means. As well as I can remember he deals with no episodes. I think that any critic examining his work minutely would find that every scene and every part of every scene adds something to the clearness with which the story is told. Among all his stories there is not one which does not leave on the mind a feeling of distress that women should ever be immodest or men dishonest, – and of joy that women should be so devoted and men so honest. How we hate the idle selfishness of Pendennis, the worldliness of Beatrix, the craft of Becky Sharp! – how we love the honesty of Colonel Newcome, the nobility of Esmond and the devoted affection of Mrs Pendennis! The hatred of evil and love of good can hardly have come upon so many readers without doing much good.

Late in Thackeray's life, – he never was an old man, but towards the end of his career, – he failed in his power of charming because he allowed his mind to become idle. In the plots which he conceived and in the language which he used I do not know that there is any perceptible change, – but in *The Virgians* and in *Philip*[3] the reader is introduced to no character with which he makes a close and undying acquaintance. And this, I have no doubt, is so because Thackeray himself had no such intimacy. His mind had come to be weary of that fictitious life which is always demanding the labour of new creation, and he troubled himself with his two Virgians and his Philip only when he was seated at his desk.

At the present moment George Eliot is the first of English novelists, and I am disposed to place her second of those of my time. She is best known to the literary world as a writer of prose fiction, and not improbably whatever of permanent fame she may acquire will come from her novels. But the nature of her intellect is very far removed indeed from that which is common to the tellers of stories. Her imagination is no doubt strong, but it acts in analysing rather than in creating. Everything that comes before her is pulled to pieces so that the inside of it shall be seen, and be seen if possible by her readers as clearly as by herself. This searching analysis is carried so far that in studying her latter writings one feels oneself to be in company with some philosopher rather than with a novelist. I doubt whether any young person can read with pleasure either *Felix Holt*, *Middlemarch* or *Daniel Deronda*. I know that they are very difficult to many that are not young.

Her personifications of character have been singularly terse and graphic, and from them has come her great hold on the public, – though by no means the greatest effect which she has produced. The lessons which she teaches remain though it is not for the sake of the lessons that her pages are read. Seth Bede, Adam Bede, Maggie and Tom Tulliver, old Silas Marner, and much above all Tito in *Romola*[4] are characters which when once known can never be forgotten. I cannot say quite so much for any of those in her later works, because in them the philosopher so greatly overtops the portrait painter that in the dissection of the mind the outward signs seem to have been forgotten. In her, as yet, there is no symptom whatever of that weariness of mind, which, when felt by the reader, induces him to declare that the author has written himself out. It is not from decadence that we do not have another Mrs Poyser, but because the author soars to things which seem to her to be higher than Mrs Poyser.

It is I think the defect of George Eliot that she struggles too hard to do work that shall be excellent. She lacks ease. Latterly the signs of this have been conspicuous in her style which has always been and is singularly correct, but which has become occasionally obscure, from her too great desire to be pungent. It is impossible not to feel the struggle, and that feeling begets a flavour of affectation. In *Daniel Deronda*, of which at this moment only a portion has been published, there are sentences which I have found myself compelled to read three times before I have been able to take home to myself all that the writer has intended. Perhaps I may be permitted here to say that this gifted woman was among my dearest and most intimate friends. As I am speaking here of novelists I will not attempt to criticise[g] George Eliot's merit as a poet.

There can be no doubt that the most popular novelist of my time, probably the most popular English novelist of any time, has been Charles Dickens. He has now been dead nearly six years, and the sale of his books goes on as it did during his life. The certainty with which his novels are found in every house, the familiarity of his name in all

English-speaking countries, the popularity of such characters as Mrs Gamp, Micawber, Pecksniff and many others whose names have entered into the English language and become well known words,[5] the grief of the country at his death, and the honours paid to him at his funeral, all testify to his popularity. Since the last book he wrote himself I doubt whether any book has been so popular as his biography by John Forster. There is no withstanding such testimony as this. Such evidence of popular appreciation should go for very much, almost for everything, in criticism on the work of a novelist. The primary object of a novelist is to please; and this man's novels have been found more pleasant than those of any other writer. It might of course be objected to this that though the books have pleased, they have been injurious; – that their tendency has been immoral and their teaching vicious; – but it is almost needless to say that no such charge has ever been made against Dickens. His teaching has ever been good. From all which there arises to the critic a question whether, with such evidence against him as to the excellence of this writer, he should not subordinate his own opinion to the collected opinion of the world of readers. To me it almost seems that I must be wrong to place Dickens after Thackeray and George Eliot, knowing as I do that so great a majority put him above those authors.

My own peculiar idiosyncrasy in the matter forbids me to do so. I do acknowledge that Mrs Gamp, Micawber, Pecksniff and others have become household words in every house, – as though they were human beings; but to my judgement they are not human beings, nor are any of the characters human which Dickens has portrayed. It has been the peculiarity and the marvel of this man's power that he has invested his puppets with a charm that has enabled him to dispense with human nature. There is a drollery about them in my estimation very much below the humour of Thackeray, – but which has reached the intellect of all while Thackeray's humour has escaped the intellect of many. Nor is the pathos of Dickens human. It is stagey and melodramatic. But it is so expressed that it touches every heart a little. There is no real life in Smike. His misery, his idiocy, his devotion for Nicholas, his love for Kate,[6] are all overdone and are incompatible with each other. But still the reader sheds a tear. Every reader can find a tear for Smike. Dickens's novels are like Boucicault's plays.[7] He has known how to draw his lines broadly so that all should see the colour.

He too in his best days always lived with his characters – and he too, as he gradually ceased to have the power of doing so, ceased to charm. Though they are not human beings we all remember Mrs Gamp and Pickwick. The Boffins and Veneerings[8] do not I think dwell in the minds of so many.

Of Dickens's style it is impossible to speak in praise. It is jerky, ungrammatical, and created by himself in defiance of rules, – almost as completely as that created by Carlyle. To readers who have taught themselves to regard language it must therefore be unpleasant. But the critic is driven to feel the weakness of his criticism when he acknowledges to himself, – as he is compelled in all honesty to do, – that with this language such as it is, the writer has satisfied the great mass of the readers of his country. Both these great writers have satisfied the readers of their own pages, – but both have done infinite harm by creating a school of imitators. No young novelist should ever dare to imitate the style of Dickens. If such a one wants a model for his language, let him take Thackeray.

Bulwer – or Lord Lytton, but I think that he is still better known by his earlier name, – was a man of very great parts. Better educated than either of those I have named before him he was always able to use his erudition, and he thus produced novels from which very much not only may be, but must be learned by his readers. He thoroughly understood the political status of his own country, a subject on which Dickens was I think marvellously ignorant, and which Thackeray had never studied. He had read extensively and was always apt to give his readers the benefit of what he knew. The result has been that very much more than amusement may be obtained from Bulwer's novels. There is also a brightness about them, the result rather of thought than of imagination, – of study and of care than of mere intellect, – which has made many of them excellent in their way. It is perhaps improper to class all his novels together, as he wrote in varied manners, making in his earlier works, such as *Pelham* and *Ernest Maltravers*, pictures of a fictitious life, – and afterwards pictures of life as he believed it to be, as in *My Novel* and *The Caxtons*.[9] But from all of them there comes the same flavour of an effort to produce effect. The effects are produced, but it would have been better[h] if the flavour had not been there.

I cannot say of Bulwer as I have of the other novelists whom I have named that he lived with his characters. He lived with his work, with the doctrines which at the time he wished to preach, thinking always of the effects which he wished to produce; but I do not think he ever knew his own personages, – and therefore neither do we know them. Even Pelham and Eugene Aram are not human beings to us, as are Pickwick and Colonel Newcome, and Mrs Poyser. [10]

In his plots Bulwer has generally been simple, facile, and successful. The reader with him never feels, as he does with Wilkie Collins, that it is all plot, or, as with George Eliot, that there is no plot. The story comes naturally without calling for too much attention, and is thus a proof of the completeness of the man's intellect. His language is clear good intelligible English, but it is defaced by mannerism. In all that he did affectation was his fault.

How shall I speak of my dear old friend Charles Lever, and his rattling, jolly, joyous, swearing Irishmen. Surely never did a sense of vitality come so constantly from a man's pen, – nor from man's voice as from his! I knew him well for many years and whether in sickness or in health I have never come across him without finding him to be running over with wit and fun. Of all the men I have encountered he was the surest fund of drollery. I have known many witty men, many who could say good things, many who would sometimes be ready to say them when wanted though they would sometimes fail; – but he never failed. Rouse him in the middle of the night and wit would come from him before he was half awake. And yet he never monopolised the talk, was never a bore. He would take no more than his own share of the words spoken, and would yet seem to brighten all that was said during the night. His earlier novels, – the latter I have not read, – are just like his conversation. The fun never flags, and to me, when I read them, they were never tedious. As to character, he can hardly be said to have produced it. Corney Delaney,[11] the old man servant, may perhaps be named as an exception.

Lever's novels will not live long, – even if they may be said to be alive now, – because it is so. What was his manner of working I do not know, but I should think it must have been very quick, and that he never troubled himself on the subject except when he was seated with a pen in his hand.

Charlotte Brontë[i] was surely a marvellous woman. If it could be right to judge the work of a novelist from one small portion of one novel, and to say of an author that he is to be accounted as strong as he shows himself to be in his strongest morsel of work, I should be inclined to put Miss Brontë very high indeed. I know no interest more thrilling than that which she has been able to throw into the characters of Rochester and the governess in the second volume of *Jane Eyre*. She lived with these[j] characters and felt with every fibre of her heart[k] the longings of the one and the sufferings of the other. And therefore, though the end of the book is weak, and the beginning not very good I venture to predict that *Jane Eyre* will be read among English novels when many whose names are now better known shall have been forgotten. *Jane Eyre* and *Esmond* and *Adam Bede* will be in the hands of our grandchildren, when *Pickwick* and *Pelham* and *Harry Lorrequer*[12] are forgotten, because the men and women depicted are human in their aspirations, human in their sympathies, and human in their actions.

In *Villette* too and in *Shirley* there is to be found human life as natural and as real, though in circumstances not so full of interest as those told in *Jane Eyre*. The character of Paul in the former of the two is a wonderful study. She must herself have been in love with some Paul when she wrote the book, and have been determined to prove to herself that she was capable of loving one whose exterior circumstances were mean and in every way unprepossessing.

There is no writer of the present day who has so much puzzled me by his eccentricities, impracticabilities, and capabilities as Charles Reade. I look upon him as endowed almost with genius, but as one who has not been gifted by nature with ordinary powers of reasoning. He can see what is grandly noble, and admire it with all his heart. He can see too what is foully vicious and hate it with equal ardour. But in the common affairs of life he cannot see what is right or wrong; and as he is altogether unwilling to be guided by the opinion of others he is constantly making mistakes in his literary career and subjecting himself to reproach which he hardly deserves. He means to be honest. He means to be especially honest, – more honest than other people. He has written a book, called *The Eighth Commandment*,[13] on behalf of honesty in literary transactions, – a wonderful work which has I believe been read by very few. I never saw a copy except that in my own library, or heard of any one who knew the book. Nevertheless it is a volume that must have taken very great labour and have been written – as indeed he declares that it was written, – without the hope of pecuniary reward. He makes an appeal to the British Parliament and the British people on behalf of literary honesty, declaring that should he fail, – 'I shall have to go on blushing for the people I was born among.' And yet, of all the writers of my day, he has seemed to me to understand literary honesty the least. On one occasion, as he tells us in this book, he bought for a certain sum from a French author the right of using a plot taken from a play, – which he probably might have used without such purchase and also without infringing any international copyright act. The French author not unnaturally praises him for the transaction, telling him that he is *'un vrai gentleman.'* The plot was used by Reade in a novel, and a critic discovering the adaptation made known his discovery to the public. Whereupon the novelist became angry, called his critic a pseud-onymuncule,[14] and defended himself by stating the fact of his own purchase. In all this he seems to me to ignore what we all mean when we talk of literary plagiarism[1] and literary honesty. The sin of which the author is accused is not that of taking another man's property, but of passing off as his own creation that which he does not himself create. When an author puts his name to a book he claims to have written all that there is therein, unless he makes direct signification to the contrary. Some years subsequently there arose another similar question in which Mr Reade's opinion was declared even more plainly, – and certainly very much more publicly. In a tale which he wrote he inserted a dialogue which he took from Swift,[15] and took without any acknowledgment. As might have been expected, one of the critics of the day fell foul of him for this barefaced plagiarism. The author, however, defended himself, with much abuse of the critic, by asserting that whereas Swift had found the jewel, he had supplied the setting, – an argument in which there was some little wit, and would have been much excellent truth had he given the words as belonging to Swift and not to himself.

On another occasion, during my absence in Australia, he took the plot of a novel of mine, and, adapting it very cleverly to the stage, brought it out, with a notice in the bills, that it was by 'Anthony Trollope and Charles Reade'. This he did without any concert with me, and without any former partnership, or even allusion to such partnership; – I may say without any word having even passed between us in reference to joint workmanship. I felt myself bound to repudiate the play by writing to the newspapers. Had Mr Reade asked me for the plot for the purpose for which he used it, I should have felt myself honoured by the request. Had it been in my line to write a play in conjunction with another writer, I know no one with whom I would more willingly have embarked[m] in such a task than with Mr Reade. But this unauthorised use of my name on a play-bill angered me. I could not, however, make him understand that he had done wrong, and could only escape from the absurdity of a personal quarrel with a man I esteemed by suggesting to him that nothing more should be said about it by either of us.[n]

The novels of a man possessed of so singular a mind, must themselves be very strange; – and they are strange. It has generally been his object to write down some abuse with which he has been particularly struck, – the harshness for instance with which paupers or lunatics are treated, or the wickedness of certain classes; and he always, I think, leaves upon his readers an idea of great earnestness of purpose. But he has always left at the same time on my mind so strong a conviction that he has not really understood his subject, that I have found myself ever taking the part of those whom he has accused. So good a heart and so wrong a head surely no novelist ever before had combined! In story-telling he has occasionally been almost great. Among his novels I would especially recommend *The Cloister and the Hearth*. I do not know that in this work, or in any, he has left a character that will remain, but he has written some of his scenes so brightly that to read them would always be a pleasure.

Of Wilkie Collins it is impossible for a true critic not to speak with admiration because he has excelled all his contemporaries in a certain most difficult branch of his art; but as it is a branch which I have not myself at all cultivated, it is not unnatural that his work should be very much lost upon me individually. When I sit down to write a novel I do not at all know and I do not very much care how it is to end. Wilkie Collins seems so to construct his, that he not only, before writing, plans everything on, down to the minutest detail, from the beginning to the end; but then, plots it all back again, to see that there is no piece of necessary dove-tailing which does not dove-tail with absolute accuracy. The construction is most minute and most wonderful. But I can never lose the taste of the construction. The author seems always to be warning me to remember that something happened exactly at half past two o'clock on Tuesday morning, or that a woman disappeared from the road just fifteen yards beyond the fourth milestone. One is constrained by mysteries and hemmed in by difficulties, knowing, however, that the mysteries will be made clear and the difficulties overcome at the end of the third volume. Such work gives me no pleasure. I am however quite prepared to acknowledge that the want of pleasure comes from fault of my intellect.

There are two ladies of whom I would fain say a word, though I feel that I am making my list too long, in order that I may declare how much I have admired their work. They are Annie Thackeray[16] and Rhoda Broughton. I have known them both, and have loved the former almost as though she belonged to me. No two writers were ever more dissimilar, – except in this that they are both feminine. Miss Thackeray's characters are sweet, charming, and quite true to human nature. In her writings she is always endeavouring to prove that good produces good, and evil evil. There is not a line of which she need be ashamed, – not a sentiment of which she should not be proud. But she writes like a lazy writer, who dislikes her work, and who allows her own want of energy to show itself in her pages.

Miss Broughton on the other hand is full of energy, – though she too, I think, can become tired over her work. She, however, does take the trouble to make her personages stand upright on the ground. And she has the gift of making them speak as men and women do speak. 'You beast', said Nancy sitting on the wall to the man who was to be her husband, – thinking that she was speaking to her brother.[17] Now Nancy, whether right or wrong, was just the girl who would, as circumstances then were, have called her brother a beast. There is nothing wooden about any of Miss Broughton's novels, – and in these days so many novels are wooden! But they are not sweet-savoured as are those by Miss Thackeray, and are therefore less true to nature. In Miss Broughton's determination not to be mawkish and missish she has made her ladies do and say things which ladies would not do and say. They throw themselves at men's heads, and when they are not accepted only think how they may throw themselves again. Miss Broughton is still so young that I hope she may live to overcome her fault in this direction.[18]

There is one other name, without which the list of the best known English novelists of my own time would certainly be incomplete, and that is the name of the present Prime Minister of England. Mr Disraeli has written so many novels, and has been so popular as a novelist, that whether for good or for ill I feel myself compelled to speak of him. He began his career as an author early in life, publishing *Vivian Grey* when he was twenty three years old. He was very young for such a work,[o] though hardly young enough to justify the excuse that he makes in his own preface that it is a book written by a boy. Dickens was, I think, younger when he wrote *The Sketches by Boz*, and as young when he was writing the *Pickwick Papers.*[19] It was hardly longer ago than the other day when Mr Disraeli brought out *Lothair*, and between the two there were eight or ten others. To me they have all had the same flavour of paint and unreality. In whatever he has written he has affected something which has been intended to strike his readers as uncommon and therefore grand. Because he has been bright and a man of genius he has carried his object as regards the young. He has struck them with astonishment and aroused in their imagination ideas of a world more glorious, more rich, more witty, more enterprising than their own. But the glory has ever been[p] the glory of pasteboard, and the wealth has been a wealth of tinsel. The wit has been the wit of hairdressers, and the enterprise has been the enterprise of mountebanks. An audacious conjurer has generally been his hero, – some youth who by wonderful cleverness can obtain success by every intrigue that comes to his hand. Through it all there is a feeling of stage properties, a smell of hair oil, an aspect of buhl,[20] a remembrance of tailors, and that pricking of the conscience which must be the general accompaniment of paste diamonds. I can understand that Mr Disraeli should by his novels have instigated many a young man and many a young woman on their way in life, but I cannot understand that he should have instigated any one to good. Vivian Grey has had probably as many followers as Jack Sheppard,[q] and has led his followers in the same direction.[21]

Lothair which is as yet Mr Disraeli's last work, – and I think undoubtedly his worst, – has been defended on a plea somewhat similar to that by which he has defended *Vivian Grey.* As that was written when he was too young, so was the other when he was too old, – too old for work of that nature, though not too old to be Prime Minister. If his mind were so occupied with greater things as to allow him to write such a work, yet his judgement should have sufficed to induce him to destroy it when written. Here that flavour of hair oil, that feeling[r] of false jewels, that remembrance of tailors comes out stronger than in all the others. Lothair is falser even than Vivian Grey and Lady Corisande,[s] the daughter of the Duchess, more inane and unwomanlike than Venetia or Henrietta Temple.[22] It is the very bathos of storytelling. I have often lamented, and have as often excused to myself, that lack of public judgement which enables readers to put up with bad work because it comes from good or from lofty hands. I never felt the feeling so strongly or was so little able to excuse it, as when a portion of the reading public received *Lothair* with satisfaction.

CHAPTER 14

On Criticism.

Literary criticism in the present day has become a profession, – but it has ceased to be an art. Its object is no longer that of proving that certain literary work is good and other literary work is bad, in accordance with rules which the critic is able to define. English criticism at present rarely even pretends to go so far as this. It attempts, in the first place, to tell the public whether a book be or be not worth public attention, and in the second place so to describe the purport of the work as to enable those who have not time or inclination for reading it to feel that by a short cut they have[a] become acquainted with its contents. Both these objects, if fairly well carried out, are salutary. Though the critic may not be a profound judge himself, though not unfrequently he be a young man making his first literary attempts, with tastes and judgements still unfixed, yet he probably has a conscience in the matter and would not have been selected for that work had he not shown some aptitude for it. Though he may not be the best possible guide to undiscerning readers, he will be better than no guide at all. Real substantial criticism must from its nature be costly, and that which the public wants should at any rate be cheap. Advice is given to many thousands which, though it may not be the best advice possible, is better than no advice at all. Then that description of the work criticised, that compressing of the much into very little, – which is the chief work[b] of many modern critics or reviewers, – does enable many to know something of what is being said, who without it would know nothing.

I do not think it is incumbent on me at present to name periodicals in which this work is well done, and to make complaints of others by which it is scamped. I should give offence and might probably be unjust. But I think I may certainly say that as some of these publications are entitled[c] to great praise for the manner in which the work is done generally, so are others open to very severe censure, – and that the praise and that the censure are chiefly due on behalf of one virtue and its opposite vice. It is not critical ability that we have a right to demand, or its absence that we are bound to deplore. Critical ability, for the price we pay, is not attainable. It is a faculty not peculiar to Englishmen; and when displayed is very frequently not appreciated. But that critics should be honest we have a right to demand and critical dishonesty we are bound to expose. If the writer will tell us what he thinks, though his thoughts be absolutely vague and useless, we can forgive him; but when he tells us what he does not think, actuated either by friendship or by animosity, then there should be no pardon for him. This is the sin in modern English criticism of which at present there[d] is most reason to complain.

It is a lamentable fact that men and women lend themselves to this practice who are neither vindictive nor ordinarily dishonest. It has become 'the custom of the trade', under the veil of which excuse so many tradesmen justify their malpractices! When a struggling author learns that so much has been done for A. by the *Barsetshire Gazette*, so much for B. by the *Dillsborough Herald*, and again so much for C. by that powerful metropolitan organ the *Evening Pulpit*, and is told also that A. and B. and C. have been thus favoured through personal interest, he also goes to work among the Editors or the Editors' wives, – or perhaps, if he cannot reach their wives, with the wives' first or second cousins. When once the feeling has come upon an Editor or a critic that he may allow himself to be influenced by other considerations than the duty he owes to the public, all sense of critical or of editorial honesty falls from him at once. *Facilis descensus Averni.*[1] In a very short time that editorial honesty becomes ridiculous to himself. It is for other purpose that he wields his power, and when he is told what is his duty and what should be his conduct, the preacher of such doctrine seems to him to be Quixotic. 'Where have you lived, my friend, for the last twenty years,' he says in spirit if not in word, 'that you come out now with stuff as old-fashioned as this?' And thus dishonesty begets dishonesty, till dishonesty seems to be beautiful. How nice to be good-natured! How glorious to assist a struggling young author,[e] especially if the young author be also a pretty woman! How gracious to oblige a friend! Then the motive, though still pleasing, departs farther from the border of what is good. In what way can the critic better repay the hospitality of his wealthy literary friend than by good-natured criticism, – or more certainly ensure for himself a continuation of hospitable favours!

Some years since a critic of the day, a gentleman well known then in literary circles, showed me the manuscript of a book recently published, – the work of a popular author of the day.[f] It was handsomely bound and was a valuable and desirable possession. It had been just given to him by the author as an acknowledgment for a laudatory review in one of the leading journals of the day. As I was expressly asked whether I did not regard such a token as a sign of grace both in giver and in receiver, I said that I thought it should neither have been given nor been taken. My theory was repudiated with scorn, and I was told that I was strait-laced, visionary and impracticable! In all that, the damage did not lie in the fact of that one present, but in the feeling on the part of the critic that his office was not debased by the acceptance of presents from those whom he criticised. This man was a professional critic, – bound by his contract with certain employers to review such books as were sent to him. How could he, when he had received a valuable present for praising one book, censure another by the same author?[2] He knew indeed that there was no question of censure, – that with an author so popular it was his duty to praise. All which makes the whole matter very much the worse.[g]

While I write this I well know that what I say, if it be ever noticed at all, will be taken as a straining at gnats,[3] as a pretence of honesty, or, at any rate, as an exaggeration of scruples. I have said the same thing before, and have been ridiculed for saying it. But not[h] the less am I sure that English literature generally is suffering much under this evil. All those who are struggling for success have forced upon them the idea that their strongest efforts should be made in touting for praise. Those who are not familiar with the lives of authors will hardly be-lieve how low will be the forms which their struggles will take; – how little presents will be sent to men who write little articles, how much flattery may be expended even on the keeper of a circulating library, with what profuse and distant genuflexions approaches are made to the outside railing of the temple which contains within it the great thunderer of some metropolitan periodical publication![4] The evil here is not only that done to the public when interested counsel is given to them, but extends to the debasement of those who have at any rate considered themselves fit to provide literature for the public.

I am satisfied that the remedy for this evil must lie in the conscience and deportment of authors themselves. If once the feeling could be produced that it is disgraceful for an author to ask for praise, – and demands for praise are I think disgraceful in every walk of life, – the practice would gradually fall into the hands of the lowest, and that which is done only by the lowest soon becomes despicable even to them. The sin when perpetrated[i] with unflagging labour brings with it at best very poor reward. That work of running after critics, Editors, publishers, the keepers of circulating libraries and their clerks is very hard and must be disagreeable. He who does it must feel himself to be dishonoured, – or she. It may perhaps help to sell an edition, but can never make an author successful.

> *Ponatur calculus, adsint*
> *Cum tabulâ pueri; numeras; sestertia quinque*
> *Omnibus in rebus; nemerentur deinde labores.*[15]

I think it may be laid down as a golden rule in literature that there should be no intercourse at all between an author and his critic. The critic, as critic, should not know his author, nor the author, as author, his critic. As censure should beget no anger, so should praise beget no gratitude. The young author should feel that criticisms fall upon him as dew or hail from heaven, – which as coming from heaven man accepts as fate. Praise let the author try to obtain by wholesome effort; censure let him avoid, if possible, by care and industry. But when they come let him take them as coming from some source which he cannot influence and with which he should not meddle.

I know no more disagreeable trouble into which an author may plunge himself than of a quarrel with his critics, or any more useless labour than that of answering them. It is wise to presume at any rate that the reviewer has simply done his duty and has spoken of the book according to the dictates of his conscience. Nothing can be gained by combating the reviewer's opinion. If the book which he has disparaged be good, his judgement will be condemned by the praise of others; – if bad, his judgement will be confirmed by others. Or if unfortunately, the criticism of the day be in so evil a condition generally that such ultimate truth cannot be expected, the author may be sure that his efforts made on behalf of his own book will not set matters right. If injustice be done him, let him bear it. To do so is consonant with the dignity of the position which he ought to assume. To shriek and scream and sputter, to threaten actions, and to swear about the town that he has been belied and defamed in that he has been accused of bad grammar or a false metaphor, of a dull chapter or even of a borrowed heroine, will leave on the minds of the public nothing but a sense of irritated impotence.

If indeed there should spring from an author's published work any assertion by a critic injurious to the author's honour, if the author be accused of falsehood, or of personal motives which are discreditable to him, then indeed he may be bound to answer the charge. It is hoped, however, that he may be able to do so with clean hands, or he will so stir the mud in the pool as to come forth dirtier than he went into it.

I have lived much among men by whom the English criticism of the day has been vehemently abused. I have heard it said that to the public it is a false guide, and that to authors it is never a trustworthy Mentor.[6] I do not concur in this wholesale censure. There is of course criticism and criticism. There are at this moment one or two periodicals to which both public and authors may safely look for guidance, though there are many others from which no spark of literary advantage can be obtained. But it is well that both public and authors should know what is the advantage which they have a right to expect. There have been critics, – and there probably will be again, though the circumstances of English literature do not tend to produce them, – with power sufficient to entitle them to speak with authority. These great men have declared, *tanquam ex cathedrâ*,[7] that such a book has been so far good and so far bad, or that it has been altogether good or altogether bad, – and the world has believed them. When making such assertions they have given their reasons, explained their causes, and have carried conviction. Very great reputations have been achieved by such critics, but not without infinite study and the labour of many years.

Such are not the critics of the day of whom we are now speaking. In the literary world as it lives at present some writer is selected for the place of critic to a newspaper, – generally some young writer, – who for so many shillings a column shall review whatever book is sent to him, and express an opinion, – reading the book through for the purpose if the amount of honorarium as measured with the amount of labour will enable him to do so. A labourer must measure his work by his pay or he cannot live. From criticism such as this must for the most part be, the general reader has no right to expect philosophical analysis or literary judgement on which confidence may be placed. But he probably may believe that the books praised will be better than the books censured, and that those which are praised by periodicals which never censure are better worth his attention than those which are not noticed. And readers will also find that by devoting an hour or two on Saturday to the criticisms of the week they will enable themselves to have an opinion about the books of the day. The knowledge so acquired will not be great nor will that little be lasting, but it adds something to the pleasure of life to be able to talk on subjects of which others are speaking, and the man who has sedulously gone through the literary notices in the *Spectator* and the *Saturday* may perhaps be justified in thinking himself as well able to talk about the new book, as his friend who has brought that new book on the *tapis*,[8] and who not improbably obtained his information from the same source.

As an author I have paid careful attention to the reviews which have been written on my own work, and I think that now I well know where I may look for a little instruction, where I may expect only greasy adulation, where I shall be cut into mincemeat for the delight of those who love sharp invective, and where I shall find an equal mixture of praise and censure, so adjusted, without much judgement, as to exhibit the impartiality of the newspaper and its staff. Among it all there is much chaff which I have learned how to throw to the winds with equal disregard whether it praises or blames, – but I have also found some corn on which I have fed and nourished myself, and for which I have been thankful.

CHAPTER 15

'The Last Chronicle of Barset' – Leaving the Post Office – 'St Paul's Magazine'.

I will now go back to the year 1867 in which I was still living at Waltham Cross. I had, some time since, bought the house there which I had at first hired and added rooms to it and made it for our purposes very comfortable. It was however a rickety old place requiring much repair and occasionally not as weather-tight as it should be. We had a domain there sufficient for the cows and for the making of our butter and hay. For strawberries, asparagus, green peas, out-of-door peaches, for roses especially, and such every day luxuries, no place was ever more excellent. It was only twelve miles from London and admitted therefore of frequent intercourse with the metropolis. It was also near enough to the Roothing country for hunting purposes. No doubt the Shoreditch station by which it had to be reached had its drawbacks. My average distance also to the Essex meets was twenty miles. But the place combined as much or more than I had a right to expect. It was within my own postal district, and had upon the whole been well chosen.

The work I did during the twelve years that I remained there, from 1859 to 1871 was certainly very great. I feel confident that in amount no other writer contributed so much during that time to English literature. Over and above my novels I wrote political articles, critical, social, and sporting articles for periodicals without number. I did the work of a Surveyor of the General Post Office, and so did it as to give the authorities of the department no slightest pretext for fault-finding. I hunted always at least twice a week. I was frequent in the Whist room at the Garrick. I lived much in society in London, and was made happy by the presence of many friends at Waltham Cross. In addition to this we always spent six weeks at least out of England. Few men I think ever lived a fuller life, and I attribute the power of doing this altogether to the virtue of early hours. It was my practice to be at my table every morning at 5.30 a.m., and it was also my practice to allow myself no mercy. An old groom[1] whose business it was to call me, and to whom I paid £5 extra a year for the duty allowed himself no mercy. During all those years at Waltham Cross he was never once late with the coffee which it was his duty to bring me. I do not know that I ought not to feel that I owe more to him than to any one else for the success I have had. By beginning at that hour I could complete my literary work before I dressed for breakfast.

All those I think who have lived as literary men, – working daily as literary labourers, – will agree with me that three hours a day will produce as much as a man ought to write. But then, he should so have trained himself that he shall be able to work continuously during those three hours, – so have tutored his mind that it shall not be necessary for him to sit nibbling his pen and gazing at the wall before him till he shall have found the words which[a] he wants to express his ideas. It had at this time become my custom, – and still is my custom, though of late I have become a little lenient to myself, – to write with my watch before me and to require from myself 250 words every quarter of an hour. I have found that the 250 words have been forthcoming as regularly as my watch went. But my three hours were not devoted entirely to writing. I always began my task by reading the work of the day before, an operation which would take me half an hour and which consisted chiefly in weighing with my ear the sound of the words and phrases. I would strongly recommend this practice to all tyros in writing. That their work should be read after it has been written is a matter of course; – that it should be read twice at least before it goes to the printers, I take to be a matter of course. But by reading what he has last written just before he recommences his task, the writer will catch the tone and spirit of what he is then saying and will avoid the fault of seeming to be unlike himself. This division of time allowed me to produce ten pages of an ordinary novel volume a day, and if kept up through ten months would have given as its results three novels of three volumes each in the year, – the precise amount which so greatly acerbated the publisher in Paternoster Row, and which must at any rate be felt to be quite as much as the novel readers of the world can want from the hands of one man.

I have never written three novels in a year, but by following the plan above described I have written more than as much as three volumes; and by adhering to it over a course of years I have been enabled to have always on hand, – for some time back now, – one or two or even three unpublished novels in my desk beside me. Were I to die now there are three such, besides *The Prime Minister* half of which only has as yet been issued. One of these has been six years finished[2] and has never seen the light since it was first tied up in the wrapper which now contains it. I look forward with some grim pleasantry to its publication after another period of six years, and to the declaration of the critics that it has been the work of a period of life at which the power of writing novels had passed from me. Not improbably, however, these pages may be printed first.

In 1866 and 1867 *The Last Chronicle of Barset* was brought out by George Smith in sixpenny monthly numbers. I do not know that this mode of publication had been tried before, or that it answered very well on this occasion. Indeed the shilling magazines had interfered greatly with the success of novels published in numbers without other accompanying matter. The public, finding that so much might be had for a shilling, in which a portion of one or more novels was always included, were unwilling to spend their money on the novel alone. Feeling that this had certainly become the case in reference to novels published in shilling numbers, Mr Smith and I determined to make the experiment with sixpenny parts. As he paid me £3000 for the use of my manuscript, the loss, if any, did not fall upon me. If I remember right the enterprise was not altogether successful.[3]

Taking it as a whole I regard this as the best novel I have written. I was never quite satisfied with the development of the plot, which consisted of the loss of a cheque, of a charge made against a clergyman for stealing it, and of absolute uncertainty on the part of the clergyman himself as to the manner in which the cheque had found its way into his hands. I cannot quite make myself believe that even such a man as Mr Crawley could have forgotten how he got it, nor would the generous friend who was anxious to supply his wants have supplied them by tendering the cheque of a third person. Such fault I acknowledge, – acknowledging at the same time that I have never been capable of constructing with complete success the intricacies of a plot that required to be unravelled. But while confessing so much I claim to have portrayed the mind of the unfortunate man with great accuracy and great delicacy. The pride, the humility, the manliness, the weakness, the conscientious rectitude and bitter prejudices of Mr Crawley were, I feel, true to nature and well described. The surroundings too are good. Mrs Proudie at the palace is a real woman, – and the poor old dean dying at the deanery[4] is also real. The Archdeacon in his rectory[b] is very real. There is a true savour of English country life all through the book. It was with many misgivings that I killed my old friend Mrs Proudie. I could not, I think, have done it but for a resolution taken and declared under circumstances of great momentary pressure. It was thus that it came about. I was sitting one morning at work upon the novel at the end of the long drawing-room of the Athenæum club, – as was then my wont when I had slept the previous night in London. As I was there two clergymen, each with a magazine in his hand, seated themselves, one on one side of the fire and one on the other, close to me. They soon began to abuse what they were reading, and each was reading some part of some novel of mine. The gravamen of their complaint lay in the fact that I re-introduced the same characters so often! 'Here,' said one, 'is that Archdeacon whom we have had in every novel he has ever written.' 'And here,' said the other, 'is the old Duke whom he has talked about till everybody is tired of him. If I could not invent new characters I would not write novels at all.' Then one of them fell foul of Mrs Proudie. It was impossible for me not to hear their words, and almost impossible to hear them and be quiet. I got up and standing between them I acknowledged myself to be the culprit. 'As to Mrs Proudie,' I said, 'I will go home and kill her before the week is over.' And so I did.[5] The two gentlemen were utterly confounded and one of them begged me to forget his frivolous observations.

I have sometimes regretted the deed, so great was my delight in writing about Mrs Proudie, so thorough was my knowledge of all the little shades of her character. It was not only that she was a tyrant, a bully, a would-be priestess, a very vulgar woman, and one who would send headlong to the nethermost pit all who disagreed with her; – but that at the same time she was conscientious, by no means a hypocrite, really believing in the brimstone which she threatened and anxious to save the souls around her from its horrors. And as her tyranny encreased so did the bitterness of the moments of her repentance encrease in that she knew herself to be a tyrant, – till that bitterness killed her. Since her time others have grown up equally dear to me, – Lady Glencora and her husband for instance; but I have never dissevered myself from Mrs Proudie, and still live much in company with her ghost.

I have in a previous chapter said how I wrote *Can You Forgive Her?* after the plot of a play which had been rejected, – which play had been called *The Noble Jilt.* Some year or two after the completion of *The Last*

Chronicle I was asked by the manager of a theatre to prepare a piece for his stage, and I did so, taking the plot of this novel. I called the comedy *Did He Steal It?* But my friend the manager did not approve of my attempt. My mind at this time was less attentive to such a matter than when dear old George Bartley nearly crushed me by his criticism, – so that I forget the reason given. I have little doubt but that the manager was right. That he intended to express a true opinion, and would have been glad to have taken the piece had he thought it suitable, I am quite sure.[c]

I have sometimes wished to see during my lifetime a combined republication of those tales which are occupied with the fictitious county of Barsetshire. These would be *The Warden, Barchester Towers, Doctor Thorne, Framley Parsonage,*[d] and *The Last Chronicle of Barset.* But I have hitherto failed. The copyrights are in the hands of four different persons, including myself; and with one of the four I have not been able to prevail to act in concert with the others.[*]

In 1867 I made up my mind to take a step in life which was not unattended with peril, which many would call rash, and which when taken I should be sure at some periods to regret. This step was the resignation of my place in the Post Office. I have described how it was that I contrived to combine the performance of its duties with my other avocations in life. I got up always very early; – but even this did not suffice. I worked always on Sundays, – as to which no scruple of religion made me unhappy, – and not unfrequently I was driven to work at night. In winter, when the hunting was going on, I had to keep myself very much on the alert. And during the London season, when I was generally two or three days of the week in town, I found the official work to be a burden. I had determined, some years previously, after due consultation[e] with my wife, to abandon the Post Office when I had put by enough to give me an income[f] equal to the pension to which I should be entitled if I remained in the department till I was sixty. That I had now done, and I sighed for liberty.

The exact time chosen, the autumn of 1867, was selected because I

---

[*] Since this was written I have made arrangements for doing as I have wished, and the first volume of the series will now very shortly be published.[6]

was then about to undertake other literary work in editing a new magazine, – of which I shall speak very shortly. But in addition to these reasons, there was another which was, I think, at last the actuating cause. When Sir Rowland Hill left the Post Office and my brother-in-law Mr Tilley became Secretary in his place, I applied for the vacant office of Under-Secretary. Had I obtained this, I should have given up my hunting, have given up much of my literary work, – at any rate would have edited no magazine, – and would have returned to the habit of my youth in going daily to the General Post Office. There was very much against such a change in life. The encrease of salary would not have amounted to above £400 a year, and I should have lost much more than that in literary remuneration. I should have felt bitterly the slavery of attendance at an office from which I had then been exempt for five and twenty years. I should too have greatly missed the sport which I loved. But I was attached to the department, had imbued myself with a thorough love of letters, – I mean the letters which are carried by the post, – and was anxious for their welfare as though they were all my own. In short I wished to continue the connexion. I did not, moreover, wish that any younger officer should again pass over my head. I believed that I had been a valuable public servant, and I will own to a feeling existing at that time that I had not been altogether well treated. I was probably wrong in this. I had been allowed to hunt, and to do as I pleased, and to say what I liked, and had in that way received my reward. I applied for the office, but Mr Scudamore[7] was appointed to it. He no doubt was possessed of gifts which I did not possess. He understood the manipulation of money and the use of figures, and was a great accountant. I think that I might have been more useful in regard to the labours and wages of the immense body of men employed by the Post Office. However Mr Scudamore was appointed, and I made up my mind that I would fall back upon my old intention and leave the department. I think I allowed two years to pass before I took the step, and the day on which I sent the letter was to me most melancholy.

The rule of the service in regard to pensions is very just. A man shall serve till he is sixty before he is entitled to a pension, – unless his health fail him. At that age he is entitled to one sixtieth of his salary for every year he has served, up to forty years. If his health do fail him, so that he is unfit for further work before the age named, then he may go with pension amounting to one sixtieth for every year he has served. I could not say that my health had failed me, and therefore I went without any pension. I have since felt occasionally that it has been supposed that I left the Post Office under pressure, – because I attended to hunting and to my literary work rather than to postal matters. As it had for many years been my ambition to be a thoroughly good servant to the public, and to give to the public much more than I took in the shape of salary, this feeling has sometimes annoyed me. And as I am still a little sore on the subject, and as I would not have it imagined after my death that I had slighted the public service to which I belonged, I will venture here to give the reply which was sent to the letter containing my resignation.

GENERAL POST OFFICE,

Oct 9 1867

Sir

I have received your letter of the 3rd Inst in which you tender your resignation as Surveyor in the Post Office Service and state as your reason for this step, that you have adopted another profession the exigencies of which have become so[g] great as to make you feel that you cannot give to the duties of the Post Office that amount of attention which you consider the Postmaster General has a right to expect.

You have for many years ranked among the most conspicuous servants[h] of the Post Office which, on several occasions, when you have been employed on large and difficult matters, has reaped much benefit from the great abilities which you have been able to place at its disposal; and in mentioning this I have been especially glad to record that, notwithstanding the many calls upon your time, you have never permitted your other avocations to interfere with your Post Office work, which has been faithfully and, indeed, energetically performed. (*There was a touch of irony in this word energetically, but still it did not displease me.*)

In accepting your resignation, which he does with much regret, the

Duke of Montrose desires me to convey to you his own sense of the value of your services and to state how alive he is to the loss which will be sustained by the Department in which you have long been an ornament and where your place will with difficulty be supplied.

(*Signed*) J. TILLEY.

Readers will, no doubt, think that this is official flummery, – and so in fact it is. I do not at all imagine that I was an ornament to the Post Office, and have no doubt that the Secretaries and Assistant Secretaries very often would have been glad to be rid of me; – but the letter may be taken as evidence that I did not allow my literary enterprises to interfere with my official work. A man who takes public money without earning it is to me so odious that I can find no pardon for him in my heart. I have known many such, and some who have craved the power to do so. Nothing would annoy me more than to think that I should even be supposed to have been among the number.

And so my connexion was dissolved with the department to which I had applied the thirty three best years of my life; – I must not say devoted because devotion implies an entire surrender, and I certainly had found time for other occupations! It is however absolutely true that during all those years I had thought very much more about the Post Office than I had of my literary work and had given to it a more unflagging attention. Up to this time I had never been angry, never felt myself injured or unappreciated, in that my literary efforts were slighted. But I had suffered very much bitterness on that score in reference to the Post Office. And I had suffered not only on my own personal behalf, but also and more bitterly when I could not procure[i] to be done the things which I thought ought to be done for the benefit of others. That the public in little villages should be enabled to buy postage stamps, that they should have their letters delivered free and at an early hour, that pillar-letter-boxes should be put up for them, – (of which accommodation in the streets and ways of England I was the originator,[8] having, however, got authority for the erection of the first at St Heliers in Jersey, –) that the Letter Carriers and sorters should not be overworked, that they should be adequately paid and have some hours to themselves especially on Sundays, above all that they should be made to earn their wages, and latterly that they should not be crushed by what I thought to be the damnable system of promotion by so-called merit,[1] – these were the matters by which I was stirred to what the Secretary was pleased to call energetic performance of my duties. How I loved, when I was contradicted, – as I was very often and no doubt properly, – to do instantly as I was bid, and then to prove that what I was doing was fatuous, dishonest, expensive, and impracticable! And then there were feuds, – such delicious feuds! I was always an Anti-Hillite, acknowledging indeed the great thing which Sir Rowland Hill had done for the country,[9] but believing him to be entirely unfit to manage men or to arrange labour. It was a pleasure to me to differ from him on all occasions; – and looking back now I think that in all such differences I was right.

Having so steeped myself, as it were, in postal waters, I could not go out from them without a regret. I wonder whether I did anything to improve the style of writing in official reports! I strove to do so gallantly, never being contented with the language of my own reports unless it seemed to have been so written as to be pleasant to be read. I took extreme delight in writing them, not allowing myself to recopy them, never having them recopied by others, but sending them up with their original blots and erasures, – if blots and erasures there were. It is hardly manly, I think, that a man should search after a fine neatness at the expense of so much waste labour, or that he should not be able to exact from himself the necessity of writing words in the form in which they should be read. If a copy be required let it be taken afterwards, – by hand or by machine as may be. But the writer of a letter, if he wish his words to prevail with the reader, should send them out, as written by himself, by his own hand, with his own marks, his own punctuation correct or incorrect, with the evidence upon them that they have come out from his own mind.

And so the cord was cut and I was a free man to run about the world where I would.

A little before the date of my resignation Mr James Virtue,[10] the printer and publisher, had asked me to edit a new magazine for him, and had offered me a salary of £1000 a year for the work, over and above what might be due to me for my own contributions. I had known something of magazines and did not believe that they were generally very lucrative. They were, I thought, useful to some publishers as bringing grist to the mill; but as Mr Virtue's business was chiefly that of a printer in which he was very successful, this consideration could hardly have had much weight with him. I very strongly advised him to abandon the project, pointing out to him that a large expenditure would be necessary to carry on the magazine in accordance with my views, – that I could not be concerned in it on any other understanding and that the chances of an adequate return to him for[k] his money were very small. He came down to Waltham, listened to my arguments with great patience, and then told me that if I would not do the work he would find some other Editor.

Upon this I consented to undertake the duty. My terms as to salary were those which he had himself proposed. The special stipulations which I demanded were: 1st that I should put whatever I pleased into the magazine or keep whatever I pleased out of it, without interference; 2nd that I should from month to month give in to him a list of payments to be made to contributors and that he should pay them, allowing me to fix the amounts, and 3rd that the arrangement should remain in force at any rate for two years. To all this he made no objection, and during the time that he and I were thus bound together he not only complied with these stipulations but also with every suggestion respecting the magazine that I made to him. If the use of large capital combined with wide liberality, and absolute confidence and perpetual good humour on the part of the proprietor, could have produced success, our magazine certainly would have succeeded.

In all such enterprises the name is the first great difficulty. There is the name which has a meaning and the name which has none, – of which two the name that has none is certainly the better as it never belies itself. *The Liberal* may cease to be liberal, or *The Fortnightly*, alas, to come out once a fortnight. But *The Cornhill* and *The Argosy* are under any set of circumstances as well adapted to these names as under any other. Then there is the proprietary name, or possibly the editorial name, – which is only amiss because the publication may change hands. *Blackwood's* has indeed remained always Blackwood's, and *Fraser's* though it has been bought and sold, still does not sound amiss.

Mr Virtue, fearing the too attractive qualities of his own name, wished the magazine to be called *Anthony Trollope's*. But to this I objected eagerly. There were then about the town, – still are about the town, – two or three literary gentlemen by whom to have had myself editored would have driven me an exile from my country. After much discussion we settled on *St Paul's* as the name for our bantling, – not as being in any way new, but as enabling it to fall easily into the ranks with many others. If we were to make ourselves in any way peculiar, it was not by our name that we were desirous of doing so.

I do not think that we did make ourselves in any way peculiar, – and yet there was a great struggle made. On the part of the proprietor I may say that money was spent very freely. On my own part I may declare that I omitted nothing which I thought might tend to success. I read all manuscripts sent to me, and endeavoured to judge impartially. I succeeded in obtaining the services of an apparently excellent[l] literary corps. During the three years and a half of my editorship I was assisted by Mr Goschen, Captain Brackenbury, Edward Dicey, Percy Fitzgerald, H.A. Layard, Allingham, Leslie Stephen, Mrs Lynn Linton, my brother T.A. Trollope and his wife, Charles Lever, E. Arnold, Austin Dobson, R.A. Proctor, Lady Pollock, G.H. Lewes, C. Mackay, Hardman (of the *Times*), George Macdonald, W.R. Greg, Mrs Oliphant, Sir Charles Trevelyan, Leoni Levi, Dutton Cook,[ll] – and others whose names would make the list too long.[m] It might have been thought that with such aid the *St Paul's* would have succeeded. I do not think that the failure, – for it did fail, – arose from bad editing. Perhaps too much editing might have been the fault. I was too anxious to be good, and did not think enough of what might be lucrative.

It did fail, for it never paid its way. It reached if I remember right, a circulation of nearly 10,000; – perhaps on one or two occasions it may have gone beyond that. But the enterprise had been set on foot on a system too expensive to be made lucrative by anything short of a very large circulation. Literary merit will hardly set a magazine afloat, though when afloat it will sustain it. Time is wanted, – or the hubbub and flurry and excitement created by ubiquitous sesquipedalian advertisement. Merit and time together may be effective, but then they must be backed by oeconomy and patience.

I think upon the whole that publishers themselves have been the best Editors of magazines, when they have been able to give time and intelligence to the work. Nothing certainly has ever been done better than *Blackwood's*. The *Cornhill* too after Thackeray had left it and before Leslie Stephen had taken it seemed to be in quite efficient hands, – those hands being the hands of the proprietor and publisher. The proprietor at any rate knows what he wants and what he can afford and is not so frequently tempted to fall into that worst of literary quicksands, – the publishing of matter, not for the sake of the reader, but for that of the writer. I did not so sin very often, – but often enough to feel that I was a coward. 'My friend, my dear friend, – this is trash!' It is so hard to speak thus, – but so necessary for an Editor! We all remember the thorn in his pillow of which Thackeray complained.[12] Occasionally I know that I did give way on behalf of some literary aspirant whose work did not represent itself to me as being good; – and, as often as I did so, I broke my trust to those who employed me. Now I think that such Editors as Thackeray and myself, – if I may for the moment be allowed to couple two men so unequal, – will always be liable to commit such faults; but that the natures of proprietors and publishers will be less soft.

Nor do I know why the pages of a magazine should be considered to be open to every aspirant who thinks that he can write an article, or why the manager of a magazine should be doomed to read all that may be sent to him. The object of the proprietor is to produce a periodical that shall satisfy the public, which he may probably best do by securing the services of writers of acknowledged ability.

CHAPTER 16

Beverley.

Very early in life, very soon after I had become a clerk at St Martin's le Grand, when I was utterly impecunious and beginning to fall grievously into debt, I was asked by an uncle of mine, who was himself a clerk in the War Office,[1] what destination I should like best for my future life. He probably meant to enquire whether I should wish to live married or single, whether to remain in the Post Office or to leave it, whether I should prefer the town or the country. I replied that I should like to be a Member of Parliament. My uncle, who was given to sarcasm, rejoined that, as far as he knew, few clerks in the Post Office did become Members of Parliament. I think it was the remembrance of this jeer which stirred me up to look for a seat as soon as I had made myself capable of holding one by leaving the public service. My uncle was dead, but if I should get a seat, the knowledge that I had done so might travel to that bourne from whence he was not likely to return,[2] and he might there feel that he had done me wrong.

Independently of this I have always thought that to sit in the British Parliament should be the highest object of ambition to every educated Englishman. I do not by this mean to suggest that every educated Englishman[a] should set before himself a seat in Parliament as a probable or even a possible career; but that the man in Parliament has reached a higher position than the man out, – that to serve one's country without pay is the grandest work that a man can do, – that of all studies the study of politics is the one in which a man may make himself most useful to his fellow creatures, – and that, of all lives, public political life is capable of the highest efforts. So thinking, though I was aware that fifty three was too late an age at which to commence a new career, I resolved with much hesitation that I would make the attempt.

Writing now at an age beyond sixty I can say that my political feelings and convictions have never undergone any change. They are now what they became when I first began to have political feelings and convictions. Nor do I find in myself any tendency to modify them as I have found generally in men as they grow old. I consider myself to be an advanced but still a conservative Liberal,[b] which I regard not only as a possible but as a rational and consistent phase of political existence. I can, I believe, in a very few words make known my political theory, and as I am anxious that any who know aught of me should know that, I will endeavour to do so.

It must, I think, be painful to all men to feel inferiority. It should, I think, be a matter of some pain to all men to feel superiority, unless when it has been won by their own efforts. We do not understand the operations of Almighty wisdom, and are therefore unable to tell the causes of the terrible inequalities that we see, – why some, why so many, should have so little to make life enjoyable, so much to make it painful, while a few others, not through their own merit, have had gifts poured out to them from a full hand. We acknowledge the hand of God, and his wisdom, but still we are struck with awe and horror at the misery of many of our brethren. We, who have been born to the superior condition, – for in this matter I consider myself to be standing on a platform with Dukes and Princes and all others to whom plenty and education and liberty have been given, – cannot, I think, look upon the inane, unintellectual, and toil-bound life of those who cannot even feed themselves sufficiently by their sweat, without some feeling of injustice, some sting^c of pain.

This consciousness of wrong has induced in many enthusiastic but unbalanced minds a desire to set all things right by a proclaimed Equality. In their efforts such men have shown how powerless they are in opposing the ordinances of the Creator. For the mind of the thinker and the student is driven to admit, though it be awe-struck by apparent injustice, that this inequality is the work of God. Make all men equal today, and God has so created them that they shall be all unequal tomorrow. The so-called Conservative, the conscientious philanthropic Conservative, seeing this, and being surely convinced that such inequalities are of divine origin, tells himself that it is his duty to preserve them. He thinks that the preservation of the welfare of the world depends on the maintenance of those distances between the Prince and the peasant by which he finds himself to be surrounded; – and, perhaps, I may add, the duty is not unpleasant as he feels himself to be one of the Princes.

But this man, though he sees something, and sees that very clearly, sees only a little. The divine inequality is apparent to him, but not the equally divine diminution of that inequality. That such diminution is taking place on all sides is apparent enough, – but it is apparent to him as an evil the consummation of which it is his duty to retard. He cannot prevent it, and therefore the society to which he belongs is in his eyes retrograding. He will even at times assist it, and will do so conscientiously, feeling that under the gentle pressure supplied by him and with the drags and holdfasts[3] which he may add, the movement would be slower than it would become if subjected to his proclaimed and absolute opponents. Such I think are Conservatives, – and I speak of men who, with the fear of God before their eyes and the love of their neighbours warm in their hearts, endeavour to do their duty to the best of their ability.

Using the term which is now common and which will be best understood, I will endeavour to explain how the equally conscientious Liberal is opposed to the Conservative. He is equally aware that these distances are of divine origin, equally averse to any sudden disruption of society in quest of some Utopian blessedness, – but he is alive to the fact that these distances are day by day becoming less, and he regards this continual diminution as a series of steps towards that human millennium of which he dreams. He is ever[d] willing to help the many to ascend the ladder a little though he knows that as they come up towards him, he must go down to meet them. What is really in his mind is – I will not say equality, for the word is offensive and presents to the imaginations of men ideas of communism, of ruin, and insane democracy, – but a tendency towards equality. In following that, however, he knows that he must be hemmed in by safeguards, lest he be tempted to travel too quickly; and therefore he is glad to be accompanied on his way by the repressive action of the conservative[e] opponent. Holding such views I think I am guilty of no absurdity in calling myself an advanced conservative Liberal. A man who entertains in his mind any political doctrine, except as a means of improving the condition of his fellows, I regard as a political intriguer, a charlatan, and a conjurer, – as one who thinks that by a certain amount of wary wire-pulling he may raise himself in the estimation of the world.

I am aware that this theory of politics will seem to many to be stilted, overstrained, and, as the Americans would say, hi-foluting. Many will declare that the majority even of those who call themselves politicians, – perhaps, even, especially of those who take an active part in politics, – are stirred by no such feelings as these and acknowledge no such motives. Men become Tories or Whigs, Liberals or Conservatives, partly by education – following their fathers, partly by chance, partly as openings come, partly in accordance with the bent of their minds, but still without any far-fetched reasonings as to distances and the diminution of distances. No doubt it is so, – and, in the battle of politics as it goes, men are led further and further away from first causes till at last a measure is opposed by one simply because it is advocated by another, and members of Parliament swarm into lobbies following the dictation of their leaders and not their own individual judgements. But the principle is at work throughout. To many, though hardly acknowledged, it is still apparent. On almost all it has its effect, – though there are the intriguers, the clever conjurers, to whom politics is simply such a game as is billiards or rackets, only played with greater results. To the minds that create, and lead, and sway political opinion some such theory is, I think, ever present.

The truth of all this I had long since taken home to myself. I had now been thinking of it for thirty years, and had never doubted. But I had always been aware of a certain visionary weakness about myself in regard to politics. A man, to be useful in Parliament, must be able to confine himself and conform himself, to be satisfied with doing a little bit of a little thing at a time. He must patiently get up everything connected with the duty on mushrooms, and then be satisfied with himself when at last he has induced a Chancellor of the Exchequer to say that he will consider the impost at the first opportunity. He must be content to be beaten six times in order that on a seventh, his work may be found to be of assistance to some one else. He must remember that he is one out of 660, and be content with 1–6th part[f] of the attention of the nation. If he have grand ideas he must keep them to himself – unless by chance he can work his way up to the top of the tree. In short he must be a practical man. Now I knew that in politics I could never become a practical man. I should never be satisfied with a soft word from the Chancellor of the Exchequer, but would always be flinging my over-taxed catchup in his face.

Nor did it seem to me to be possible that I should ever become a good speaker. I had no special gifts that way and had not studied the art early enough in life to overcome natural difficulties. I had found that with infinite labour I could learn a few sentences by heart and deliver them, monotonously indeed, but clearly. Or, again, if there were something special to be said I could say it in a common place fashion, – but always as though I were in a hurry, and with the fear before me of being thought to be prolix. But I had no power of combining, as a public speaker should always do, that which I had studied with that which occurred to me at the moment. It must be all lesson, – which I found to be best; or else all impromptu, – which was very bad indeed unless I had something special on my mind. I was thus aware that I could do no good by going into Parliament, – that the time for it, if there could have been a time, had gone by. But still I had an almost insane desire to sit there, and be able to assure myself that my uncle's scorn had not been deserved.

In 1867 it had been suggested to me that in the event of a dissolution I should stand for one division of the County of Essex, and I had promised that I would do so, – though the promise at that time was as rash a one as a man could make. I was instigated to this by the late Charles Buxton,[4] a man whom I greatly loved, and who was very anxious that the county for which his brother had sat and with which the family were connected should be relieved from what he regarded as the thraldom of Toryism. But there was no dissolution then. Mr Disraeli passed his reform bill by the help of the liberal member for Newark[5] and the summoning of a new parliament was postponed till the next year. By this reform bill Essex was portioned out into three instead of two electoral divisions, one of which, that adjacent to London, would it was thought be altogether liberal. After the promise which I had given, the performance of which would have cost me a large sum of money absolutely in vain, it was felt by some that I should be selected as one of the candidates for the new division, – and as such I was proposed by Mr Charles Buxton. But another gentleman, who would have been bound by previous pledges to support me, was put forward by what I believe to have been the dissenting[g] interest, and I had to give way. At the election this gentleman, with another Liberal who had often stood for the county were returned without a contest. Alas, alas! They were both unseated at the next election, when the great conservative reaction took place.

In the spring of 1868 I was sent to the United States on a postal mission of which I will speak presently. While I was absent the dissolution took place. On my return I was somewhat too late to look out for a seat. But I had friends who knew the weakness of my ambition and it was not likely therefore that I should escape the peril of being put forward for some impossible borough, as to which the liberal party would not choose that it should go to the Conservatives without a struggle. At last, after one or two others, Beverley was proposed to me, and to Beverley I went.

I must, however, exculpate the gentleman who acted as my agent from undue persuasion exercised towards me. He was a man who thoroughly understood Parliament, having sat there himself – and he sits there, now at this moment. He understood Yorkshire, – or at least the East Riding of Yorkshire in which Beverley is situated, – certainly better than any one alive. He understood all the mysteries of canvassing, and he knew well the traditions, the condition, and the prospects of the liberal party. I will not give his name, but they who knew Yorkshire in 1868 will not be at a loss to find it.[6] 'So,' said he, 'you are going to stand for Beverley!' I replied gravely that I was thinking of doing so. 'You don't expect to get in!' he said. Again I was grave. I would not, I said, be sanguine, but nevertheless I was disposed to hope the best. 'Oh no,' continued he, with good humoured raillery, 'you won't get in. I don't suppose you really expect it. But there is a fine career open to you. You will spend £1000, and lose the election. Then you will petition and spend another £1000. You will throw out the elected members; there will be a commission, and the borough will be disfranchised. For a beginner such as you are that will be a great success.' And yet, in the teeth of this from a man who knew all about it, I persisted in going to Beverley!

The borough, which returned two members, had long been represented by Sir Henry Edwards, of whom I think I am justified in saying that he had contracted a close intimacy with it for the sake of the seat. There had been many contests, many petitions, many void elections, many members, but, through it all, Sir Henry had kept his seat, if not permanently, still with a fixity of tenure next door to permanence. I fancy that with a little management between the parties the borough might at this time have returned a member of each colour quietly; –

but there were spirits there who did not love political quietude, and it was at last decided that there should be two liberal and two conservative candidates. Sir Henry was joined by a young man of fortune in quest of a seat,[7] and I was grouped with Mr Maxwell the eldest son of Lord Herries, a Scotch Roman Catholic peer who lives in the neighbourhood.

When the time came I went down to canvass and spent, I think, the most wretched fortnight of my manhood. In the first place I was subject to a bitter tyranny from grinding vulgar tyrants. They were doing what they could, or said that they were doing so, to secure me a seat in Parliament and I was to be in their hands for at any rate[h] the period of my candidature. On one day both of us, – Mr Maxwell and I, – wanted to go out hunting. We proposed to ourselves but the one holyday during this period of intense labour; but I was assured, as was he also, by a publican who was working for us that if we committed such a crime he and all Beverley would desert us. From morning to evening every day I was taken round the lanes and bye ways of that uninteresting town, canvassing every voter, exposed to the rain, up to my knees in slush, and utterly unable to assume that air of triumphant joy with which a jolly successful candidate should be invested. At night, every night, I had to speak somewhere, – which was bad, and to listen to the speaking of others, – which was much worse. When on one Sunday I proposed to go to the Minster Church I was told that was quite useless as the Church party were all certain to support Sir Henry! 'Indeed,' said the publican, my tyrant, 'he goes there in a kind of official procession[i] and you had better not allow yourself to be seen in the same place.' So I stayed away and omitted my prayers. No Church of England church in Beverley would on such an occasion have welcomed a liberal candidate. I felt myself to be a kind of Pariah in the borough to whom was opposed all that was pretty, and all that was nice and all that was – ostensibly – good.

But perhaps my strongest sense of discomfort arose from the conviction that my political ideas were all leather and prunella[8] to the men whose votes I was soliciting. They cared nothing for my doctrines, and could not even be made to understand that I should have any. I had been brought to Beverley either to beat Sir Henry Edwards,

– which, however, no one probably thought to be feasible, – or to cause him the greatest possible amount of trouble, inconvenience and expense. There were, indeed, two points on which a portion of my wished-for supporters seemed to have opinions, and on both these two points I was driven by my opinions to oppose them. Some were anxious for the Ballot,[9] – which had not then become law, and some desired the Permissive Bill.[10] I hated, and do hate, both these measures, thinking it to be unworthy of a great people to free itself from the evil results of vicious conduct by unmanly restraints. Undue influence on voters is a great evil from which this country had already done much to emancipate itself by extended electoral divisions and by an encrease of independent feeling. These, I thought, and not secret voting, were the weapons by which electoral intimidation should be overcome. And as for drink, – I believe in no parliamentary restraint, but I do believe in the gradual effect of moral teaching and education. But a Liberal, to do any good at Beverley, should have been able to swallow such gnats[11] as those. I would swallow nothing, and was altogether the wrong man.

I knew, from the commencement of my candidature how it would be. Of course that well-trained gentleman who condescended to act as my agent, had understood the case, and I ought to have taken his thoroughly kind advice. He had seen it all and had told himself that it was wrong that one so innocent in such ways as I, so utterly unable to fight such a battle, should be carried down into Yorkshire merely to spend money and to be annoyed. He could not have said more than he did say, and I suffered for my obstinacy. Of course I was not elected. Sir Henry Edwards[j] and his comrade became members for Beverley, and I was at the bottom of the poll. I paid £400 for my expenses, and then returned to London.

My friendly agent, in his raillery, had of course exaggerated the cost. He had, when I arrived at Beverley, asked me for a cheque for £400 and told me that that sum would suffice. It did suffice. How it came to pass that exactly that sum should be required I never knew, but such was the case. Then there came a petition, – not from me, but from the town. The enquiry was made, the two gentlemen were unseated, the borough was disfranchised, Sir Henry Edwards was put on his trial for some kind of parliamentary offence and was acquitted. In this way Beverley's privilege as a borough, and my parliamentary ambition, were brought to an end at the same time.

When I knew the result I did not altogether regret it. It may be that Beverley might have been brought to political confusion and Sir Henry Edwards relegated to private life without the expenditure of my hard-earned money and without that fortnight of misery; but, connecting the things together, as it was natural that I should do, I did flatter myself that I had done some good. It had seemed to me that nothing could be worse, nothing more unpatriotic, nothing more absolutely opposed to the system of representative government, than the time-honoured practices of the borough of Beverley. It had come to pass that political cleanliness was odious to the citizens. There was something grand in the scorn with which a leading Liberal there turned up his nose at me when I told him that there should be no bribery, no treating, – not even a pot of beer on one side! It was a matter for study to see how at Beverley politics were appreciated because they might subserve electoral purposes, and how little it was understood that electoral purposes, which are in themselves a nuisance, should be endured in order that they may subserve politics. And then the time, the money, the mental energy which had been expended in making the borough a secure seat for a gentleman who had realised the idea that it would become him to be a member of Parliament! This use of the borough seemed to be relished[k] and approved in the borough generally! The inhabitants had taught themselves to think that it was for such purposes that boroughs were intended! To have assisted in putting an end to this even in one town was to a certain extent a satisfaction.

CHAPTER 17

The American Postal Treaty – Four More Novels.

In the spring of 1868, – before the affair of Beverley which as being the first direct result of my resignation of office has been brought in a little out of its turn, – I was requested to go over to the United States and make a postal treaty at Washington. This, as I had left the service, I regarded as a compliment, and of course I went. It was my third visit to America and I have made two since. As far as the Post Office work was concerned it was very far from being agreeable. I found myself located at Washington, a place I do not love, and was harassed by delays, annoyed by incompetence, and opposed by what I felt to be personal and not national views. I had to deal with two men,[1] – with one who was a working officer of the American post office, than whom I never met a more zealous, or, as far as I could judge, a more honest public servant. He had his views and I had mine, each of us having at heart the welfare of the service in regard to his own country; – each of us also having certain orders which we were bound to obey. But the other gentleman who was in rank the superior, – whose executive position was dependent on his official status as is the case with our own Ministers, – did not recommend himself to me equally. He would make appointments with me and then not keep them, – which at last offended me so grievously that I declared at the Washington Post Office that if this treatment were continued I would write home to say that any further action on my part was impossible. I think I should have done so, had it not occurred to me that I might in this way serve his purposes rather than my own, or the purposes of those who had sent me. The treaty, however, was at last made, – the purport of which was that everything possible should be done, at a heavy expenditure on the part of England, to expedite the mails from England to America, and that nothing should be done by America to expedite the mails from thence to us. The expedition, I believe, to be now equal both ways; but it could not be maintained as it is without the payment of a heavy subsidy from Great

Britain, whereas no subsidy is paid by the States. This was a state of things which may probably have appeared to American politicians to be exactly that which they should try to obtain. The whole arrangement has again been altered since the time of which I have spoken.[a]

I had also a commission from the Foreign Office, for which I had asked, to make an effort on behalf of an international copyright between the United States and Great Britain, – the want of which is the one great impediment to pecuniary success which still stands in the way of English successful authors. I cannot say that I have never had a shilling of American money on behalf of reprints of my work; but I have been conscious of no such payments. Having found many years ago, – in 1861 when I made a struggle on the subject being then in the States, the details of which are sufficiently amusing* – that I could not myself succeed in dealing with American booksellers, I have sold all foreign right to the English publishers; and though I do not know that I have raised my price against them on that score, I may in this way have had some indirect advantage from the American market. But I do know that what the publishers have received here is very trifling. I doubt whether Messrs Chapman & Hall, my present publishers, get for early sheets sent to the States as much as 5 per cent on the price they pay me for my manuscript. But the American readers are more numerous than the English, and, taking them all through, are probably more wealthy. If I can get £1000 for a book here, (exclusive of their market) I ought to be able to get as much there. If a man supply 600 customers with shoes in place of 300, there is no question as to such result. Why not then if I can supply 60,000 readers instead of 30,000?

I fancied that I knew that the opposition to an international copy-

* In answer to a question from myself, a certain American publisher, he who usually reprinted my works,[2] promised me *that if any other American publisher republished my work on America before he had done so,* he would not bring out a competing edition, though there would be no law to hinder him. I then entered into an agreement with another American publisher, stipulating to supply him with early sheets, and he stipulating to pay me a certain royalty on his sales and to supply me with accounts half yearly. I sent the sheets with energetic punctuality, and the work was brought out with equal energy and precision, – by my old American publishers. The gentleman who made the promise had not broken his word. No other American Edition had come out before his. I never got any account, and, of course, never received a dollar.

right was by no means an American feeling, but was confined to the bosoms of a few interested Americans. All that I did and heard in reference to the subject on this further visit, – and having a certain authority from the British Secretary of State with me, I could hear and do something, – altogether confirmed me in this view. I have no doubt that if I could poll American readers, or American Senators, – or even American Representatives, if the polling could be unbiassed, – or American booksellers,* that an assent to an international copyright would be the result. The state of things as it is is crushing to American authors, as the publishers will not pay them on a liberal scale, knowing that they can supply their customers with modern English literature without paying for it. The English amount of production so much exceeds the American, that the rate at which the former can be published rules the market. It is equally injurious to American booksellers, – except to two or three of the greatest houses. No small man can now acquire the exclusive right of printing and selling an English book. If such a one attempt it the work is reprinted instantly by one of the leviathans, – who alone are the gainers. The argument of course is that American readers are the gainers, – that as they can get for nothing the use of certain property they would be cutting their own throats were they to pass a law debarring themselves from the power of such appropriation. In this argument all idea of honesty is thrown to the winds. It is not that they do not approve of a system of copyright, – as many great men have disapproved, – for their own law of copyright is as stringent as is ours. A bold assertion is made that they like to appropriate the goods of other people, and that as in this case they can do so with impunity, they will continue to do so. But the argument, as far as I have been able to judge, comes, not from the people, but from the bookselling leviathans and from those politicians whom the leviathans are able to attach to their interests. The ordinary American purchaser is not much affected by the slight variations in price. He is at any rate too high-hearted to be affected by the prospect of such variation. It is the man who wants to make money, not he who fears that he

---

* I might also say American publishers if I might count them by the number of heads and not by the amount of work done by the firms.

may be called on to spend it, who controls such matters as this in the United States. It is the large speculator who becomes powerful in the lobbies of the House and understands how wise it may be to incur a great expenditure either in the creation of a great business or in protecting that which he has created from competition.

Nothing was done in 1868, – and nothing has been done since (up to 1876). A Royal Commission on the Law of Copyright is now about to sit in this country, of which I have consented to be a member, and the question must then be handled, though nothing done by a Royal Commission here can affect American legislators. But I do believe that if the measure be consistently and judiciously urged, the enemies to it in the States will gradually be overcome. Some years since we had some quasi private meetings under the Presidency of Lord Stanhope, in Mr John Murray's dining room, on the subject of international copyright. At one of these I discussed this matter of American international copyright with Charles Dickens who strongly declared his conviction that nothing would induce an American to give up the power he possesses of pirating British literature. But he was a man who, seeing clearly what was before him, would not realise the possibility of shifting views. Because, in this matter, the American decision had been according to his thinking dishonest, therefore no other than dishonest decision was to be expected from Americans. Against that idea I then protested and now protest. American dishonesty is rampant, but it is rampant only among a few.[b] It is the great misfortune of the community that those few have been able to dominate so large a portion of the population among which all men can vote but so few can understand for what they are voting.

Since this was written the Commission on the Law of Copyright has sat and made its report.[3] With the great body of it I agree, and could serve no reader by alluding here at length to matters which are discussed there. But in regard to this question of international copyright with the United States I think that we were incorrect in the expression of an opinion that fair justice, – or justice approaching to fair, – is now done by American publishers to English authors by payments made by them for early sheets. I have just found that £20 was paid to my publisher in England for the use of the early sheets of a novel for which I received £1600 in England. When asked why he accepted so little he assured me that the firm with whom he dealt would not give more. 'Why not go to another firm?' I asked. No other firm would give a dollar, because no other firm would care to run counter to that great firm which had assumed to itself the right of publishing my books. I soon after received a copy of my own novel in the American form and found that it was published for 7½d. That a great sale was expected can be argued from the fact that without a great sale the paper and printing necessary for the republication of a three volume novel could not be supplied. Many thousand copies must have been sold. But from these the author received not one shilling. I need hardly point out that the sum of £20 would not do more than compensate the publisher for his trouble in making the bargain. The publisher here no doubt might have refused to supply the early sheets, but he had no means of exacting a higher price than that offered. I mention the circumstance here because it has been boasted on behalf of the American publishers that though there is no international copyright they deal so liberally with English authors as to make it unnecessary that the English Author should be so protected. With the fact of the £20 just brought to my knowledge, and with the copy of my book published at 7½d. now in my hands, I feel that an international copyright is very necessary for my protection.[c]

They among Englishmen who best love and most admire the United States feel themselves tempted to use the strongest language in denouncing the sins of Americans. Who can but love their personal generosity, their active and far-seeking philanthropy, their love of education, their hatred of ignorance, the general convictions in the minds of all of them that a man should be enabled to walk upright, fearing no one and conscious that he is responsible for his own actions? In what country have grander efforts been made by private munificence to relieve the sufferings of humanity? Where is there a wider hospitality?[d] Where can the English traveller find any more anxious to assist him than the normal American when once the American shall have found the Englishman to be neither sullen nor fastidious? Who, lastly, is so much an object of heart-felt admiration of the American man and the American woman as the well-mannered and well-educated English woman or English man? These are the ideas which I say spring uppermost in the mind of the unprejudiced English traveller, as he makes acquaintance with these near relatives. Then he becomes cognisant of their official doings, of their politics, of their municipal scandals, of their great ring-robberies,[4] of their lobbyings and bribings and the infinite baseness of their public life. There at the top of everything he finds the very men who are the least fit to occupy high places. American public dishonesty is so glaring that the very friends he has made in the country are not slow to acknowledge it, – speaking of public life as a thing apart from their own existence, as a state of dirt, in which it would be an insult to suppose that they are concerned! In the midst of it all the stranger who sees so much that he hates and so much that he loves hardly knows how to express himself.

'It is not enough that you are personally clean,' he says with what energy and courage he can command, – 'not enough, though the clean outnumber the foul as greatly as those gifted with eyesight outnumber the blind, if you that can see allow the blind to lead you. It is not by the private lives of the millions that the outside world will judge you, but by the public career of those units whose venality is allowed to debase the name of your country. There never was plainer proof given than is given here that it is the duty of every honest citizen to look after the honour of his State.'

Personally I have to own that I have met Americans, – men but more frequently women, – who have in all respects come up to my ideas of what men and women should be, energetic, having opinions of their own, quick in speech, with some dash of sarcasm at their command, always intelligent, sweet to look at (I speak of the women), fond of pleasure, and each with a personality of his or her own, which makes no effort on my own part necessary in remembering the difference between Mrs Walker and Mrs Green, or between Mr Smith and Mr Johnson. They have faults. They are self-conscious, and too prone to prove by ill-concealed struggles that they are as good as you, – whereas you perhaps have been long acknowledging to yourselves that they are much better. And there is sometimes a pretence at personal dignity among those who think themselves to have risen high in the world which is deliciously ludicrous. I remember two old gentlemen, –

the owners of names which stand deservedly high in public estimation, – whose deportment at a public funeral turned the occasion for
me into[e] one for irresistible comedy.[5] They are suspicious at first, and
fearful of themselves. They lack that simplicity of manners which with
us has become a habit from our childhood. But they are never fools,
and I think that they are seldom ill-natured.

There is an American woman,[f6] of whom not to speak in a work
purporting to be a[g] memoir of my own life, would be to omit all allusion to one of the chief pleasures which has graced my later years. In
the last fifteen years she has been, out of my family, my most chosen
friend. She is a ray of light to me from which I can always strike a spark
by thinking of her. I do not know that I should please her or do any
good by naming her. But not to allude to her in these pages would
amount almost to a falsehood. I could not write truly of myself without saying that such a friend had been vouchsafed to me. I trust that
she may live to read the words I have now written, and to wipe away a
tear as she thinks of my feeling while I write them.

I was absent on this occasion something over three months, and on
my return I went back with energy to my work at the *St Paul's Magazine*. The first novel in it from my own pen was called *Phineas Finn* in
which I commenced a series of semi-political tales. As I was debarred
from expressing my opinions in the House of Commons, I took this
method of declaring myself. And as I could not take my seat on those
benches where I might possibly have been shone upon by the Speaker's
Eye, I had humbly to crave his permission for a seat in the gallery so
that I might thus become conversant with the ways and doings of the
House in which some of my scenes were to be placed. The Speaker
was very gracious and gave me a running order for, I think, a couple of
months. It was enough at any rate to enable me often to be very tired,
– and, as I have been assured by members, to talk of the proceedings
almost as well as though Fortune had enabled me to fall asleep within
the House itself.

In writing *Phineas Finn* and also some other novels which followed it
I was conscious that I could not make a tale pleasing chiefly, or perhaps in any part, by politics. If I write politics for my own sake, I must
put in love and intrigue, social incidents with perhaps a dash of sport,

for the sake of my readers. In this way I think I made my political hero interesting. It was certainly a blunder to take him from Ireland, – into which I was led by the circumstance that I created the scheme of the book during a visit to Ireland.[7] There was nothing to be gained by the peculiarity, and there was an added difficulty in obtaining sympathy and affection for a politician belonging to a nationality whose politics are not respected in England. But in spite of this Phineas succeeded. It was not a brilliant success, – because men and women not conversant with political matters could not care much for a hero who spent so much of his time either in the House of Commons, or in a public office. But the men who would have lived with Phineas Finn read the book, and the women who would have lived with Lady Laura Standish read it also. As this was what I had intended I was contented. It is all fairly good, except the ending, – as to which till I got to it I made no provision. As I fully intended to bring my hero again into the world, I was wrong to marry him to a simple pretty Irish girl, who could only be felt as an encumbrance on such return. When he did return I had no alternative but to kill the pretty simple Irish girl which was an unpleasant and awkward necessity.

In writing *Phineas Finn* I had constantly before me the necessity of progression in character, – of marking the changes in men and women which would naturally be produced by the lapse of years. In most novels the writer can have no such duty, as the period occupied is not long enough to allow of the change of which I speak. In *Ivanhoe*, all the incidents of which are included in less than a month, the characters should be, as they are, consistent throughout. Novelists who have undertaken to write the life of a hero or heroine have generally considered their work completed at the interesting period of marriage and have contented themselves with the advance in taste and manners which are common to all boys and girls as they become men and women. Fielding no doubt did more than this in *Tom Jones*, which is one of the greatest novels in the English language, for there he has shown how a noble and sanguine nature may fall away under temptation and be again strengthened and made to stand upright. But I do not think that novelists have often set before themselves the state of progressive change, – nor should I have done it had I not found myself so frequently allured back to my old friends. So much of my inner life was passed in their company that I was continually asking myself how this woman would act when this or that event had passed over her head or how that man would carry himself when his youth had become manhood or his manhood declined to old age. It was in regard to the old Duke of Omnium, of his nephew and heir, and of his heir's wife Lady Glencora that I was anxious to carry out this idea; – but others added[h] themselves to my mind as I went on, and I got round me a circle of persons as to all of whom[i] I knew not only their present characters but how those characters were to be affected by years and circumstances. The happy motherly life of Violet Effingham which was due to the girl's honest but long-restrained love, the tragic misery of Lady Laura which was equally due to the sale which she made of herself in her wretched marriage, and the long suffering but final success of the hero of which he had deserved the first by his vanity, and the last by his constant honesty, had been foreshadowed to me from the first. As to the incidents of the story, the circumstances by which these personages were to be affected, I knew nothing. They were created for the most part as they were described. I never could arrange a set of events before me. But the evil and the good of my puppets, and how the evil would always lead to evil, and the good produce good, – that was clear to me as are the stars on a summer night.

Lady Laura Standish is the best character in the two books,[j] – of which I will speak here together. They are in fact but one novel, though they were brought out at a considerable interval of time and in different forms. The first was commenced in the *St Paul's Magazine* in 1867, and the other was brought out in the *Graphic* in 1873.[k8] In this there was much bad arrangement, as I had no right to expect that novel readers would remember the characters of a story after an interval of six years, or that any little interest which might have been taken in the career of my hero could then have been renewed. I do not know that such interest was renewed. But I found that the sequel enjoyed the same popularity as the former part and among the same class of readers. Phineas and Lady Laura, and Lady Chiltern – as Violet had become, and the old Duke, whom I killed gracefully, and the new duke and the young duchess, either kept their old friends, or made new friends for themselves. Phineas Finn I certainly think was successful from first to last. I am aware however that there was nothing in it to touch the heart like the abasement of Lady Mason when confessing her guilt to her old lover, or any approach in delicacy of delineation to the character of Mr Crawley.

Phineas Finn, the first part of the story, was completed in May 1867. In June and July I wrote *Linda Tressel*, for *Blackwood's Magazine*, of which I have already spoken. In September and October I wrote a short novel, called *The Golden Lion of Granpere*, which was intended also for *Blackwood*, – with a view of being published anonymously; – but Mr Blackwood did not find the arrangement to be profitable, and the story remained on my hands unread and unthought of for a few years. It appeared subsequently in *Good Words*. It was written on the model of *Nina Balatka* and *Linda Tressel* but is very inferior to either of them. In November of the same year, 1867, I began a very long novel which I called *He Knew He Was Right*, and which was brought out by Mr Virtue, the proprietor of *St Paul's Magazine*, in sixpenny numbers every week. I do not know that in any literary effort I ever fell more completely short of my own intention than in this story. It was my purpose to create sympathy for an[1] unfortunate man who, while endeavouring to do his duty to all around him, should be led constantly astray by his unwillingness to submit his own judgement to the opinion of others. The man is made to be unfortunate enough and the evil which he does is apparent. So far I did not fail, but the sympathy has not been created yet. I look upon the story as being nearly altogether bad. It is in part redeemed by certain scenes in the house and vicinity of an old maid in Exeter. But a novel which in its main parts is bad cannot in truth be redeemed by the vitality of subordinate characters.

This work was finished while I was at Washington in the spring of 1868, and on the day after I finished it I commenced *The Vicar of Bullhampton*, a novel which I wrote for Messrs Bradbury & Evans. This I completed in November 1868, and at once began *Sir Harry Hotspur of Humblethwaite*, a story which I was still writing at the close of the year. I look upon these two years, 1867 and 1868, of which I have given a somewhat confused account in this and the two preceding chapters as the busiest in my life. I had indeed left the Post Office, but though I had left it I had been employed by it during a considerable portion of the time. I had established the *St Paul's Magazine* in reference to which I had read an enormous amount of manuscript, and for which, independently of my novels, I had written articles almost monthly. I had stood for Beverley, and had made many speeches. I had also written five novels, – and had hunted three times a week during each of the winters. And how happy I was with it all! I had suffered at Beverley, – but I had suffered as a part of the work which I was desirous of doing, and I had gained my experience. I had suffered at Washington with that wretched American Postmaster; – and with the mosquitoes, not having been able to escape from that capital till July; but all that had added to the activity of my life. I had often groaned over those manuscripts, – but I had read them, considering it perhaps foolishly, to be part of my duty as Editor. And, though in the quick production of my novels I had always ringing in my ears that terrible condemnation and scorn pronounced[m] by the great man in Paternoster Row,[9] I was nevertheless proud of having done so much. I had always had a pen in my hand. Whether crossing the seas, or fighting with American officials, or tramping about the streets of Beverley, I could do a little, and generally more than a little. I had long since convinced myself that in such work as mine the great secret consisted in acknowledging myself to be bound to rules of labour similar to those which an artisan or a mechanic is forced to obey. A shoemaker when he has finished one pair of shoes does not sit down and contemplate his work in idle satisfaction. 'There is my pair of shoes, – finished at last! What a pair of shoes it is!' The shoemaker who so indulged himself would be without wages half his time. It is the same with a professional writer of books. An author may, of course, want time to study a new subject. He will at any rate assure himself that there is some good reason why he should pause. He does pause and will be idle for a month or two while he tells himself how beautiful is that last pair of shoes which he has finished! Having thought much of all this, and having made up my mind that I could be really happy only when I was at work, I had now quite accustomed myself to begin a second pair as soon as the first was out of my hands.

CHAPTER 18

'The Vicar of Bullhampton' – 'Sir Harry Hotspur'
'An Editor's Tales' – 'Caesar'.

In 1869 I was called on to decide, in council with my two boys and their mother, what should be their destination in life. In June of that year the elder who was then twenty three was called to the Bar; and as he had gone through the regular courses of lecturing, tuition, and study it might be supposed that his course had been already decided. But, just as he was called, there seemed to be an opening for him in another direction, and this, joined to the terrible uncertainty of the Bar, the terror of which was not in his case lessened by any peculiar forensic aptitudes, induced us to sacrifice dignity in quest of success. Mr Frederic Chapman, who was then and now is the sole[a] representative of the publishing house known as Messrs Chapman & Hall, wanted a partner, and my son Henry went into the firm. He remained there three years and a half; but he did not like it, nor do I think he made a very good publisher. At any rate he left the business, with perhaps more pecuniary success than might have been expected from the short period of his labours, and has since taken himself to literature as a profession. Whether he will work at it so hard as his father, and write as many books, may be doubted.

My second son, Frederic, had very early in life gone out to Australia, having resolved on a colonial career when he found that boys who did not grow as fast as he did got above him at school. This departure was a great pang to his mother and me; but it was permitted on the understanding that he was to come back when he was twenty one, and then decide whether he would remain in England or return to the Colonies. In the winter of 1868 he did come to England, and had a season's hunting in the old country; but there was no doubt in his own mind as to his settling in Australia. His purpose was fixed and in the spring of 1869, he made his second journey out. As I have, since that date, made two journeys to see him, – of one of which at any rate I

shall have to speak as I wrote a long book on the Australasian Colonies, – I shall have an opportunity of saying a word or two further of
him and his doings.

The Vicar of Bullhampton was written in 1868 for publication in *Once a
Week*, a periodical then belonging to Messrs Bradbury & Evans. It was
not to come out till 1869, and I, as was my wont, had made my terms
long previously to the proposed date. I had made my terms and written my story and sent it to the publisher long before it was wanted, –
and so far my mind was at rest. The date fixed was the 1st of July, – which
date had been named in accordance with the exigencies of the Editor
of the periodical.[1] An author who writes for these publications is
bound to suit himself to these exigencies and can generally do so
without personal loss or inconvenience, if he will only take time by the
forelock. With all the pages that I have written for magazines I have
never been a day late, nor have I ever caused inconvenience by sending less or more matter than I had stipulated to supply. But I have
sometimes found myself compelled to suffer by the irregularity of
others. I have endeavoured to console myself by reflecting that such
must ever be the fate of virtue. The industrious must feed the idle.
The honest and simple will always be the prey of the cunning and
fraudulent. The punctual who keep none waiting for them are doomed
to wait perpetually for the unpunctual. But these earthly sufferers
know that they are making their way heavenwards, – and their oppres-
sors their way elsewards. If the former reflexion does not suffice for
consolation, the deficiency is made up by the second. I was terribly aggrieved on the matter of the publication of my new Vicar, and had to
think very much of the ultimate rewards of punctuality and its opposite. About the end of March 1869 I got a dolorous letter from the
Editor. All the *Once a Week* people were in terrible trouble. They had
bought the right of translating one of Victor Hugo's modern novels,
L'Homme qui rit;[2] they had fixed a date, relying on positive pledges
from the French publishers; and now the great French author had
postponed his work from week to week and from month to month, and
it had so come to pass that the Frenchman's grinning hero would have
to appear exactly at the same time as my clergyman. Was it not quite
apparent to me, the Editor asked, that *Once a Week* could not hold the

two? Would I allow my clergyman to make his appearance in the *Gentleman's Magazine*[3] instead?

My disgust at this proposition was, I think, chiefly due to my dislike of Victor Hugo's[b] latter novels, which I regard as pretentious and untrue to nature. To this perhaps was added some feeling of indignation that I should be asked to give way to a Frenchman. The Frenchman had broken his engagement. He had failed to have his work finished by the stipulated time. From week to week and month to month he had put off the fulfilment of his duty. And because of these *laches*[4] on his part, – on the part of this sententious French Radical, – I was to be thrown over! Virtue sometimes finds it difficult to console herself even with the double comfort. I would not come out in the *Gentleman's Magazine*, and as *The Grinning Man* could not be got out of the way my novel was published in separate numbers.

The same thing has occurred to me more than once since. 'You, no doubt are regular,' a publisher has said to me. 'But Mr — is irregular. He has thrown me out, and I cannot be ready for you till three months after the time named.' In these emergencies I have given, perhaps, half what was wanted, and have refused to give the other half. I have endeavoured to fight my own battle fairly, and at the same time not to make myself unnecessarily obstinate. But the circumstances have impressed on my mind the great need there is that men engaged in literature should feel themselves to be bound to their industry, as men know that they are bound in other callings. There does, I fear, exist a feeling that authors, because they are authors, are relieved from the necessity of paying attention to every day rules. A writer, if he be making[c] £800 a year, does not think himself bound to live modestly on £600, and put by the remainder for his wife and children. He does not understand that he should sit down at his desk at a certain hour. He imagines that publishers and booksellers should keep all their engagements with him to the letter, – but that he, as a brain-worker and conscious of the subtle nature of the brain, should be able to exempt himself from bonds when it suits him. He has his own theory about inspiration which will not always come, – especially will not come if wine-cups overnight have been too deep. All this has ever been odious to me, – as being unmanly. A man may be frail in health, and therefore unable to do as he has contracted in whatever grade of life. He who has been blessed with physical strength to work day by day, year by year, – as has been my case, – should pardon deficiencies caused by sickness or infirmity. I may in this respect have been a little hard on others, – and, if so, I here record my repentance. But I think that no allowance should be given to claims for exemption from punctuality made if not absolutely on the score still with the conviction of intellectual superiority.

The Vicar of Bullhampton was written chiefly with the object of exciting not only pity but sympathy for a fallen woman, and of raising a feeling of forgiveness for such in the minds of other women. I could not venture to make this female the heroine of my story. To have made her a heroine at all would have been directly opposed to my purpose. It was necessary therefore that she should be a second rate personage in the tale; – but it was with reference to her life that the tale was written, and the hero and the heroine with their belongings are all subordinate. To this novel I affixed a preface, – in doing which I was acting in defiance of an old-established principle. I do not know that any one read it; but as I wish to have it read, I will insert it here again.

'I have introduced[d] in the *Vicar of Bullhampton* the character of a girl whom I will call, – for want of a truer word that shall not in its truth be offensive, – a castaway. I have endeavoured to endow her with qualities that may create sympathy, and I have brought her back at last from degradation at least to decency. I have not married her to a wealthy lover, and I have endeavoured to explain that though there was possible to her a way out of perdition, still things could not be with her as they would have been had she not fallen.

'There arises, of course, the question whether a novelist, who professes to write for the amusement of the young of both sexes, should allow himself to bring upon his stage a character such as that of Carry Brattle. It is not long since, – it is well within the memory of the author, – that the very existence of such a condition of life, as was hers, was supposed to be unknown to our sisters and daughters, and was, in truth, unknown to many of them. Whether that ignorance was good may be questioned; but that it exists no longer is beyond question. Then arises the further question, – how far the condition of such unfortunates should be made a matter of concern to the sweet young hearts of those whose delicacy and cleanliness of thought is a matter of pride to so many of us. Cannot women, who are good, pity the sufferings of the vicious, and do something perhaps to mitigate and shorten them, without contamination from the vice? It will be admitted probably by most men who have thought upon the subject that no fault among us is punished so heavily as that fault, often so light in itself but so terrible in its consequences to the less faulty of the two offenders, – by which a woman falls. All her own sex is against her, – and all those of the other sex in whose veins runs the blood which she is thought to have contaminated, and who, of nature, would befriend her were her trouble any other than it is.

'She is what she is, and she remains in her abject, pitiless, unutterable misery, because this sentence of the world has placed her beyond the helping hand of Love and Friendship. It may be said, no doubt, that the severity of this judgement acts as a protection to female virtue, – deterring, as all known punishments do deter, from vice. But this punishment, which is horrible beyond the conception of those who have not regarded it closely, is not known beforehand. Instead of the punishment there is seen a false glitter of gaudy life, – a glitter which is damnably false, – and which, alas, has been more often portrayed in glowing colours, for the injury of young girls than have those horrors which ought to deter, with the dark shadowings which belong to them.

'To write in fiction of one so fallen as the noblest of her sex, as one to be rewarded because of her weakness, as one whose life is happy, bright, and glorious, is certainly to allure to vice and misery. But it may perhaps be possible that if the matter be handled with truth to life, some girl, who would have been thoughtless, may be made thoughtful, or some parent's heart may be softened.'

These were my ideas when I conceived the story, and with that feeling I described the characters of Carry Brattle and of her family. I have not introduced her lover on the scene, nor have I presented her to the reader in the temporary enjoyment of any of those fallacious luxuries the longing for which is sometimes more seductive to evil than love itself. She is introduced as a poor abased creature who hardly knows how false were her dreams, with very little of the Magdalen about her, – because though there may be Magdalens they are not often found, –

but with an intense horror of the sufferings of her position. Such being her condition, will they who naturally are her friends protect her? The vicar, who has taken her by the hand, endeavours to excite them to Charity, – but father and brother and sister are alike hard-hearted. It had been my purpose at first that the hand of every Brattle should be against her, but my own heart was too soft to enable me to make the mother cruel, – or the unmarried sister who had been the early companion of the forlorn one.

As regards all the Brattles the story is I think, well told. The characters are true, and the scenes at the mill are in keeping with human nature. For the rest of the book I have little to say. It is not very bad, and it certainly is not very good. As I have myself forgotten what the heroine does and says, – except that she tumbles into a ditch, – I cannot expect that any one else should remember her. But I have forgotten nothing that was done or said by any of the Brattles.

The question brought in argument is one of fearful importance. As to the view to be taken first there can I think be no doubt. In regard to a sin common to the two sexes almost all the punishment and all the disgrace is heaped upon the one who in nine cases out of ten has been the least sinful. And the punishment inflicted is of such a nature that it hardly allows room for repentance. How is the woman to return to decency to whom no decent door is opened? Then comes the answer. It is to the severity of the punishment alone that we can trust to keep women from falling. Such is the argument used in favour of the existing practice, and such the excuse given for their severity by women who will relax nothing of their harshness. But in truth the severity of the punishment is not known beforehand; – it is not in the least understood by women in general except by those who suffer it. The gaudy dirt, the squalid plenty, the contumely of familiarity, the absence of all good words and all good things, the banishment from honest labour, the being compassed round with lies, the flaunting glare of fictitious revelry, the weary pavement, the horrid slavery to some horrid tyrant, – and then the quick depreciation of that one ware of beauty, the substituted paint, garments bright without but foul within like painted sepulchres,⁵ hunger, thirst, and strong drink, life without a hope, without the certainty even of a morrow's breakfast, utterly friendless, disease, starvation, and a quivering fear of that coming hell which still can hardly be worse than all that is suffered here! This is the life to which we doom our erring daughters when, because of their error, we close our door upon them! But for our erring sons we find pardon easily enough.

Of course there are houses of refuge, – from which it has been thought expedient to banish anything pleasant, as though the only repentance to which we can afford to give a place must necessarily be one of sackcloth and ashes. It is hardly thus that we can hope to recall those to decency who, if they are to be recalled at all, must be induced to obey the summons before they have reached the last stage of that misery which I have attempted to describe. To me the mistake which we too often make seems to be this, – that the girl who has gone astray is put out of sight, out of mind if possible, at any rate out of speech, as though she had never existed, and that this ferocity comes not only from hatred of the sin but in part also from a dread of the taint which the sin brings with it. Very low as is the degradation to which a girl is brought when she falls through love or vanity, or perhaps from a longing for luxurious ease, – still much lower is that to which she must descend perforce when, through the hardness of the world around her, she converts that sin into a trade. Mothers and sisters, when the misfortune comes upon them of a fallen female from among their number, should remember this, and not fear contamination so strongly as did Carry Brattle's married sister and sister-in-law.

In 1870 I brought out three books, – or rather of the latter of the three I must say that it was brought out by others for I had nothing to do with it except to write it. These were *Sir Harry Hotspur of Humblethwaite*, *An Editor's Tales* and a little volume on Julius Caesar. *Sir Harry Hotspur* was written on the same plan as *Nina Balatka*, and *Linda Tressel*, and had for its object the telling of some pathetic incident in life rather than the portraiture of a number of human beings. *Nina* and *Linda Tressel* and *The Golden Lion* had been placed in foreign countries, and this was an English story. In other respects it is of the same nature, and was not, I think, by any means a failure. There is much of pathos in the love of the girl and of paternal dignity and affection in the father.

It was published first in *Macmillan's Magazine*, – by the intelligent proprietor of which I have since been told that it did not make either his fortune or that of his magazine. I am sorry that it should have been so, – but I fear that the same thing may be said of a good many of my novels. When it had passed through the magazine, the subsequent use of it was sold to other publishers by Mr Macmillan, and then I learned that it was to be brought out by them as a novel in two volumes. Now it had been sold by me as a novel in one volume, and hence there arose a correspondence.

I found it very hard to make the purchasers understand that I had reasonable ground for objection to the process. What was it to me? How could it injure me if they stretched my pages by means of lead and margin into double the number I had intended? I have held the same argument on other occasions. When I have pointed out that in this way the public would have to suffer, seeing that they would have to pay Mudie for the use of two volumes in reading that which ought to have been given to them in one, I have been assured that the public are pleased with literary short measure, that it is the object of novel readers to get through novels as fast as they can, and that the shorter each volume is the better! Even this, however, did not overcome me, and I stood to my guns. *Sir Harry* was published in one volume, containing something over the normal 300 pages with an average of 220 words to a page, – which I had settled with my conscience to be the proper length of a novel volume. I may here mention that on one occasion and on one occasion only, a publisher got the better of me in a matter of volumes. He had a two-volume novel of mine running through a certain magazine, and had it printed complete in three volumes, before I knew where I was, – before I had seen a sheet of the letter press. I stormed for a while, but I had not the heart to make him break up the type.[6]

The *Editor's Tales* was a volume republished from the *St Paul's Magazine*, and professed to give an Editor's experience of his dealings with contributors. I do not think that there is a single incident in the book which could bring back to any one concerned the memory of a past event. And yet there is not an incident in it the outline of which was not presented to my mind by the remembrance of some fact; – how an ingenious gentleman got into conversation with me, I not knowing that he knew me to be an Editor, and pressed his little article on my notice, – how I was addressed by a lady with a becoming pseudonym and with much equally becoming audacity; how I was appealed to by the dearest of little women, whom here I have called Mary Gresley; – how in my own early days there was a struggle over an abortive periodical which was intended to be the best thing ever done; – how terrible was the tragedy of a poor drunkard, who, with infinite learning at his command, made one sad final effort to reclaim himself, and perished while he was making it; and, lastly, how a poor weak Editor was driven nearly to madness by threatened litigation from a rejected contributor. Of these stories *The Spotted Dog* with the struggles of the drunkard-scholar, is the best. I know now however, that when the things were good they came out too quick, one upon another, to gain much attention; – and so also, luckily, when they were bad.

The *Caesar* was a thing of itself. My friend, John Blackwood,[7] had set foot a series of small volumes called *Ancient Classics for English Readers*, and had placed the editing of them and the compiling of many of them in the hands of William Lucas Collins,[8] a clergyman who, from my connexion with the series, became a most intimate friend. The *Iliad* and *Odyssey* had already come out when I was in Edinburgh with John Blackwood, and, on my expressing my very strong admiration for those two little volumes, – which I here recommend to all young ladies as the most charming tales they can read, – he asked me whether I would not undertake one myself. Herodotus was in the press, – but if I could get it ready, mine should be the next. Whereupon I offered to say what might be said to the readers of English on the *Commentaries of Caesar*.

I at once went to work and in three months from that day the little book had been written. I began by reading through the *Commentaries* twice which I did without any assistance either by translation or English notes. Latin was not so familiar to me then as it has since become, – for from that date I have almost daily spent an hour with some latin author, and on many days many hours. After the reading what my author had left behind him, I fell into the reading of what others had written about him, in Latin, in English, and even in French, – for I went through much of that most futile book by the late Emperor of the

French.[9] I do not know that for a short period I ever worked harder. The amount I had to write was nothing. Three weeks would have done it easily. But I was most anxious in this soaring out of my own peculiar line not to disgrace myself. I do not think that I did disgrace myself. Perhaps I was anxious for something more. If so I was disappointed.

The book I think to be a good little book. It is readable by all, old and young, and it gives, I believe, accurately both an account of Caesar's *Commentaries*, – which of course was the primary intention, – and the chief circumstances of the great Roman's life. A well-educated girl who had read it and remembered it would, perhaps, know as much about Caesar and his writings as she need know. Beyond the consolation of thinking as I do about it I got very little gratification from the work. Nobody praised it. One very old and very learned friend to whom I sent it, thanked me for my 'comic Caesar',[10] but said no more. I do not suppose that he intended to run a dagger into me. Of any suffering from such wounds, I think, while living I never showed a sign, – but still I have suffered occasionally. There was, however, probably present to my friend's mind and to that of others a feeling that a man who had spent his life writing English novels could not be fit to write about Caesar. It was as when an amateur gets a picture hung on the walls of the Academy. What business had I there? *Ne sutor ultra crepidam*.[11] In the press it was faintly damned by most faint praise. Nevertheless, having read the book again within the last month or two, I make bold to say that it is a good book. The series, I believe, has done very well. I am sure that it ought to do well in years to come for, putting aside Caesar, – the work has been done with infinite scholarship and very generally with a light hand. With the leave of my sententious and sonorous friend, who had not endured that subjects which had been grave to him should be treated irreverently, I will say that such a work, unless it be light, cannot answer the purpose for which it is intended. It was not exactly a school book that was wanted, but something that would carry the purposes of the school room even into the leisure hours of adult pupils. Nothing was ever better suited for such a purpose than the *Iliad* and *Odyssey*, as done by Mr Collins. The *Virgil* also done by him, is very good, and so is the *Aristophanes* by the same hand.

CHAPTER 19

'Ralph the Heir' – 'The Eustace Diamonds' – 'Lady Anna' – 'Australia'.

In the spring of 1871 we, – I and my wife, – had decided that we would go to Australia to visit our shepherd son. Of course before doing so I made a contract with a publisher for a book about the Colonies. For such work as this I had always been aware that I could not fairly demand more than half the price that would be given for the same amount of fiction; – and as such books have an indomitable tendency to stretch themselves, so that more is given than what is sold, and as the cost of travelling is heavy, the writing of them is not remunerative. This tendency to stretch comes, not, I think, generally from the ambition of the writer, but from his inability to comprise the different parts in their allotted spaces. If you have to deal with a country, a colony, a city, a trade, or a political opinion, it is so much easier to deal with it in twenty than in twelve pages! I also made an engagement with the Editor of a London daily paper to supply him with a series of articles, – which were duly written, duly published, and duly paid for.[1] But, with all this, travelling with the object of writing is not a good trade. If the travelling author can pay his bills he must be a good manager on the road.

Before starting there came upon us the terrible necessity of coming to some resolution about our house at Waltham. It had been first hired and then bought, primarily because it suited my Post Office avocations. To this reason had been added other attractions, – in the shape of hunting, gardening, and suburban hospitalities. Altogether the house had been a success, and the scene of much happiness. But there arose questions as to expense. Would not a house in London be cheaper? There could be no doubt that my income would decrease and was decreasing. I had thrown the Post Office as it were away, and the writing of novels could not go on for ever. Some of my friends already told me that at fifty five I ought to give up the fabrication of love stories. The hunting, I thought, must soon go, and I would not therefore allow that to keep me in the country. And then why should I live at Waltham Cross now, seeing that I had fixed on that place in reference to the Post Office? It was therefore determined that we would flit, and as we were to be away for eighteen months we determined also to sell our furniture. So there was a packing up, with many tears, and consultations as to what should be saved out of the things we loved. As must take place on such occasions there was some heart-felt grief. But the thing was done, and orders were given for the letting or sale of the house. I may as well say here that it never was let and that it remained unoccupied for two years before it was sold. I lost by the transaction about £800. As I continually hear that other men make money by buying and selling houses I presume that I am not well adapted for transactions of that sort. I have never made money by selling anything except a manuscript. In matters of horseflesh I am so inefficient that I have generally given away horses that I have not wanted.

When we started from Liverpool in May 1871 *Ralph the Heir* was running through the *St Paul's*. This was the novel of which Charles Reade afterwards took the plot and made on it a play. I have always thought it to be one of the worse[a] novels I have written, and almost to have justified that dictum that a novelist after fifty should not write love stories. It was in part a political novel, and that part which appertains to politics and which recounts the electioneering experiences of the candidates at Percycross is well enough. Percycross and Beverley were of course one and the same place. Neefit the breeches-maker and his daughter are also good in their way, – and Moggs, the daughter's lover, who was not only lover but one of the candidates at Percycross as well. But the main thread of the story, – that which tells of the doings of the young gentlemen and young ladies, – the heroes and the heroines, – is not good. Ralph the heir has not much life about him; while Ralph who is not the heir, but is intended to be the real hero, has none. The same may be said of the young ladies, – of whom she who was meant to be the chief has passed utterly out of my mind without leaving a trace of remembrance behind.[b]

I also left in the hands of the Editor of the *Fortnightly*, ready for production on the 1st of July following, a story called *The Eustace Diamonds*. In that I think that my friend's dictum was disproved. There is not much love in it, but what there is is good. The character of Lucy Morris is pretty, and her love is as genuine and as well told as that of Lucy Robarts or Lily Dale. But *The Eustace Diamonds* achieved the success which it certainly did attain not as a love story but as the record of a cunning little woman of pseudo-fashion, to whom, in her cunning, there came a series of adventures unpleasant enough in themselves, but pleasant to the reader. As I wrote the book the idea constantly presented itself to me that Lizzie Eustace was but a second Becky Sharp, – but in planning the character I had not thought of this, and I believe that Lizzie would have been just as she is though Becky Sharp had never been described. The plot of the diamond necklace is I think well arranged, though it produced itself without any forethought. I had no idea of setting thieves after the bauble till I had got my heroine to bed in the inn at Carlisle, nor of the disappointment of the thieves till Lizzie had been wakened in the morning with the news that her door had been broken open. All these things, and many more, Wilkie Collins would have arranged before, with infinite labour, preparing things present so that they should fit in with things to come. I have gone on the very much easier plan of making everything as it comes fit in with what has gone before. At any rate, the book was a success, and did much to repair the injury which I felt had come to my reputation in the novel market by the works of the last few years. I doubt whether I had written anything so successful as *The Eustace Diamonds* since *The Small House at Allington*. I had written what was much better, – as for instance *Phineas Finn* and *Nina Balatka*; – but that is by no means the same thing.

I also left behind, in a strong box, the manuscript of *Phineas Redux*, a novel of which I have already spoken, and which I subsequently sold to the proprietors of the *Graphic* Newspaper. The Editor of that paper greatly disliked the title, assuring me that the public would take Redux for the gentleman's surname, – and was dissatisfied with me when I replied that I had no objection to them doing so. The introduction of a latin word or of a word from any other language into the title of an English novel is undoubtedly in bad taste; but, after turning the matter much over in my own mind I could find no other suitable name.

I also left behind me, in the same strong box, another novel, called *An Eye for an Eye*, which then had been some time written, and of which as it has not even yet been published, I will not further speak.[c] It will probably be published some day, though looking forward I can see no room for it at any rate for the next two years.

If therefore the 'Great Britain' in which we sailed for Melbourne had gone to the bottom I had so provided that there would be new novels ready to come out under my name for some years to come. I do not know how many posthumous books the public would receive from an author's pen, one after the other, when the author had been long buried. That one novel should be accepted, as was the case with *Kenelm Chillingly*[2] I can understand; but I fear that the number appearing month after month, and year after year, with persistent regularity, when the man who wrote them was by all forgotten, – would weary the British public. From the shade of Dickens they would have been accepted, but not, I fear, from mine.[d]

This consideration, however, did not keep me idle while I was at sea. When making long journeys I have always succeeded in getting a desk put up in my cabin and this was done ready for me in the 'Great Britain', so that I could go to work the day after we left Liverpool. This I did; and before I reached Melbourne I had finished a story called *Lady Anna*. Every word of this was written at sea during the two months required for our voyage and was done day by day, – with the intermission of one day's illness, – for eight weeks, at the rate of sixty six pages of manuscript in each week, every page of manuscript containing 250 words.[e] Every word was counted. I have seen work come back to an author from the press with terrible deficiencies as to the amount supplied. Thirty two pages have perhaps been wanted for a number, and the printers with all their art could not stretch the matter to more than twenty eight or nine! That work of filling up must be very dreadful. I have sometimes been ridiculed for the methodical details of my business. But by these contrivances I have been preserved from many troubles; and I have saved others with whom I have worked, Editors, publishers, and printers from much trouble also.

A month or two after my return home, *Lady Anna* appeared in the *Fortnightly*, following *The Eustace Diamonds*. In it a young girl, who is really a lady of high rank and great wealth though in her youth she enjoyed none of the privileges of wealth or rank, marries a tailor who had been good to her and whom she had loved when she was poor and neglected. A fine young noble lover is provided for her, and all the charms of sweet living with nice people are thrown in her way in order that she may be made to give up the tailor. And the charms are very powerful with her. But the feeling that she is bound by her troth to the man who had always been true to her overcomes everything, – and she marries the tailor. It was my wish of course to justify her in doing so, and to carry my readers along with me in my sympathy with her. But every body found fault with me for marrying her to the tailor. What would they have said if I had allowed her to jilt the tailor and marry the good-looking young lord? How much louder then would have been the censure! The book was read, and I was satisfied. If I had not told my story well there would have been no feeling in favour of the young lord. The horror which was expressed to me at the evil thing I had done in giving the girl to the tailor was the strongest testimony I could receive of the merits of the story.

I went to Australia chiefly in order that I might see my son among his sheep. I did see him among his sheep and remained with him for four or five very happy weeks. He was not making money, nor has he made money since. I grieve to say that several thousands of pounds which I had squeezed out of the pockets of perhaps too liberal publishers, have been lost on the venture. But I rejoice to say that this has been in no way due to any fault of his. I never knew a man work with more persistent honesty at his trade than he has done.

I had however the further intention of writing a book about the entire group of Australasian Colonies, and in order that I might be enabled to do that with sufficient information I visited them all. Making my head quarters at Melbourne, I went to Queensland, New South Wales, Tasmania, then to the very little known territory of Western Australia, to South Australia and then,[f] last of all, to New Zealand. I was absent in all eighteen months, and think that I did succeed in learning much of the political, social, and material condition of these countries. I wrote my book as I was travelling, and brought it back with me to England all but completed in December 1872.[g]

It was a better book than that which I had written eleven years before on the American States, but not so good as that on the West

Indies in 1859. As regards the information given there was much more to be said about Australia than the West Indies. Very much more is said, – and very much more may be learned from the latter than from the former book. I am sure that any one who will take the trouble to read the book on Australia will learn much from it. But the West Indian volume was readable. I am not sure that either of the other works are so in the proper sense of that word. When I go back to them I find that the pages drag with me; – and if so with me, how must it be with others who have none of that love which a father feels even for his ill-favoured offspring. Of all the needs a book has the chief need is that it be readable.

Feeling that these volumes on Australia were dull and long I was surprised to find that they had an extensive sale. There were, I think, 2000 copies circulated of the first expensive edition, and then the book was divided into four little volumes which were published separately and which again had a considerable circulation. That some facts were stated inaccurately I do not doubt; that many opinions were crude I am quite sure; that I failed to understand much which I attempted to explain is possible. But, with all these faults, the book was a thoroughly honest book, and was the result of unflagging labour for a period of fifteen months. I spared myself no trouble in enquiry, no trouble in seeing, and no trouble in listening. I thoroughly imbued my mind with the subject and wrote with the simple intention of giving trustworthy information on the state of the Colonies. Though there be inaccuracies, – those inaccuracies to which work quickly done must be always subject, – I think I did give much valuable information.

I came home across America, from San Francisco to New York, visiting Utah and Brigham Young[3] on the way. I did not achieve great intimacy with the great polygamist of the Salt Lake City. I called upon him, sending to him my card, apologising for doing so without an introduction, and excusing myself by saying that I did not like to pass through the territory without seeing a man of whom I had heard so much. He received me in his door way, not asking me to enter, and enquired whether I were not a miner. When I told him that I was not a miner he asked me whether I earned my bread. I told him I did. 'I guess you're a miner,' said he. I again assured him I was not. 'Then how do you earn your bread?' I told him that I did so by writing books. 'I'm sure you're a miner,' said he. Then he turned upon his heel, went back into the house, and closed the door. I was properly punished, as I had been vain enough to conceive that he would have heard my name.

I got home in December 1872, and in spite of any resolution made to the contrary, my mind was full of hunting as I came back. No real resolutions had in truth been made, for out of a stud of four horses I kept three, two of which were absolutely idle through the two summers and winters of my absence. Immediately on my arrival I bought another and settled myself down to hunting from London three days a week. At first I went back to Essex, my old country but finding that to be inconvenient, I took my horses to Leighton Buzzard and became one of that numerous herd of sportsmen who rode with the 'Baron' and Mr Selby Lowndes.[4] In those days Baron Meyer was alive, and the riding with his hounds was very good. I did not care so much for Mr Lowndes. During the winters of 1873, 1874, and 1875, I had my horses back in Essex, and went on with my hunting, always trying to resolve that I would give it up. But still I bought fresh horses, and, as I did not give it up, I hunted more than ever. Three times a week the cab has been at my door in London very punctually, and not unfrequently before seven in the morning. In order to secure this attendance, the man has always been invited to have his breakfast in the hall. I have gone to the Eastern Counties Railway,[h] – ah, so often with the fear that frost would make all my exertions useless, and so often too with that result! – and then, from one or another station, have travelled on wheels at least a dozen miles. After the day's sport the same toil has been necessary to bring me home to dinner at eight. This has been work for a young man and a rich man but I have done it as an old man and comparatively a poor man. Now at last, in April 1876, I do think that my resolution has been taken. I am giving away my old horses and any body is welcome to my saddles and horse-furniture.

> *Singula de nobis anni prædantur euntes;*
> *Eripuere jocos, venerem, convivia, ludum;*
> *Tendunt extorquere poëmata.*[5]

Our years keep taking toll as they move on;
My feast, my frolics are already gone,
And now, it seems, my verses must go too.

This is Conington's translation, but it seems to me to be a little flat.

Years, as they roll, cut all our pleasures short;
Our pleasant mirth, our loves, our wine, our sport.
And then they stretch their power and crush at last
Even the power of singing of the past.

I think that I may say with truth that I rode hard to my end.

Vixi puellis nuper idoneus,
Et militavi non sine gloriâ;
Nunc arma defunctum que bello[1]
Barbiton, hic paries habebit.[6]

I've lived about the covert side;
I've ridden straight, and ridden fast.
Now breeches, boots and scarlet pride
Are but mementoes of the past.

CHAPTER 20

'The Way We Live Now' and 'The Prime Minister' – Conclusion.

In what I have said at the end of the last chapter about my hunting I have been carried a little in advance of the date at which I had arrived. We returned from Australia in the winter[a] of 1872 and early in 1873 I took a house in Montagu Square, – in which I hope to live and hope to die. Our first work in settling here, was to place upon new shelves the books which I had collected round myself at Waltham. And this work which was in itself great entailed also the labour of a new catalogue. As all who use libraries know a catalogue is nothing unless it show the spot on which every book is to be found, – information which every volume also ought to give as to itself. Only those who have done it know how great is the labour of moving and arranging a few thousand volumes. At the present moment I own about 5000 volumes, and they are dearer to me even than the horses which are going, or than the wine in the cellar which is very apt to go and upon which I also pride myself.

When this was done and the new furniture had got into its place, and my little book room was settled sufficiently for work I began a novel to the writing of which I was instigated by what I conceived to be the commercial profligacy of the age. Whether the world does or does not become more wicked as years go on is a question which probably has disturbed the minds of thinkers since the world began to think. That men have become less cruel, less violent, less selfish, less brutal there can be no doubt; – but have they become less honest? If so can a world retrograding from day to day in honesty be considered to be in a state of progress. We know the opinion on this subject of our philosopher Mr Carlyle. If he be right, we are all going, straight away, to darkness and the dogs. But then we do not put very much faith in Mr Carlyle, – nor in Mr Ruskin[1] and his other followers. The loudness and extravagance of their Lamentations,[b] the wailing and gnashing of teeth[2] which comes from them over a world which is supposed to have gone altogether shoddy-wards, are so contrary to the convictions of men who cannot but see how comfort has been encreased, how health has been improved, and education extended, that the general effect of their teaching is the opposite of what they have intended. It is regarded simply as Carlylism to say that the English-speaking world is growing worse from day to day. And it is Carlylism to opine that the general grand result of encreased intelligence is a tendency to deterioration. Nevertheless, a certain class of dishonesty, dishonesty magnificent in its proportions and climbing into high places, has become at the same time so rampant and so splendid that there seems to be reason for fearing that men and women will be taught to feel that dishonesty, if it can become splendid, will cease to be abominable. If dishonesty can live in a gorgeous palace with pictures on all its walls, and gems in all its cupboards, with marble and ivory in all its corners, and can give Apician dinners[3] and get into Parliament and deal in millions, then dishonesty is not disgraceful, and the man dishonest after such a fashion is not a low scoundrel. Instigated, I say, by some such reflexions as these I sat down in my new house to write *The Way We Live Now*. And as I had ventured to take the whip of the satirist into my hand I went beyond the iniquities of the great speculator who robs everybody, and made an onslaught also on other vices, – on the intrigues of girls who want to get married, on the luxury of young men who prefer to remain single, and on the puffing propensities of authors who desire to cheat the public into buying their volumes.

The book has the fault which is to be attributed to almost all satires, whether in prose or verse. The accusations are exaggerated. The vices implied are coloured so as to make effect rather than to represent truth. Who when the lash of objurgation is in his hands, can so moderate his arm as never to strike harder than justice would require? The spirit which produces the satire is honest enough, but the very desire which moves the satirist to do his work energetically, makes him dishonest. In other respects *The Way We Live Now* was, as a satire, powerful and good. The character of Melmotte is well maintained. The Beargarden is amusing, – and not untrue. The Longestaffe girls and their friend Lady Monogram are amusing, – but exaggerated. Dolly Longestaffe is I think very good. And Lady Carbury's literary efforts are, I am sorry to say, such as are too frequently made. But here, again, the young lady with her two lovers is weak and vapid. I almost doubt whether it be not impossible to have two absolutely distinct parts in a novel, and to imbue them both with interest. If they be distinct the one will seem to be no more than padding to the other. And so it was in *The Way We Live Now*. The interest of the story lies among the wicked and foolish people, with Melmotte and his daughter, with Dolly, and his family, with the American woman, Mrs Hurtle, and with John Crumb and the girl of his heart. But Roger Carbury, Paul Montague, and Henrietta Carbury are uninteresting. Upon the whole I by no means look upon the book as one of my failures; – nor was it taken as a failure by the public or the press.

While I was writing *The Way We Live Now* I was called upon by the proprietors[c] of the *Graphic* for a Christmas story. I feel with regard to literature somewhat as I suppose an upholsterer and undertaker feels when he is called upon to supply a funeral. He has to supply it, however distasteful it may be. It is his business and he will starve if he neglect it. So have I felt that when anything in the shape of a novel was required I was bound to produce it. Nothing can be more distasteful to me than to have to give a relish of Christmas to what I write. I feel the humbug implied by the nature of the order. A Christmas story in the proper sense should be the ebullition of some mind anxious to instil others with the desire for Christmas religious thought, or Christmas festivities, – or, better still, with Christmas charity. Such was the case with Dickens when he wrote his two first Christmas stories. But since that the things written annually, all of which have been fixed to Christmas like children's toys to a Christmas tree, have had no real savour of Christmas about them. I had done two or three before. Alas, at this very moment I have one to write which I have promised to supply within three weeks of this time, – the picture-makers always require a long interval, – as to which I have in vain been cudgelling my brain for the last month. I can't send away the order to another shop, but I do not know how I shall ever get the coffin made.

For the *Graphic* in 1873 I wrote a little story about Australia. Christmas at the antipodes is of course midsummer, and I was not loth to describe the troubles to which my own son had been subjected by the mingled accidents of heat and bad neighbours on his station in the bush. So I wrote *Harry Heathcote of Gangoil* and was well through my labour on that occasion. I only wish I may have no worse success in that which now hangs over my head.

When *Harry Heathcote* was over I returned with a full heart to Lady Glencora and her husband. I had never yet drawn the completed picture of such a Statesman as my imagination had conceived. The personages with whose names my pages had been familiar, and perhaps even the minds of some of my readers, the Brocks, De Terriers, Monks, Greshams and Daubeneys, had been more or less portraits, not of living men, but of living political characters. The strong-minded, thick-skinned, useful ordinary member either of the Government or of the opposition, had been very easy to describe and had required no imagination to conceive. The character reproduces itself from generation to generation and, as it does so, becomes shorn in a wonderful way of those little touches of humanity which would be destructive of its purposes. Now and again there comes a burst of human nature as in the quarrel between Burke and Fox;[4] but, as a rule, the men submit themselves to be shaped and fashioned, and to be formed into tools which are used either for building up or pulling down, and can generally bear to be changed from this box into the other without, at any rate, the appearance of much personal suffering. Four and twenty gentlemen will amalgamate themselves into one whole, and work for one purpose, having, each of them, to set aside his own idiosyncrasy, and to endure the close personal contact of men who must often be personally disagreeable, having been thoroughly taught that in no other way can they serve either their country or their own ambition. These are the men who are publicly useful, and whom the necessities of the age supply, – as to whom I have never ceased to wonder that stones of such strong calibre should be so quickly worn down to the shape and smoothness of rounded pebbles.

Such have been to me the Brocks and the Mildmays about whom I have written with great pleasure, having had my mind much exercised in watching them. But I had also conceived the character of a Statesman of a different nature, – of a man who should be in something, perhaps, superior but in very much inferior to these men, of one who could not become a pebble, having too strong an identity of his own. To rid oneself of fine scruples, to fall into the traditions of a party, to feel the need of subservience not only in acting but also even in thinking, to be able to be a bit, and at first only a very little bit, – these are the necessities of the growing Statesman. The time may come, the glorious time when some great self-action shall be possible and shall be even demanded, as when Peel gave up the Corn Laws; but the rising man as he puts on his harness should not allow himself to dream of this. To become a good round smooth hard useful pebble is his duty, and to achieve this he must harden his skin and swallow his scruples. But every now and again we see the attempt made by men who cannot get their skins to be hard, – who after a little while generally fall out of the ranks. The Statesman of whom I was thinking, of whom I had long thought, was one who did not fall out of the ranks even though his skin would not become hard. He should have rank, and intellect, and parliamentary habits by which to bind him to the service of his country, – and he should also have unblemished, unextinguishable, unexhaustible love of country. That virtue I attribute to our Statesmen generally. They who are without it are, I think, mean indeed. This man should have it as the ruling principle of his life, and it should so rule him that all other things should be made to give way to it. But he should be scrupulous, and, being scrupulous, – weak. When called to the highest place in the council of his Sovereign[5] he should feel with true modesty his own insufficiency; but not the less should the greed of power grow upon him when he had once allowed himself to taste and to enjoy it. Such was the character I endeavoured to depict in describing the triumph, the troubles, and the failure of my Prime Minister. And I think that I have succeeded. What the public may think, or the press may say, I do not yet know, the work having as yet run but half its course.*

That the man's character should be understood as I understand it, – or of his wife, the delineation of which has also been a matter of much happy care to me, – I have no right to expect, seeing that the operation of describing has not been confined to one novel, which might perhaps be read through by the majority of those who commenced it. It has been carried on through three or four, – each of which will be forgotten even by the most zealous reader almost as soon as read. In *The Prime Minister* my Prime Minister will not allow his wife to take office among, or even over, those ladies who are attached by office to the Queen's Court. 'I should not choose,' he says to her, 'that my wife should have any duties unconnected with our joint family and home.' Who will remember in reading those words that in a former story, published some years before, he tells his wife, when she has twitted him

---

* Writing this note in 1878 after a lapse of nearly three years, I am obliged to say that as regards the public *The Prime Minister* was a failure. It was worse spoken of by the Press than any novel I had written. I was specially hurt by a criticism on it in the *Spectator*. The critic who wrote the notice I know to be a good critic,[6] inclined to be more than fair to me; – but in this case I could not agree with him, so much do I love the man whose character I had endeavoured to portray.

with his willingness to clean the Premier's shoes, that he would even allow her to clean them, if it were for the good of the country? And yet it is by such details as these that I have, for many years past, been manufacturing within my own mind the characters of the man and his wife.

I think that Plantagenet Palliser, Duke of Omnium, is a perfect gentleman. If he be not then am I unable to describe a gentleman. She is by no means a perfect lady; – but if she be not all over a woman, then am I not able to describe a woman. I do not think it probable that my name will remain among those who in the next century will be known as the writers of English prose fiction; – but if it does, that permanence of success will probably rest on the characters of Plantagenet Palliser, Lady Glencora, and the Revd. Mr Crawley.

I have now come to the end of that long series of books written by myself with which the public is already acquainted. Of those which I may hereafter be able to add to them of course I cannot speak; – though I have an idea that I shall even yet once more have recourse to my political hero as the mainstay of another story.[7] When *The Prime Minister* was finished I at once began another novel which is now completed in three volumes, and which is called *Popenjoy*. There are two Popenjoys in the book, one succeeding to the title held by the other, but as they are both babies and do not in the course of the story progress beyond babyhood, the future readers, should the tale ever be published, will not be much interested in them. Nevertheless the story, as a story, is not I think amiss. Since that I have written still another three-volume novel to which, very much in opposition to my publisher, I have given the name of *The American Senator*.* It is to appear in *Temple Bar*, and is to commence its appearance on the first of next month. Such being its circumstances I do not know that I can say anything else about it here.

And so I end the record of my literary performances, – which I think are more in amount than the works of any other living English

* *The American Senator* and *Popenjoy* have both appeared, each with fair success. Neither of them have encountered that reproach which, in regard to *The Prime Minister*, seemed to tell me that my work as a novelist should be brought to a close. And yet I feel assured that they are very inferior to *The Prime Minister*.

author. If any English authors not living have written more, – as may probably have been the case, – I do not know who they are. I find that, taking the books which have appeared under our names, I have published more than twice as much as Carlyle. I have also published considerably more than Voltaire, even including his letters. I do not know the writer who has been more voluminous.[d] We are told that Varro[8] at the age of eighty had written 480 volumes, and that he went on writing for eight years longer. I wish I knew what was the length of Varro's volumes. I comfort myself by reflecting that the amount of manuscript described as a book in Varro's time was not much. Varro too is dead, and Voltaire, – whereas I am still living, and may add to the pile.

The following is a list of the books I have written, with the dates of publication and the sums I have received for them. The dates given are the years in which the works were published as a whole, most of them having appeared before in some serial form.

Names of Works	Date of publication	Total sums received		
The Macdermots of Ballycloran	1847	£ 48	6	9
The Kellys and O'Kellys	1848	123	19	5
La Vendee	1850	20	0	0
The Warden	1855	727	11	3
Barchester Towers	1857			
Three Clerks	1858	250	0	0
Doctor Thorne	1858	400	0	0
The West Indies and Spanish Main	1859	250	0	0
The Bertrams	1859	400	0	0
Castle Richmond	1860	600	0	0
Framley Parsonage	1861	1,000	0	0
Tales of All Countries – 1st Series	1861	1,830	0	0
" " " " 2d "	1863			
" " " " 3d "	1870			
Orley Farm	1862	3,135	0	0
North America	1862	1,250	0	0
Rachel Ray	1863	1,645	0	0

Names of Works	Date of publication	Total sums received		
Small House at Allington	1864	3,000	0	0
Can You Forgive Her?	1864	3,525	0	0
Miss Mackenzie	1865	1,300	0	0
The Belton Estate	1866	1,757	0	0
The Claverings	1867	2,800	0	0
The Last Chronicle of Barset	1867	3,000	0	0
Nina Balatka	1867	450	0	0
Linda Tressel	1868	450	0	0
Phineas Finn	1869	3,200	0	0
He Knew He Was Right	1869	3,200	0	0
Brown, Jones, and Robinson	1870	600	0	0
Vicar of Bullhampton	1870	2,500	0	0
An Editor's Tales	1870	378	0	0
Caesar (Ancient Classics)	1870*	0	0	0
Sir Harry Hotspur of Humblethwaite	1871	750	0	0
Ralph the Heir	1871	2,500	0	0
The Golden Lion of Granpere	1872	550	0	0
Eustace Diamonds	1873	2,500	0	0
Australia and New Zealand	1873	1,300	0	0
Phineas Redux	1874	2,500	0	0
Harry Heathcote of Gangoil	1874	450	0	0
Lady Anna	1874	1,200	0	0
The Way We Live Now	1875	3,000	0	0
The Prime Minister	1876	2,500	0	0^e
The American Senator	1877	1,800	0	0
Popenjoy	1878	1,600	0	0
South Africa	1878	850	0	0
John Caldigate	1879	1,800	0	0
Sundries		7,800	0	0

£68,939 17 5

* This was given by me as a present to my friend John Blackwood.

It will not I am sure be thought, that, in making my boast as to quantity, I have endeavoured to lay claim to any literary excellence. That in the writing of books quantity without quality is a vice and a misfortune has been too manifestly settled to leave a doubt on such a matter. But I do lay claim to whatever merit should be accorded to me for persevering diligence in my profession. And I make the claim not with a view to my own glory, but for the benefit of those who may read these pages when young and may intend to follow the same career. *Nulla dies sine lineâ.*[9] Let that be their motto. And let their work be to them as is his common work to the common labourer. No gigantic efforts will then be necessary. He need tie no wet towels round his brow nor sit for thirty hours at his desk without moving, – as men have sat or said that they have sat. More than nine-tenths of my literary work has been done in the last twenty years, and during twelve of those years I followed another profession. I have never been a slave to this work, giving due time if not more than due time to the amusements I have loved. But I have been constant, – and constancy in labour will conquer all difficulties.[10] *Gutta cavat lapidem non vi, sed sæpe cadendo.*[11]

It may interest some if I state that during the last twenty years I have made by literature something near £70,000. As I have said before in these pages I look upon the result as comfortable, but not splendid.[f]

It will not, I trust, be supposed by any reader that I have intended in this so-called autobiography to give a record of my inner life. No man ever did so truly, – and no man ever will. Rousseau probably attempted it,[12] but who doubts but that Rousseau has confessed in much the thoughts and convictions rather than the facts of his life? If the rustle of a woman's petticoat has ever stirred my blood, if a cup of wine has been a joy to me, if I have thought tobacco at midnight in pleasant company to be one of the elements of an earthly Paradise, if now and again I have somewhat recklessly fluttered a £5 note over a card table, of what matter is that to any reader? I have betrayed no woman. Wine has brought me to no sorrow. It has been the companionship of smoking that I have loved rather than the habit. I have never desired to win money and I have lost none. To enjoy the excitement of pleasure, but to be free from its vices and ill effects; to have the sweet and to leave the bitter untasted, – that has been my study. The preachers tell us that this is impossible. It seems to me that hitherto I have succeeded fairly well. I will not say that I have never scorched a finger, – but I carry no ugly wounds.

For what remains to me of life I trust for my happiness still chiefly to my work, – hoping that when the power of work be over with me God may be pleased to take me from a world in which according to my view there can be no joy; – secondly to the love of those who love me, and then to my books. That I can read and be happy while I am reading is a great blessing. Could I have remembered,[g] as some men do, what I read I should have been able to call myself an educated man. But that power I have never possessed. Something is always left, – something dim and inaccurate, – but still something sufficient to preserve the taste for more. I am inclined to think that it is so with most readers.

Of late years, putting aside the latin classics, I have found my greatest pleasure in our old English dramatists, – not from any excessive love of their work which often irritates me by its want of truth to nature, even while it charms[h] me by its language, – but from curiosity in searching their plots and examining their characters.[i] If I live a few years longer I shall, I think leave in my copies of these dramatists, down to the close of the time of James I, written criticisms on every play. No one who has not looked closely into it, knows how many there are.

Now I stretch out my hand and from the further shore I bid adieu to all who have cared to read any among the many words that I have written.

THE END

TEXTUAL NOTES

Chapter One

a   In MS this chapter is in Florence Bland's hand, with one insertion in AT's hand.

b   'Court' deleted in MS, and 'Square' substituted.

c   In MS 'showy' is crossed out, and 'sorry' substituted in Florence Bland's hand.

d   This sentence is an insertion in AT's hand.

Chapter Two

a   1883: the then unknown

b   1883: many troubles

c   1883: published it

d   1883: intrusted

Chapter Three

a   1883: written by me, called

b   1883: building, – which

c   MS and 1883: great indeed;

d   1950: but it existed

e   1883: insure

f   1883: requiring culture

g   1883: being idle.

h   In MS 'allowed' is struck through and 'introduced' substituted.

i   1883: beloved Mrs Clayton Freeling

j   MS: into her that

k   1883: I had often breakfast to pay

l   MS: him

m   1883 and 1950: loft and were

n   1883 and 1950: complaints

Chapter Four

a   In MS, 'degradation' is crossed out, and 'de-gradation' substituted.

b   MS uses both the Scottish and the Irish spelling for Irish whiskey, while 1883 and 1950 use the Scottish spelling 'whisky' throughout.

c Marginal note in MS: This latter is in Lotta Schmidt

d 1883: me about it.

e 1883 and 1950: economical

f 1883 and 1950: pennyworth

g 1883: remember

h MS: drank

i 1883: twenty members

j 1883 and 1950: would

k 1883: on by Messrs.

l MS: course said

m Cancelled in MS: 'I never received any account from Mr Colburn, and do not doubt but that he lost his money by the transaction.' An underscoring which elsewhere indicates the end of a chapter is here also cancelled. The remainder of the chapter appears to represent AT's second thoughts.

n 1883: food though

o MS, throughout: La Vendee

p 1883: would bet

Chapter Five

a Cancelled from MS: – , and did give me, –

b An earlier draft in MS reads: the only one I ever saw on the book.

c 1883 and 1950: succeeded

d 1883 and 1950: by the Government

e 1883 and 1950: hands

f 1883: he belonged

g 1883 and 1950: that eagerness

h 1883 and 1950: paper

i 1883: Government at

j MS: their

k 1883: sent my

l This paragraph is an insertion on a separate sheet, numbered in MS '90.B'.

m 1883: job of special official

n 1883: a habit

o MS: week, to

p 1883: the

q 1883: there one

r Passage cancelled in MS: In the treatment of subjects the ephemeral writers of the day were apt to study – or in slang phraseology to get up, – the subject matter of which they are writing, than to take up a subject which they have studied. So it was with me.

s   1883: no work
t   In MS a second 'every' is erroneously inserted.
u   This paragraph is followed by an underscoring in MS, as though the chapter was at first intended to end here.

Chapter Six

a   1883: assuming upon myself more
b   1883 and 1950: on the road
c   MS: Literature
d   1883 and 1950: content
e   1883: governed
f   This paragraph is underscored, and the underscoring is cancelled, as though the chapter was at one time to end here.
g   MS, here and throughout: Dr Thorne
h   1883: to some other
i   Cancelled in MS: the sin of plagiarism

Chapter Seven

a   MS: Improbus [indicating a new line in Virgil]
b   MS: drank
c   MS: had
d   1883: my own experience
e   1883 and 1950: that
f   1883: my head
g   1883: and
h   MS: that
i   1883 and 1950: relieved
j   1883: a week on

Chapter Eight

a   1883: into
b   MS: his
c   1883 and 1950 substitute the more recent spelling 'draft'.
d   MS and 1883: is first
e   1883 corrects this to: It was in January.
f   1883 omits 'Russell of the "Times"'.
g   MS, here and throughout, except in one deleted passage: The Small House of Allington
h   1883 and 1950: than his
i   Here and elsewhere MS misspells 'Elliott'.

j 1883: did

k MS: acuse; after consultation between Henry Trollope and J.M. Langfield (see Note on the Text), 1883 omits the following passage and that defined in note l: – but hardly a staff . . . accuse him.

l 1883 omits: He has fallen . . . much of him.

m The following paragraph is repeatedly crossed through in MS:

I do not know whether I did not put an end to these dinners by an indiscretion of my own. It was I think at the first of them that Thackeray, sitting opposite to his host, asked whether Dr Johnson was getting his dinner behind the screen. The old story is too well known to require any further telling here. Our munificent publisher being engaged with his neighbour did not hear the question, and Thackeray, naturally anxious for his little joke, repeated it. Whereupon Mr Smith, who was still very eager with the friend at his elbow, replied across the table that he did not think there was anybody of the name of Johnson in the room. There was not much fun in it, but, what there was, consisted in Thackeray's vain attempts to have his allusion recognized. On the next morning I unfortunately told the story to a friend; – but I told it also in the presence of a man to whom nothing could be told quite safely. He was, though I did not know it then, a literary gutter-scraper, – one who picked up odds and ends of scandal from chance sources, and turning them with a spice of malice into false records, made his money of them among such newspapers as would pay him. This story, altogether be-devilled and twisted from the truth, – crammed with bitterness, both against Thackeray & Smith, loaded with poison, – was sent to an American newspaper. That alone would not have mattered much because American newspapers are not much read in this country. But The Saturday, – which everybody reads, or which at least everybody then read, – got hold by chance of this American paper, and, *more suo*,* tore everybody concerned to pieces. Why were such dinners given? Why were such stories told? Was it creditable to anybody that the conversation of a private table in London should be made gossip to satisfy the evil cravings of New York readers? This article afflicted Thackeray much. It annoyed Mr Smith greatly. I taxed the gutter-scraper** with his offence, and he owned his sin, praying to be

___

* *more suo*: 'after its fashion' (Latin).

** *the gutter-scraper* The 'literary gutter-scraper' before whom Trollope unwisely spoke was already known to him, being Edmund Yates (1831–94), a Post Office colleague and minor man of letters, who is reputed to have been the first ever newspaper 'gossip columnist'. Yates sold his story to *The New York Times* ('Echoes from London Clubs', May 1860), and the *Saturday Review*, ever eager to discredit the *Cornhill Magazine*, repeated the forgiven. I confessed my fault to the others; – for it was a fault to have told anything in the presence of such a man. I was pardoned, but there were no more Cornhill dinners.

n   This last sentence was added in MS after AT had underscored the chapter in his customary way.

Chapter Nine

a   1883: men's
b   1883: for
c   1883: Bromley Davenport
d   1883: Huguessen
e   MS: health'
f   MS: or amusement
g   1883: believe
h   1883: during
i   MS: him.
j   1883: marked, the overtures
k   Passage cancelled in MS: And now came the question of abandoning it. At this moment I have not decided whether this season should be the last, – it

_____

story, ostensibly to illustrate how shocking it was that such things should appear in the public press. The story to which Thackeray was alluding is one Boswell tells of Dr Johnson dining behind a screen because he was ashamed of his shabby coat. The brouhaha was greater than it might otherwise have been because Yates and Thackeray had already been at odds in 1858, when they had fallen out over the former's supposedly 'ungentlemanly' behaviour in attacking the latter, a fellow member of the Garrick Club, in a penny paper. Dickens had sided with Yates, and much of the literary world had split into two camps each supporting one of the great novelists, with relations probably becoming more acrimonious as Thackeray's party showed their disapproval of Dickens's conduct in leaving his wife for a young actress. The affair had ended with Yates being expelled from the Garrick, and Dickens and his supporters leaving the club in protest. Although Trollope was not at that time part of the London literary scene, his sympathies would have lain with Thackeray's party, and his attitude to Dickens in *An Autobiography* shows his disapproval of the Inimitable's standards of behaviour. It is usually supposed that 'young Grubstreet' and 'Tom Garbage' in Chapters 35 and 43 of Thackeray's *The Virginians* (1858–9) are attacks on Yates. In 1860, Thackeray's revenge on Yates was a more mildly phrased attack in the sixth of his monthly *Roundabout Papers* in the *Cornhill*, 'On Screens in Dining-Rooms', on a 'Mr Nameless', who spies on the private lives of gentlemen, and who, clearly no gentleman himself, is bid 'leave gentlemen alone'.

is now February 1876, – or whether another year should be added. But, as I
have gone along the fields alone, I have made my own epitaph [– ?]

> 'I have lived about the covert side
> I have ridden straight, and have ridden fast.
> Now breeches, boots and scarlet pride
> Are but mementoes of the past.'

Perhaps after all I shall not hang them on their pegs till another year
shall have passed. [Note: In the margin Trollope has scored through
the Latin original, which he has identified as 'Horace 3d book 26
ode –' This translation, slightly improved, is incorporated at the end of
Chapter 19.]

Chapter Ten

a 1883: may be
b Passage deleted in MS: Of Can You Forgive Her I cannot speak with too
   great affection, though I do not know that of itself it did very much to establish my reputation. [When this sentence reappears two paragraphs later,
   'establish' has been changed to 'encrease'.]
c 1883: French
d 1883 and 1950: predominant
e 1883: should it
f 1883: weaknesses
g 1883: with
h This passage is not marked in MS as a footnote.
i The chapter originally ended here, but a paragraph was added in MS.

Chapter Eleven

a 1883: written I have
b 1883: Fitz-James
c 1883: will be
d MS: al the same; 1883 and 1950: at the same time
e 1883: pretend to read
f At the request of John Blackwood 1883 omitted the passage: ; – no doubt . . .
   price [See Note on the Text.]

Chapter Twelve

a 1883: as to point
b 1883: except

c Passage cancelled in MS: As I write this there is still living among us one, venerable in age and venerable in position, whom I have ever revered as a thinker and valued as an author; whom I esteem as a man, and from whom I have myself learned very much. I was astounded when I first came across the following words from him. It is thus that Mr Carlyle has written of the novel-writers of his day. '"How knowest thou", may the distressed novel-wright exclaim, "that I here where I sit, am the foolishest of existing mortals; that this my long ear of a fictitious biography shall not find one and the other into whose still longer ears it may be the means of instilling somewhat." We answer, "No one knows; none can certainly know. Therefore write on, worthy brother, even as thou canst, even as it is given thee".'

I was at first confounded and as it were convicted of being a windbag. I and my friends, – those whom I so greatly loved and esteemed, whose works were to me the objects of such close criticism and scrutiny, – were all windbags.

d In MS this passage is the result of several cancellations and insertions. The final version is confused, and contains the words: 'sift this saying of such men'. A reconstruction of an earlier version of the passage reads: But when, by degrees, I dared to examine and sift this saying of Carlyle, in which he has so strongly confirmed [?] that metaphor of the ass's ears, I found [?...] silly and arrogant. Our dear old pious Homer nods sometimes, and had nodded here. But words such as these from such a man do not pass by one like the wind.

e The 1883 version of this sentence is printed here, and has semicolons where MS has commas.

f 1883 and 1950: and the grass

g 1883: pleasant reading

h 1883: great English novelists

i 1883 and 1950: most stirs

j 1883: for

k 1883: the

l 1883: thinks

m 1883: ought

n 1883 and 1950: There once used

o 1883 and 1950: to the purity

p 1883: continuation

q 1883: for the purposes

r 1883: writing has

s MS: been the writer

t 1883: myself for discontinuing

u 1883: creatures

v 1883 and 1950: creations

w 1883 and 1950: would

x 1883: that

y MS: one battery to battery

z 1883 and 1950: will

aa 1883 and 1950: in order that familiarity

ab 1883 and 1950: the same. He knows

ac MS: of readers

ad 1883 and 1950: does so

ae 1883: men and women

af 1883 and 1950: his readers

Chapter Thirteen

a 1883 and 1950: the

b MS, 1883 and 1950 consistently spell 'Newcombe'.

c 1883: of whom so

d 1883 and 1950: than of

e 1883 and 1950: until

f MS: Beckey Sharp; 1883 and 1950: Becky Sharpe. In all but one instance, MS spells 'Sharp', and in a majority of instances 'Beckey'.

g 1883 and 1950: speak of

h MS: have better

i 1883 and 1950: Bronte

j 1883 and 1950: those

k 1883: felt every fibre of the heart

l 'plagiary' changed in MS to 'plagiarism'

m MS: willingly embarked

n After consultation between Henry Trollope and J.M. Langford this paragraph was omitted in 1883.

o 1883 and 1950: such work

p 1883: has been

q MS: Shepherd

r 1883: flavour

s MS: Corysand

Chapter Fourteen

a 1883: can

b 1883: the work

c 1883 and 1950: periodicals are certainly entitled

d 1883: which there
e 1883 and 1950: assist struggling young authors
f 1883: author.
g 1883 and 1950 omit: He knew . . . the worse.
h 1883: none
i 1883: perpetuated
j This quotation is omitted in 1883.

Chapter Fifteen

a 1883 and 1950: words with which ['with' deleted in MS.]
b 1883: victory
c Paragraph cancelled in MS: Of the copyright of 'The Last Chronicle' I did
   not sell the whole as I had done of all my works since Barchester Towers.
   This came to pass in accordance with a proposition made by the publisher[s?], and not by myself. The half which I hold has however never
   brought me sixpence. Why this should be, seeing that Messrs. Longmans
   pay me annually some small sum for Barchester Towers I do not quite
   understand. I think it is because the publisher does not care to create a sale.
   It is the feeling of disappointment coming from such uncertainty as this
   which has induced me to part with so many of my copyrights. I cannot but
   think that the sale of 'The Last Chronicle' during the last eight years ought
   to have produced some profit.
d 'The Small House at Allington' (correctly named) cancelled in the MS. In
   the next sentence, 'hitherto' is an insertion, and may have been made at the
   same time as the footnote was added to the same page.
e 1883 and 1950: consideration
f 1883: put by an income
g 1883: which are so
h 1883: members
i 1883: promise
j 1883: system of so-called merit
k 1883: of
l 1883: an excellent
m In MS three of these names are abbreviated: Ed. Dicey, Geo. Macdonald,
   and Sir C. Trevelyan.

Chapter Sixteen

a On each occurrence, 'educated Englishman' is a substitution in the MS in
   AT's hand for 'Briton'.
b 1883: Conservative-Liberal

c 1883: feeling

d 1883 and 1950: even

e 1883 and 1950: Conservative. 1883 capitalizes 'Conservative' and 'Liberal' throughout this chapter, and 1950 follows 1883, except in the case of 'conservative Liberal'. The present editor assumes that since Trollope was careful about his capitalization in 'conservative Liberal', it is unwise to regularize all other occurrences, for fear some distinction in sense gets lost.

f 1883: 650 . . . 650th part

g 1883: defeating

h MS: for rate

i 1883: profession

j MS: Sir Edward

k 1883 and 1950: realised

Chapter Seventeen

a 1883 and 1950 print 'This was a state of things . . . spoken.' as a footnote. In MS the passage is an addition, cued into the text with an 'insert' symbol. The footnotes to the following paragraphs, in contrast, are clearly cued as footnotes in MS.

b This word is obscure in MS. 1883 and 1950: few

c This paragraph, which is a later addition, is presented in MS as a note. For ease of reading, the present edition follows 1883 and 1950 in printing it as part of the main text.

d 1883 omits 'Where is . . . hospitality?'

e 1883: occasion into

f 1883: a woman

g MS: to a

h In MS there is a short illegible word between 'others' and 'added'.

i 1883: to whom

j 1883: in *Phineas Finn* and its sequel *Phineas Redux*

k 1883 and 1950 correct MS's '1872' to '1873'.

l 1883 and 1950: the

m 1883: produced

Chapter Eighteen

a 1883: then the sole

b 1883: to Victor Hugo's

c MS: he making

d From this point in MS, the preface to *The Vicar of Bullhampton* is copied in Rose Trollope's hand.

Chapter Nineteen

a   1883 and 1950: worst

b   Cancelled in MS: I doubt whether I have produced any other character of whom I cannot call to mind the name.

c   Cancelled in MS: I have not read it since it was finished and, as it has not been impressed on my memory by its passage through the press, hardly know whether it is good or bad.

d   1883 omits three sentences: I do not know ... from mine.

e   The following passage is cancelled in MS: I may say here that for twenty years I have had every word I have written counted, so that I might not get into the habit of putting less into a page of manuscript than a page was supposed to contain.

f   1883: Western Australia, and then

g   MS: 1873

h   1883: Great Eastern Railway

i   MS: chordis

Chapter Twenty

a   MS: summer

b   1883 and 1950: lamentations

c   MS: by proprietors

d   1883 omits 'I do not know ... voluminous.'

e   Trollope's original list ends here, with the sum of £7,000 appended 'for other literary work'. *An American Senator, Is He Popenjoy?* and *An Eye for an Eye* are listed as 'not yet published'. The following five lines and the final totals are added later.

f   An underscoring, which often indicates the end of a chapter in MS, is here cancelled.

g   1883: I remember

h   1883: shames

i   1883: character

EXPLANATORY NOTES

Details of the publication of Trollope's works are given where they clarify the text. Other bibliographical information can be found in *Bibliography*, *Letters* and Tingay (see below).

List of works cited

Bibliography: Michael Sadleir, *Trollope: A Bibliography* (London: Constable, 1928)

Commentary: Michael Sadleir, *Trollope: A Commentary* (London: Constable, 1927)

Hall: N. John Hall, *Trollope: A Biography* (Oxford: Oxford University Press, 1991)

Letters: N. John Hall (ed.), *The Letters of Anthony Trollope* (Stanford, Calif: Stanford University Press, 1983)

Mullen: Richard Mullen, *Anthony Trollope: A Victorian in His World* (London: Duckworth, 1990)

Skilton: David Skilton, *Anthony Trollope and His Contemporaries: A Study in the Theory and Conventions of Mid-Victorian Fiction* (London: Longman, 1972; London: Macmillan, 1996)

Smalley: Donald Smalley (ed.), *Anthony Trollope: The Critical Heritage* (London: Routledge and Kegan Paul, 1969)

Super: R. H. Super, *The Chronicler of Barsetshire: A Life of Anthony Trollope* (Ann Arbor: University of Michigan Press, 1988)

Tingay: L. Tingay *et al.*, *Anthony Trollope: A Collector's Catalogue 1847–1990* (London: Trollope Society, 1992)

Preface

1 *This letter was dated 30th April 1876*: printed in its entirety in *Letters*, pp. 685–6.

2 *has been omitted*: Henry Trollope's omissions are printed in the Textual Notes.

3 *the 'Mastiff', one of Mr John Burns' steam-ships*: John Burns (1829–1901), later Lord Inverclyde, chairman of the Cunard Steamship Company.

4 *He had lived there for sixteen years*: in fact he was based in Ireland from 1841 to 1859, but was away from his Irish home for much of 1858–9.

5 *fully completed the whole tale*: this is not true. Both *Can You Forgive Her?* (1864–5) and *The Belton Estate* (1865–6) began to appear some months before they were completely written.

Chapter One

1 *set down naught in malice*: see *Othello* V.ii.340–41: 'Speak of me as I am; nothing extenuate,/Nor set down aught in malice'

2 *Lord Northwick*: in 1813 Thomas Anthony Trollope had leased Ilotts Farm from Lord Northwick, at £600 per annum. The house 'Julians' was built on the farmland by Trollope senior in 1818. ('Julians' was the name not only of one of the fields on the Harrow estate, but also of the Hertfordshire estate that Thomas Anthony at this time stood to inherit. See Hall, pp. 10–15.)

3 *a 't'other school' for Winchester*: school which a Wykehamist has previously attended is known as 't'other school'. It was unusual for 't'other school' to be an establishment as prestigious as Harrow, rather than a preparatory school.

4 *Orley Farm ... delineated by ... John Millais*: financial considerations prompted the Trollopes to let 'Julians', and to return to the old farmhouse. After its enlargement, the building was rechristened 'Julian Hill'. Trollope suggested to Millais that the artist use the farmhouse for the frontispiece of *Orley Farm* (1861–2). After the novel's publication, the then owner of the property, one Edward Hastings, who was using the building as a preparatory school, asked Trollope for permission to rename Julian Hill 'Orley Farm'. Trollope acceded, and Orley Farm School exists to this day (although on different premises).

5 *the curled darlings of the school*: see *Othello* I.ii.67: 'the wealthy, curled darlings of our nation'.

6 *lily-livered curs*: see *Macbeth* V.iii.15: 'thou lily-liver'd boy'.

7 *he lost the great glory of a Wykamist*: Winchester and New College being sister foundations, there were closed scholarships at New College available to Wykehamists.

8 *all Italian subjects*: Thomas Adolphus Trollope (1810–92), was nearly as prolific a writer as his youngest brother. His publications included *The Girlhood of Catherine de'Medici* (1856), *A Decade of Italian Women* (1859), *History of the Commonwealth of Florence* (1865) and *The Papal Conclaves as They Were and as They Are* (1876).

9 *the theories of Draco*: in ancient Athenian tradition, Draco was a lawgiver in the seventh century BC, who is said to have specified the death penalty for most offences, arguing that small offences deserved death, and that he knew no greater penalty for greater crimes.

10 *a Sizar at a Cambridge college*: an undergraduate receiving an allowance from his college because of his poverty, and – in former years at least – having to perform menial tasks in return.

a Bible clerk at Oxford: a student having the duty of reading the lessons in chapel, and in some cases of saying grace in hall.

11 *I am not making a false boast*: confirmation of the story of his 'great fight' with a boy named James Lewis, son of a book-binder, comes from Thomas Henry Baylis, quoted in T. H. S. Escott, *Anthony Trollope: His Work, Associates, and Literary Originals* (London, 1913), pp. 16–17.

12 *so many hearts*: Thomas Anthony Trollope's *Encyclopædia Ecclesiastica* suffered the indignity of having only its first volume published. It appeared in 1834, published by subscription only, under the imprint of John Murray.

13 *Gradus: Gradus ad Parnassum* ('A Step to Parnassus'), a dictionary of prosody, used in public schools as an aid to Latin versification.

14 *Cooper's ... The Prairie ... Hookham's library*: James Fenimore Cooper's *The Prairie* was first published in 1827; Thomas Hookham's library was one of the most fashionable circulating libraries, which lent novels at a standard charge per volume.

15 *Dr Butler ... Archbishop of Canterbury*: former headmasters of Harrow School. George Butler (1774–1853), was Dean of Peterborough from 1842 until his death; Charles Thomas Longley was Archbishop of Canterbury from 1862 to 1868. Trollope had a certain fondness for the latter: the even-tempered and warm-hearted Bishop Yeld, in *The Way We Live Now* (1875) is an affectionate portrait of Longley (Trollope's working diary for the novel reveals that the bishop was originally to have been called 'Yelgnol').

16 *I never got a prize*: perhaps in the Classics, but according to Frederick Ponsonby he did receive a prize for English composition. See Mullen, p. 56.

Chapter Two

1 *Chollerton*: Cecilia Tilley (1816–49) published her austere High Church novel, *Chollerton, A Tale of Our Own Times*, anonymously in 1846.

2 *The family of Estienne*: the Estienne printing firm was founded by the scholar-printer Henri Estienne in about 1502. The Estienne dynasty was responsible for many of the landmarks of Western literature, including the first printed editions of many works by ancient Greek and Roman authors, and an edition of the Greek New Testament (1551), in which the present division of the text into verses occurs for the first time.

3 *the persecution of Lord Byron*: the great poet, Lord Byron (1788–1824), earned the government's disapproval when his *The Vision of Judgement*, a satire on Southey's encomium on the death of George III, published in Leigh Hunt's magazine the *Liberal*, prompted a charge against the publisher for wounding George IV's feelings. After Byron's death in 1824, his body was refused burial in Westminster Abbey. However, Trollope may be referring

to a more localized persecution: after the death in 1822 of Byron's daughter Allegra, the rector of Harrow, J. W. Cunningham, refused permission for a memorial tablet to be installed in Harrow church. Trollope's mother was prompted by the incident to write 'Salmagundi', a satirical mock-epic poem about the incident, in which she pilloried Cunningham.

the then unknown Scott: the anonymous author of the 'Waverley Novels' was not revealed to be Sir Walter Scott (1771–1832) until 1827.

the triumphs of Miss Edgeworth: the Irish novelist Maria Edgeworth (1767–1849) had her greatest successes with *Castle Rackrent* (1800) and *The Absentee* (1809). Her other works include: *Letters for Literary Ladies* (1795); *Belinda* (1801); and *The Modern Griselda* (1804).

4 *Mathias, Henry Milman, and Miss Landon*: James Mathias (1754?–1835), author of the verse collection *Pursuits of Literature* (1794–7); Letitia Elizabeth Landon (1802–38), poet and novelist, whose works include *The Fate of Adelaide* (1821), *Improvisatrice* (1824), and *The Venetian Bracelet* (1829); the Revd Henry Milman, poet, and son of Sir Francis Milman (1746–1821), physician to George III. The widowed Lady Milman lived in nearby Pinner.

5 *Miss Wright*: Frances Wright (1795–1852), the young Scottish reformer and republican, whose *Views of Society and Manners in America* was published in 1821.

6 *the time of her death*: 1863.

7 *two novels, and then a work on Belgium and Western Germany*: the novels were *The Refugee in America* (1832) and *The Abbess* (1833). The travel book was *Belgium and Western Germany in 1833* (1834). In 1833 she also published anonymously *The Mother's Manual, or Illustrations of Matrimonial Economy: an Essay in Verse*.

8 *doing it with a troubled spirit killed Sir Walter Scott*: writing to pay off the debts of the publishing house of Ballantyne after its bankruptcy in 1826 is said to have hastened the novelist's death in 1832.

9 *usher*: an assistant schoolmaster.

William Drury at Brussels: Drury established the school in Brussels after he and his father Mark had fled Britain in 1826, to avoid their creditors (to whom it was alleged they owed some £40,000).

10 *Sir Francis Freeling ... ruled the Post Office*: Sir Francis Freeling (1764–1836) Secretary of the Post Office. The system of patronage endemic to the Civil Service, and satirized by Dickens through the Barnacle family in *Little Dorrit* (1855–7), was effectively abolished by the reforms recommended by the Northcote–Trevelyan report of 1853–5, and effected in 1855. Trollope's own *The Three Clerks* details and satirizes the implementation of the reforms. See also note 12 to Chapter 6.

11 *that false-tongued hope which knows the truth, but will lie lest the heart should faint*:
the uncharacteristic phrasing suggests that this is a quotation or translation, which I have been unable to trace.

12 *It was about this period of her career that her best novels were written*: Trollope is
presumably thinking of *Tremordyn Cliff* (1835), *Jonathan Jefferson Whitlaw*
(1836), *The Vicar of Wrexhill* (1837), *The Widow Barnaby* (1839), and *Michael
Armstrong, the Factory Boy* (1839).

Chapter Three

1 *one of the opening chapters of ... The Three Clerks*: the scene is described in
Chapter 2 of *The Three Clerks* (1857), 'The Internal Navigation'.

2 *the rule of three*: an arithmetic method of finding a fourth number from three
given numbers, of which the first is in the same proportion to the second as
the third is to the unknown fourth – i.e. a method of solving $p/q=r/x$,
without the use of algebra.

3 *Esmond*: Trollope would have known *Pride and Prejudice* (1813) and *Ivanhoe*
(1819) in his childhood, while Thackeray's *Esmond* was published in 1852.

4 *Antinous*: the Emperor Hadrian's favourite, famed for his beauty, who on
his death in 130 was deified by his master.

5 *Colonel Maberly*: William Leader Maberly (1798–1855), Secretary of the Post
Office from 1836 to 1854.

6 *écarté*: a game of cards for two persons, in which the cards from two to six
are excluded from play. It was fashionable in the first half of the nineteenth
century.

7 *marry the young lady*: a version of this event also appears in *The Three Clerks*,
in Chapter 27 ('Excelsior').

8 *Mecklenburgh Square*: this location figures as the address of the money-
lender M'Ruen in *The Three Clerks*. The cry of 'Do be punctual' is the de-
fining characteristic of M'Ruen, and of Trollope's other fictional money-
lenders, Magruin (*Can You Forgive Her?*) and Clarkson (*Phineas Finn*, 1867–9).

9 *Johnson ... spoke sneeringly of Lycidas*: Dr Johnson's attack on Milton, in his
Life of Milton (1779) is an infamous example of prejudice: 'In this poem
there is no nature, for there is no truth; there is no art, for there is nothing
new. Its form is that of a pastoral, easy, vulgar, and therefore disgusting ...'

10 *John Merivale ... Herman Merivale ... Charles Merivale ... one W.A. ... John
Tilley ... Peregrine Birch*: John Merivale (1815–86), barrister and Commis-
sioner in Bankruptcy; Herman Merivale (1806–74), political economist and
Under-Secretary for India; Charles Merivale (1808–93), historian and Dean
of Ely; one W.A., identified by biographers as Walter Awdry (1812–?69).
Awdry, writes Hall, 'was educated at Winchester and Oxford, became a

school usher, took holy orders late in life, never advanced beyond cur-
acies, and died in poverty' (Hall, p. 61); John Tilley (1813–98), Post Office
official who rose to become Secretary in 1864, and who married Trollope's
sister Cecilia in 1839; Peregrine Birch (1817–98), Clerk in the House of
Lords.

Chapter Four

1 *Sin aliquem ... vitam*: Virgil, *Æneid* VIII.578–9: the Loeb translation reads:
'But if, O Fortune, thou threatenest some dread mischance, now, oh now
may I break the thread of cruel life.'

2 *a dear old cousin, our family lawyer*: this was John Young, second cousin once
removed from Trollope on his father's mother's side.

3 *Banagher ... though it had heretofore conquered everything, including the Devil*:
'that beats Banagher' is a proverbial expression for disbelief when tall stories are told, such as improbable tales of heroism.

4 *the Secretary of the Irish Post Office*: Augustus Godby. The Godbys, like the
Freelings, were a family whose members held a number of positions in the
Post Office.

5 *a horse ... Charles Buxton ... one of the members for Surrey*: Charles Buxton
(1823–71), MP for East Surrey from 1865 until his death. The incident re-
ferred to here is the episode of 'Nappie's Grey Horse', which features in
Chapter 38 of *The Eustace Diamonds* (1871–3).

6 *Rose Heseltine*: Rose was born in Hull, on 13 December 1820, the daughter of
Edward Heseltine, a Rotherham bank manager. She died on 25 May 1917.

7 *And waste its sweetness on the desert air*: Thomas Gray, 'Elegy Written in a
Country Churchyard' xiv: 'Full many a flower is born to blush unseen ...
[etc.]'

8 *the potato disease, the famine, and the Encumbered Estates Bill*: the famine consequent upon the potato blight of the mid-1840s was a major determinant
of British policy in Ireland, while the Encumbered Estates Bill was passed
in order to provide relief to landowners.

9 *her father was the manager of a bank*: Heseltine had been manager of the
Rotherham branch of Sheffield and Rotherham Joint Stock Company from
1836 to 1853. In 1854 it was discovered that he had embezzled between four
and five thousand pounds, whereupon he absconded to the continent,
dying in Le Havre in 1855.

10 *Home Rule ... less bloody than Fenianism ... any one remedy*: Trollope is alluding
to key moments in Irish history since 1790 in order to explain his support
for Gladstone's Home Rule measure: the insurrection of 1798, which
prompted Pitt to draft the Act of Union (1800); Daniel O'Connell (1775–

1847), the great Irish political leader, held his 'monster meetings' in the 1840s; the nationalist William Smith O'Brien (1803–64) instigated an abortive national rebellion, which ended in a battle in the Widow McCormack's cabbage-garden at Ballingarry, Co. Tipperary; the Fenian Brotherhood, which was set up in 1858 by James Stephens (1825–1901), and committed a number of terrorist acts in Ireland, Britain and the United States. 'Mr Butt' is Isaac Butt (1813–79), barrister, Irish politician, and leader of the Home Rule party in the House of Commons from 1871. See note 15 below.

11 *nor have I ever read a word of my own writing aloud – even to her*: a glance at Dickens, and the famous picture of him reading to an admiring group in John Forster's rooms in Lincoln's Inn Fields; see note 6 to Chapter 5.

12 *one exception: Doctor Thorne*, for which his brother, Thomas Adolphus, supplied the plot. See also page 77.

13 *Mr Newby*: Thomas Cautley Newby (1798?–1882), publisher given to sharp practice, who tried to mislead the public into thinking that *The Macdermots of Ballycloran* was by the famous Mrs Trollope rather than her obscure son (and tried to cause similar confusion that year by trying to pass off *Wuthering Heights* as the work of 'Currer Bell' [Charlotte Brontë] rather than 'Ellis' [Emily]).

14 *If there was any notice taken of it by any critic of the day, I did not see it*: in fact, there were at least seven reviews of *The Macdermots*. See Smalley, pp. 546–52.

15 *In Ireland I think that no one knew that I had written a novel*: this is not true. The *Kerry Evening Post* of 28 July 1849 carried a transcript of Trollope's cross-examination by Isaac Butt during the prosecution of a local girl who worked at the Tralee post office, and who was accused of theft. Butt made much of Trollope's embryonic career as a novelist, trying to demonstrate that as a writer of fiction (which is false by definition), Trollope's veracity could not be trusted:

> Mr Butt – [reading from *The Macdermots*]: 'He told them what he had to say would be very brief, and considering he was a lawyer and a barrister, he kept his word with tolerable fidelity' (loud laughter). You pictured to yourself a model cross-examiner?
> Mr Trollope: I dreamed of someone like you in cross-examination (laughter).

(see Hall, pp. 106–8)

16 *Mr Colburn . . . Mr Bentley*: Henry Colburn (d. 1855), Fanny Trollope's main publisher; Richard Bentley (1794–1871), another of Mrs Trollope's publishers, and ex-partner of Colburn, who later published Trollope's *The*

Three Clerks when the novelist rejected with Longman's offer of half profits.

17 *Facilis descensus Averni:* a Latin proverb which occurs, for example, in Virgil's *Æneid* VI.126: 'The descent to Avernus is easy' – i.e. coming back up is not. Avernus was a lake near Puteoli, which, because of its extreme depth and noxious exhalations, was anciently believed to lead to the underworld.

18 *a little coarse*: the review in question appeared on 7 September 1848. Perhaps unsurprisingly, Trollope misremembered it slightly:

> In one of the recent number of *Punch* there is a woodcut representing a gentleman discussing a culinary question with his footmen. He contends that the leg of mutton he has provided for their dinner is substantial fare. This point is conceded by the spokesman of the flunkies, who, however, maintains his objection to the viand by declaring that it is 'corse – very corse.' Mr A. Trollope's novel of the 'Kelleys and the O'Kelleys' may be likened to the leg of mutton according to the two estimates of the master and his servants. There is a native humour and a bold reality in the delineation of the characters, which honourably distinguish it from a host of abstract insipidities, and therefore it may be pronounced 'substantial', while there is that predilection for the ruder manifestations of Irish life, taken rough as they come, that no great injustice will be done to the fare if we call it 'very corse.'

Chapter Five

1 *As far as I can remember this morsel of criticism is the only one that was ever written on the book*: in fact there were at least two reviews of *La Vendée*, one appearing in the *Examiner*, 15 June 1850, 373–4, and the second in the *Athenaeum*, 6 July 1850, 708.

2 *Sir Robert Peel . . . Indian corn*: repeal of the Corn Laws, which kept the price of corn artificially high, finally came in 1846. The Tory prime minister, Sir Robert Peel (1788–1850) was subsequently forced to resign, when Tory protectionists joined with the Whigs to defeat an Irish coercion bill. Lord John Russell (1792–1878), leader of the Whigs, was his successor. Peel's government had secretly bought stocks of cheap Indian meal in the United States, late in 1845. It was the distribution of this meal to the Irish, supervised and effected by Russell's administration, that Trollope refers to here.

3 *S.G.O. (Lord Sydney Godolphin Osborne) was at that time denouncing the Irish scheme of the Administration in the Times*: Lord Sydney Godolphin Osborne (1808–89), Dorset clergyman and philanthropist, infamous in the mid-century for taking up various social abuses in letters to *The Times*.

4 *'an arbitrary cove'*: John Forster (1812–76), biographer and miscellaneous

writer, most famous for his *Life of Charles Dickens* (1872–4). The incident with the cabman has not been traced.

5 *Bentley and Gifford*: Richard Bentley (1662–1742), the classical scholar famous for his inclusion in Pope's *Dunciad*, and William Gifford (1756–1826), editor of the *Anti-Jacobin* and the *Quarterly Review*, were noted for their severity towards modern literature.

6 *that reading of which there is an illustration with portraits in the second volume of his life*: Maclise's sketch 'At 58, Lincoln's Inn Fields, Monday the 2nd of December 1844', which appears facing page 149 of the second volume of Forster's *The Life of Charles Dickens*, shows a youthful and resplendent Dickens reading *The Chimes* to a rapt audience.

7 *in writing them*: Trollope's first letter to the *Examiner* on government action in Ireland appeared on 25 August 1849, entitled 'Irish Distress'; subsequently, the newspaper published five letter-articles by Trollope, between 30 March and 15 June, entitled 'The Real State of Ireland'.

8 *George Bartley ... stage manager of one of the great theatres*: George Bartley (1782?–1858), famed comic actor of the early to mid-nineteenth century, and stage manager of Covent Garden from 1829 to 1843. A full account of *The Noble Jilt* is to be found in Robert H. Taylor's foreword to the Arno Press edition of the play (New York: 1981).

9 *Mr John Murray ... a handbook for Ireland*: John Murray (1778–1843), publisher who founded the *Quarterly Review*, and who initiated a successful series of *Travellers' Guidebooks*.

10 *an Irish groom ... in my service for thirty five years*: this was Barney, the Irish groom whom Trollope paid £5 extra per annum for waking him up every morning to ensure his early start at his writing-desk. He left Trollope's employ shortly after these words were written.

11 *never lived in any Cathedral city ... no peculiar intimacy with any clergyman*: this is disingenuous on Trollope's part: not only had he been schooled at Winchester, but both his grandparents had been clergymen (his maternal grandfather, the Revd William Milton, died in 1824), as was his uncle Henry Trollope; moreover, his mother counted numerous clerics amongst her acquaintance.

12 *my moral consciousness must again have been very powerful*: the review Trollope refers to here appeared in *The Times*, 13 August 1857, p. 5:

The remarks ... [Trollope] has made on the influence exerted by the conductors of the newspaper press on public appointments are too insignificant to be seriously criticized; yet as this is the second clerical novel published within a very short period (the other is the

Perversion of the Rev. W. Conybeare) in which an account of newspaper management is given by persons who know absolutely nothing
about it, we beg to suggest that if any one hereafter chooses to write
on the subject he will first of all study it and have the charity to admit
that among the conductors and the writers of the public press it is
possible to find men who are not only men of talent, but also men of
honour and of conscience.

The reviewer was the great *Times* journalist and man of letters, Eneas
Sweetland Dallas (1828–79). He seems to have interpreted Trollope's por-
trayal of Tom Towers as a direct attack upon the editor of *The Times*, John
Thaddeus Delane (1817–79), a figure who inspired great loyalty in his staff.
For perceived and actual resemblances between the *Jupiter* and *The Times*,
see '*The Warden*, E. S. Dallas, John Delane and *The Times*', in *The Warden*,
ed. Osborne and Skilton (Everyman Paperback, London: J. M. Dent &
Sons Ltd, 1994), pp. 214–18.

Chapter Six

1 *Charles Merivale's History of the Romans under the Empire*: the first two volumes of Merivale's work appeared in 1850; it was finally completed in 1864.
According to Trollope, it was this work that inspired his own *Life of Cicero*
(1880): '[M]y work . . . was first suggested to me as I was reviewing the earlier volumes of Dean Merivale's *History of the Romans under the Empire*. In an
article on the Dean's work . . . I inserted an apology for the character of
Cicero which was found to be too long as an episode, and was discarded by
me, not without regret. From that time the subject has grown in my estimation till it has reached its present dimension' (*Life of Cicero*, Chapter 1).

2 *a little book*: this was *The Commentaries of Caesar*, published by Blackwood in
1870, in the series *Ancient Classics for English Readers*.

3 *Bismarck*: Otto von Bismarck (1815–98), first chancellor of the German
empire. The Franco-Prussian War of 1870–71 had awoken British fears
about Bismarck's possible policy of German expansionism, as victory in
that conflict had led to the establishment of the German empire.

4 *crossed the Rubicon*: Caesar's leading of his troops across the Rubicon, the
boundary between his province of Cisalpine Gaul and Italy proper, was
the first aggressive act in the civil war that ravaged the Roman world from
49 to 45 BC. That it was an act open to varying interpretations, as Trollope
states here, is due to the fact that it helped clarify the vexed question of
whether it was better for Rome to be misgoverned by the incompetent
Roman senate, or effectively governed by an autocracy.

5 *appeared in the Dublin University Magazine*: Trollope's review of the first two

volumes of Merivale's *History* appeared in May 1851; his review of volumes three and four appeared in July 1856.

6 *for that and some other article*: Trollope's article 'The Civil Service' appeared in the *Dublin University Magazine* for October 1855.

7 *Carlyle has since told me that a man when travelling should not read, but 'sit still and label his thoughts'*: this highly characteristic comment of Carlyle's has not been traced. Thomas Carlyle (1795–1881), of course, was the hugely influential Scottish historian, scholar and essayist, whose works include: *Life of Schiller* (1823–5); *Sartor Resartus* (1833–34); *History of the French Revolution* (1837); *On Heroes, Hero Worship and the Heroic in History* (1841); *Past and Present* (1843); *Latter-Day Pamphlets* (1850); and his six-volume *History of Frederick the Great* (1858–65). Trollope seems to have been at best ambivalent about Carlyle; nearly all references to him in *An Autobiography* are negative: in his fiction, Trollope lampoons Carlyle at least twice: *Past and Present* is parodied in Chapter 15 of *Doctor Thorne* (1858), and Trollope famously caricatured Carlyle as 'Dr Pessimist Anticant' in Chapter 15 of *The Warden* (1855). See also 'An Essay on Carlylism' in the second number (December 1867) of Trollope's *St Paul's Magazine*.

8 *Mr W Longman*: William Longman (1813–77) had become a partner in the family firm (established 1724) in 1839.

a most laborious and voluminous criticism: Longman's archives were destroyed by enemy action during the Second World War, but fortunately part of the reader's report in question is transcribed in *Commentary*, pp. 169–70:

> It is very difficult for me to convey to you a distinct impression of my opinion of this work, since my own impressions of it are themselves very indistinct. And no wonder; for the execution is so unequal, that while there are parts of it that I would be disposed to place on a level with the best morsels by contemporary novelists, there are others – and unfortunately these preponderate – the vulgarity and exaggeration of which, if they do not unfit them for publication, are at least likely to be repulsive to the reader.
>
> Viewed as a whole the work is inferior to *The Warden*, to which it is a sequel. You have the old characters again in action, with the addition of a weak bishop and his managing wife, Mr. Slope, the bishop's chaplain (a low-minded Low Churchman), an Oxford don, some real grandees and their dependents [sic], besides the dean and chapter and all the other odds and ends of a Cathedral town, in which High and Low Church are struggling for mastery.

Plot there is none, the main part of the story turning upon the [?giving] up of the office of Warden and the intrigues arising out of it. These give full scope for a display of the author's best powers and his subtle analysis of the motives that actuate his dramatis personæ, while the style is easy and natural and correct (not so the orthography). The grand defect of the work, I think, as a work of art is the low-mindedness and vulgarity of the chief actors. There is hardly a 'lady' or 'gentleman' among them. Such a bishop and his wife as Dr. and Mrs. Proudie have certainly not appeared in our time, and prebendary doctor Stanhope's lovely daughter, who is separated from her husband – an Italian brute who has crippled her for life – is a most repulsive, exaggerated and unnatural character. A good deal of the progress of the tale depends upon this lady, whose beauteous countenance makes sad havoc of the virtuous feelings of the clergymen and others who come in contact with her. The character is a great blot on the work.

But in noticing these defects I am far from saying that it is uninteresting. On the contrary, there is a fatal facility in the execution that makes you fancy that the author is playing with his reader, showing how easy it is for him to write a novel in three volumes, very much in the same way as [?Aytoun] proved how easy it was to [?rival] the 'spasmodic' poets.* It would be quite possible to compress the three volumes into one without much detriment to the whole. If you will read Vol. 2, chapters 1, 2 and 3, you will discover specimens of the author's merits, and if you wish to have a notion of what I consider his defects you will find a specimen in Vol. 1, page 177 seq. – 'Mrs. Proudie Reception' – and Vol. 2, page 173 seq. – 'A Love Scene.'

* William Edmonstoune Aytoun (1813–65), Scottish poet and humorist, composed *Firmilian, a Spasmodic Tragedy* (1854) under the pen- name T. Percy Jones, as a satire on such so-called 'Spasmodic' poets as Sydney Dobell, Philip James Bailey and Alexander Smith.

Trollope vehemently rejects the notion of compressing his fiction into two volumes, but makes a good number of changes at the suggestion of Longman's reader, and when the work is already set up he is approving further modifications for the sake of 'decency': 'At page 93 by all means put out "foul breathing" and page 97 alter "fat stomach" to "deep chest."' – *Letters*, p. 54.

9 *last infirmity of noble minds*: See Milton, 'Lycidas', 70–72:

Fame is the spur that the clear spirit doth raise
(That last infirmity of noble mind)
To scorn delights, and live laborious days ...

10 *the august columns of Paternoster Row*: Longman's London office, near St Paul's Cathedral.

11 *the great apostle*: the reforms proposed by Sir Charles Trevelyan (1807–86) consisted of: i) the establishment of the Civil Service Commission, to regulate appointments to official posts; ii) the division of labour into intellectual and routine work, with different recruitment procedures for each stream; iii) the appointment of senior posts to be made on the basis of general intellectual attainment, rather than on specialized knowledge. The Civil Service Commission was established in 1855, and all the proposed reforms gradually introduced.

12 *now Chancellor of the Exchequer*: after his work on Civil Service reform with Trevelyan, Sir Stafford Northcote (1818–87) entered Parliament in 1855, becoming President of the Board of Trade in 1866, Secretary of State for India in 1867, and Chancellor of the Exchequer in 1874.

13 *Coire*: Chur, in Switzerland.

14 *diligence*: a public stage-coach on the continent.

15 *Medical Venus ... the Uffizzi, but I fear he was disappointed*: the Galleria degli Uffizi in Florence houses the Medici collection.

16 *Milan ... the Austrian authorities*: the visit took place in August to September 1856, when Lombardy was occupied by Austrian forces.

17 *twenty zwanzigers*: the Zwanziger was an Austrian coin, in circulation in Austrian-occupied Lombardy and Veneto at the time.

18 *The Three Clerks*: written from spring to 18 August 1857, and published by Bentley, in three volumes in November 1857 (although the date on the first edition reads 1858).

19 *Doctor Thorne*: written from 20 October 1857 to 1 April 1858, and published by Chapman & Hall, in three volumes, in 1858.

20 *Charles Merewether, the present Member for Northampton*: Charles George Merewether (1823–84), barrister and MP for Northampton from 1874 to 1880.

21 *the Pasha*: Ismail Pasha (1830–95), Ottoman khedive of Egypt from 1879.

22 *Mr Edward Chapman*: Edward Chapman (1804–80), co-founder in 1830 of Chapman & Hall, and publisher of many of Trollope's novels, starting with *Doctor Thorne*. Trollope's main contact at the firm, however, was Frederick Chapman (1823–95), who became a partner in 1847, and head of the firm, upon his cousin Edward's retirement, in 1864.

Chapter Seven

1 *Labor omnia vincit improbus*: 'unremitting toil overcomes all difficulties' –
a conventional misquotation in the present tense of Virgil, *Georgics*
I.145–6: 'Labor omnia vicit/Improbus', which carries the sense 'has
overcome'.

2 *I have always prepared a diary*: Trollope seems to have begun this practice
during the writing of *Barchester Towers* in 1856. The diaries for most of Trollope's novels are now housed in the Bodleian.

3 *the water-drop that hollows the stone*: see note 11 to Chapter 20.

4 *the shoemaker*: Trollope's comparison of the craft of writing a novel with the
making of shoes is famous, and may originally have been a response to an
attack from the *Saturday Review* in 1860:

> Mr. Trollope has reached the stage in which he may justly claim the
> character of an excellent literary workman (though the style of his
> workmanship is certainly open to some criticism) but that he has also
> arrived at the point when he makes a novel just as he might make a
> pair of shoes, with a certain workmanlike satisfaction in turning out a
> good article, but with little of the freshness and zest which marked
> his earlier productions. (Review of *Castle Richmond, Saturday Review*
> 9 [19 May 1860], 643–4.)

Robert Lowell gives a brief account of Trollope's use of the analogy in a
letter of 20 September 1861 to an unidentified correspondent: 'I dined the
other day with Anthony Trollope ... He says he goes to work on a novel
"just like a shoemaker on a shoe, only taking care to make honest stitches".'
(Reprinted in R. C. Terry, ed., *Trollope: Interviews and Recollections*, London:
Macmillan, 1987, p. 77)

See also Lytton's slightly different use of the comparison of the novelist
and the shoemaker: 'The first essential to success in the art you practise is
respect for the art itself. Who could ever become a good shoemaker if he
did not have a profound respect for the art of making shoes? There is an
ideal even in the humblest mechanical craft. A shoemaker destined to excel
his rivals will always have before his eye the vision of a perfect shoe, which
he is always striving to realise, and never can' (Edward Bulwer Lytton, 'On
Certain Principles of Art in Works of Imagination', '*Caxtoniana: a Series of
Essays on Life, Literature, and Manners.* – Part XVI', *Blackwood's Magazine*, 93
[May 1863], 554–5).

5 *Mens sana in corpore sano*: 'a sound mind in a healthy body' (Latin).

6 *Nubar Bey*: Trollope's presumption that 'Nubar Pasha' is the person with
whom he negotiated the 1858 postal treaty between Britain and Egypt is

correct: Nubar Pasha Nubarian (1825–99), Egyptian statesman of Armenian descent, became prime minister of Egypt in 1878, and from 1884 to 1888. He successfully resolved the dispute that was slowing construction of the Suez Canal in the mid-1860s.

7 *Amelia ... Burley ... Meg Merrilies*: characters in Fielding's *Amelia* (1751), and Scott's *Old Mortality* (1816) and *Guy Mannering* (1815).

8 *Augean stables*: one of the labours of Hercules was to cleanse the Augean stables, in which 3,000 oxen were stalled, and which had not been cleaned for thirty years. He accomplished the task by diverting the rivers Alpheus and Peneus through the stables.

9 *currente calamo*: 'with running pen' (Latin).

10 *the Times newspaper ... three articles ... he had written them*: the critic in question was E. S. Dallas. See Skilton, p. 162. Two reviews of *The West Indies* appeared in *The Times*: 6 January 1860, p. 4, and 18 January 1860, p. 12. We know from a letter of Dallas's to John Blackwood, dated 5 September 1855, that he had already been rebuked by Mowbray Morris, manager of *The Times*, for revealing his authorship of anonymous reviews in that paper: 'I cannot tell you how sorry I am that I did not sufficiently see the importance of entire secrecy in writing for so powerful an organ as *The Times*.' See also note 12 to Chapter 5 and note 2 to Chapter 14.

Chapter Eight

1 *Mr Rowland Hill ... Penny Post*: Rowland Hill (1795–1879), Secretary of the Post Office from 1854 to 1864. Best remembered for the introduction of the Penny Post in 1840, following widespread acceptance of arguments first put forward in his *Post Office Reform* (1837).

2 *a lecture on the Civil Service*: delivered at St Martin's-le-Grand on 4 January 1861, and published as 'The Civil Service as a Profession' in the *Cornhill Magazine* 3 (February 1861), 214–28.

3 *the Postmaster General*: E. J. Stanley (1802–69), 1st Lord Stanley of Alderley, Postmaster General 1860–66.

4 *my Penates*: household gods; the guardian spirits of the family larder.

5 *the Cornhill Magazine ... under the editorship of Thackeray*: according to Thackeray, 'I am only a sham editor. Mr Smith, the publisher [George Smith (1824–1901), head of Smith, Elder & Co.], does most of the work and likes it. He has no confidence in my judgment, and a great deal in his.' See Hall, pp. 190–94.

6 *a principle with me ... that no part of a novel should be published till the entire story was completed*: since *Framley Parsonage* was Trollope's first serial fiction, such scruples had previously been irrelevant.

7 *Dickens, Thackeray, and Mrs Gaskell died with unfinished novels of which portions had been already published*: *Edwin Drood* (1870), *Denis Duval* (1864) and *Wives and Daughters* (1864–6) respectively.

8 *Servetur ad imum/Qualis ab incepto processerit*: 'Let it be to the end/as it has from the first appeared' – Horace, *Ars Poetica*, 126–7.

9 *Your Achilles . . . impatient, fiery, ruthless, keen*: see Horace, *Ars Poetica*, 120–22:

> scriptor honoratum si forte reponis Achillem,
> impiger, iracundus, inexorabilis, acer,
> iura neget sibi nata, nihil non arroget armis.

The Loeb translation reads: 'If haply, when you write, you bring back to the stage the honouring of Achilles, let him be impatient, passionate, ruthless, fierce; let him claim that laws are not for him, let him ever make appeal to the sword.'

10 *Davus*: a roguish slave in Terence's *Andria*, used as an example in Horace's *Ars Poetica*, I.ii.23: 'Davus sum, non Oedipus' – 'I am only Davus, not Oedipus [the solver of riddles].'

11 *I have never broken it since*: Trollope seems to have forgotten that both *Can You Forgive Her?* and *The Belton Estate* began to appear some months before they were completely written.

12 *Nathaniel Hawthorne . . . success anywhere*: Nathaniel Hawthorne (1804–64), American novelist whose works include *The Scarlet Letter* (1850), *The Blithedale Romance* (1852) and *The Marble Faun* (1860). The letter of 11 February 1860 in which this piece of criticism appears was addressed to James T. Fields (1817–81), of the Boston publishers Ticknor and Fields, and editor of the *Atlantic Monthly*. Fields first published an extract from the letter in 'Our Whispering Gallery', *Atlantic Monthly*, February 1871, p. 257, and subsequently in *Yesterdays with Authors* (1872), p. 63.

13 *Flora Macdonald*: Scottish Jacobite heroine (1722–90), who aided the escape of Bonnie Prince Charlie after the Battle of Culloden, 1746. Trollope is perhaps confusing her with Flora MacIvor, the more passionate of the two heroines of Scott's *Waverley*.

14 *Pall Mall Gazette*: as a tribute to Thackeray, the *PMG* was named after the fictional periodical in *Pendennis* (1848–50).

15 *Thackeray, Charles Taylor (Sir) . . . Robert Bell, G. H. Lewes . . . and John Everett Millais*: William Makepeace Thackeray (1811–63), one of the giants of the Victorian literary scene, greatly admired by Trollope (as the repeated appreciations in *An Autobiography* make clear); Sir Charles Taylor (1817–76), noted sportsman and bon vivant; Robert Bell (1800–67), journalist and man of letters, author of a two-volume *Lives of the English Poets*, which appeared

in *Lardner's Cabinet Cyclopedia* from 1830; George Henry Lewes (1817–78), noted journalist and intellectual, partner of Marion Evans (Geroge Eliot), and first editor of the *Fortnightly Review* (1865), which he helped to found, whose works include novels, theatre criticism, biography, popular science and philosophy; John Everett Millais (1829–96), artist and one of the founder members of the Pre-Raphaelite Brotherhood. After illustrating a number of Trollope's books, he became firm friends with the novelist.

16 *Monckton Milnes' 'unspoken dialogue'*: Richard Monckton Milnes (1809–85), later Lord Houghton, poet whose works include: *Memorials of a Tour in Some Parts of Greece* (1834); *Poems of Many Years* (1838); and *Palm Leaves* (1844). He was largely responsible for the rehabilitation of Keats's critical reputation, publishing his *Life, Letters and Literary Remains of John Keats* in 1848. 'Unspoken Dialogue', published in the *Cornhill Magazine* in 1860, is dated 1850.

17 *Canning*: George Canning (1770–1827), English statesman, prominent in the second ministry of Lord Liverpool, and prime minister in 1827.

18 *the Literary Fund Committees*: the Royal Literary Fund was established in 1790 to relieve indigent authors and their families. Trollope was heavily involved for over twenty years, becoming one of its three Treasurers in 1869 until his death.

19 *to hear the chimes go at midnight . . . to have ginger hot in his mouth*: Trollope is drawing a parallel between Bell and some of Shakespeare's most celebrated carousers, Sir John Falstaff and Justice Shallow in *2 Henry IV* (III.ii.229) and Sir Toby Belch and Sir Andrew Aguecheek in *Twelfth Night* (II.iii.117).

20 *'Billy Russell' . . . Charles Lever*: Sir William Howard Russell (1820–1907), journalist on *The Times* and *Daily Telegraph*; Charles Lever (1806–72), novelist and diplomat, whose works include: *Harry Lorrequer* (1839); *Charles O'Malley* (1841); *Arthur O'Leary* (1844); *Roland Cashel* (1850); and *The Daltons* (1852).

21 *He has fallen away latterly among Princes*: see Psalm 82.6–7, in the Book of Common Prayer; 'I have said, ye are gods: and ye are all children of the most Highest./But ye shall die like men: and fall like one of the princes.'

22 *Albert Smith . . . Higgins . . . George Augustus Sala . . . Fitzjames Stephen*: Albert Richard Smith (1816–60), author; Matthew James Higgins (1810–68), leading journalist of the period, writing as 'Jacob Omnium'; George Augustus Sala (1828–96), journalist and man of letters, editor of *Temple Bar*; Sir James Fitzjames Stephen (1829–94), judge and legal authority, and regular contributor to the *Cornhill* and *Pall Mall Gazette*.

Chapter Nine

1 *I much doubt whether anything so hard was said of it then as that which I have said here*: in fact reviews appeared in the *Athenaeum*, the *British Quarterly Review*,

the *Saturday Review* and the *Spectator*. The reception was mixed: the *Saturday*, for example, was as 'hard' as Trollope himself, objecting to the book's 'monstrosities' which 'cannot be justified by any principle of artistic propriety'. See Skilton, pp. 22–3 and 153–60.

2 *the young tyrant of my household*: Florence Nightingale Bland (b. 1855), Rose Trollope's niece, came to live with the Trollopes in 1863, when she was orphaned by the death of her father Joseph, widowed husband of Rose's sister Isabella. She later acted as Trollope's amanuensis.

3 *my custom always in the afternoon*: compare ''tis a custom with him /I'th'afternoon to sleep.' *The Tempest* III.ii.85–6.

4 *'swear off', as Rip Van Winkle says*: see Washington Irving's famous story, in *The Sketchbook of Geoffrey Crayon, Gent.* (1819–20).

5 *Lord Stanhope*: Philip Henry Stanhope (1805–75), 5th Earl Stanhope, historian and President of the Royal Literary Fund from 1863.

6 *Jacob Omnium, Monckton Milnes, Tom Hughes, William Stirling, Henry Reeve, Arthur Russell, Tom Taylor*: for Jacob Omnium, see note 22 to Chapter 8; for Monckton Milnes, see note 16 to Chapter 8; Thomas Hughes (1822–96), English reformer and novelist, best known for *Tom Brown's Schooldays* (1856); Sir William Stirling-Maxwell (1818–78), historical writer; Henry Reeve (1813–95), journalist, editor of the *Edinburgh Review* from 1855 to 1895, and long-serving member on the Committee of the Royal Literary Fund; Arthur Russell (1825–92), nephew and one-time secretary (1849–54) of Lord John Russell; Tom Taylor (1817–80), editor of *Punch* (1874–80), and popular dramatist. His works include: *Still Waters Run Deep* (1855); *The Ticket-of-Leave Man* (1863); and *Lady Clancarty* (1874).

7 *Lord Ripon, Lord Stanley, William Forster, Lord Enfield, Lord Kimberley, George Bentinck, Vernon Harcourt, Davenport Bromley, Knatchbull Hugessen*: G. F. B. Robinson (1827–1909), 2nd Earl of Ripon and later 1st Marquis of Ripon; William Edward Forster (1818–86) politician, Liberal MP for Bradford (1861–86), and contributor to the *Pall Mall Gazette*: George Henry Charles Byng (1836–98), Viscount Enfield, later 3rd Earl of Strafford, MP for Middlesex (1857–74); John Wodehouse, 1st Earl of Kimberly (1826–1902), statesman; Lord George Bentinck (1802–48), Tory politician and noted devotee of racing and field-sports, son of the 4th Duke of Portland; Sir William George Granville Venables Vernon Harcourt (1827–1904), statesman, Whewell Professor of International Law at Cambridge, MP for Oxford (1868–80), Home Secretary (1880–84); William Bromley Davenport (1821–1884), politician, MP for North Warwickshire (1864–84); Sir Edward Hugessen Knatchbull-Hugessen (1829–93), MP for Sandwich 1857–80, created Baron Brabourne 1880.

8 *sub silentio*: 'in silence' (Latin). *The Struggles of Brown, Jones, and Robinson: by One of the Firm* appeared as a serial in the *Cornhill Magazine* from August 1861 to March 1862 inclusive. The first authorized book edition was published by Smith, Elder in 1870, but Harpers of New York produced a pirated edition in 1862.

9 *I do not know that it was ever criticised or ever read*: in fact reviews appeared in the *British Quarterly Review* and the *Westminster Review*, while the *Saturday Review* attacked it in its notice of *Miss Mackenzie*. See Skilton, pp. 90, 156 and 163.

10 *Messrs Slidell and Mason . . . Commodore Wilkes . . . Mr Seward . . . Mr Sumner . . . throughout the war*: Captain Charles Wilkes (1798–1877), of the USS *San Jacinto*, stopped the British ship, the *Trent*, on 8 November 1861, to detain James Mason and John Slidell, representatives of the Confederate South who were *en route* for Europe. War between Britain and the North seemed a possibility, with Union politicians like William Henry Seward (1801–72) and Charles Sumner (1811–74) divided over the question of the handing over of the men to Britain.

Chapter Ten

1 *not single spies, but in battalions*: Hamlet IV.v.78–9.

2 *to do her duty in the position to which she was called*: the Catechism contains the promise 'to do my duty in that state of life, unto which it shall please God to call me'.

3 *a letter from a distinguished dignitary of our Church*: the 'distinguished dignitary' has not been traced, but *Letters* (p. 316) prints Trollope's reply:

> I must . . . beg you to believe that I do not write without thinking very much of what may be the effects of what I write, – and that I do my work with a most anxious wish & with much effort that what I produce may at least not do harm. Were I to believe that any young persons could be led into evil ways by what I have published I should be very unhappy.
>
> The subject of adultery is one very difficult of discussion. You have probably found it so in preaching. It is a sin . . . [of] which it is difficult to speak because of the incidents to adultery which are not only sinful, but immodest & in some degrees indecent . . .
>
> But the bible does not scruple to speak to us of adultery as openly as of other sins. You do not leave out the seventh Commandment. The young girl for whom I or you are so tender is not ignorant of the

sin; – and, as I think, it would not be well that she should be ignorant of it.

The education of our daughters is a subject on which at present many of us Englishmen differ greatly. Thinking as I do that ignorance is not innocence I do not avoid, as you would wish me to do, the mention of things which are to me more shocking in their facts than in their names. I do not think that any girl can be injured by reading the character whose thoughts I have endeavoured to describe in the novel to which you have alluded.

4 *There is some dancing ... one man's food is another man's poison*: Trollope is being disingenuous, another ground for Macleod's objection being the satire on Mr Prong, the Evangelical clergyman, whose name Macleod puns on in his letter to the author: 'You hit right & left – give a wipe here, a sneer there, & thrust a nasty *prong* into another place ... and glory over balls till 4 in the morning' (see *Letters*, pp. 222–4).

5 *the well-known French publication*: Revue des Deux Mondes.

6 *a paper advocating the signature of the authors to periodical writing*: 'On Anonymous Literature', *Fortnightly Review* 1 (1 July 1865), 491–8.

7 *Mr Freeman ... quoting from Cicero*: E. A. Freeman's 'The Morality of Field Sports' appeared in the *Fortnightly Review* on 1 October 1869, 353–85; Trollope's reply, 'Mr Freeman on the Morality of Hunting', was published on 1 December 1869, 616–25. Freeman quoted Cicero on the subject of the public slaughter of animals on the stage for amusement. See Hall, p. 346.

8 *various articles for it since ... Cicero*: Trollope published three further articles in the *Fortnightly*: 'The Kaffir Land', February 1878, 191–206; 'Iceland', August 1878, 175–90; and 'George Henry Lewes', January 1879, 15–24.

Chapter Eleven

1 *a further novel of mine in a separate form*: The Last Chronicle of Barset came out in thirty-two weekly parts from 1 December 1866 to 8 July 1867, and in two volumes in March and July 1867. See also note 3 to Chapter 15.

2 *a fictitious periodical, which was the offspring of Thackeray's brain*: see note 14 to Chapter 8.

3 *Hannay ... Lord Houghton, Lord Strangford ... Greenwood the present Editor, Greg*: James Hannay (1827–73), journalist; for Lord Houghton see note 16 to Chapter 8; Percy Ellen Frederick William Smythe, 8th Viscount Strangford (1826–69), linguist and travel writer; Richard Greenwood (1830–1909), journalist and editor of the *Pall Mall Gazette* from 1865 to 1880, and nominally editor of the *Cornhill Magazine* in the mid-1860s; according to Hall, 'Greenwood was angered by Trollope's failure to credit him in this

passage as the originator of the *Pall Mall Gazette* and furious that he should
have written of George Smith as "chief editor" in the paper's early days' (p.
280n); W. R. Greg (1809–81), a leading essayist of the period.

4 *the revelations of a visitor to one of the casual wards in London*: the 'casual ward'
of a workhouse offered overnight shelter to the homeless. James Greenwood's 'A Night in a Casual Ward' appeared in the *Pall Mall Gazette*, 12, 13
and 15 January 1866.

5 *much on the subject of the American War*: these and Trollope's other contributions to periodicals are listed in Tingay.

6 *a great Dean of that period*: Henry Alford, Dean of Canterbury. His article,
'Mr Anthony Trollope and the English Clergy', appeared in the *Contemporary Review* 2 (June 1866), 240–62.

the Metropolitan Moon: The offensive passage from *Clergyman of the Church of
England* appears in the essay 'The Normal Dean of the Present Day': 'The
dean ... who is never called upon to discharge expensive duties in London,
though he may revisit the glimpses of the metropolitan moon for a month,
perhaps, in the early summer, showing his new rosette at his club, – seems
indeed to have had his lines given to him in very pleasant places' (reprinted in Osborne and Skilton, eds., *Barchester Towers*, Everyman Paperback, London: J. M. Dent & Sons Ltd, 1994, pp. 501–71).

7 *a gentleman ... conduct in the public service*: the gentleman in question was Ri-
chard Bethell (1800–73), first Baron Westbury, and Lord Chancellor 1861–5.
The scandal concerned the nepotistic appointment of his son and a rela-
tive of his wife (Ellinor Mary, *née* Abraham, d. 1863) to vacancies arising
from the resignation of Leonard Edmunds, Clerk to the Commissioner of
Patents. Trollope's three articles on the subject, 'What is a Job?', 'Lord
Westbury and Mr. Edmunds' and 'The Lord Chancellor', appeared in the
Pall Mall Gazette on 28 March, 8 May and 28 June 1865 respectively.

8 *Exeter Hall*: the building in the Strand where missionary societies held their
meetings.

9 *A Zulu in search of a religion*: *Pall Mall Gazette*, 10 May 1865.

10 *Mr Hutton of the Spectator ... generally the most eulogistic*: Richard Holt Hutton
(1826–97), critic, Unitarian theologian, Professor of Mathematics at Bedford
College, London, and Literary Editor of the *Spectator*. In an unsigned notice
of *Nina Balatka* in the *Spectator* (23 March 1867, xl, 329–30) the reviewer, who
is probably Hutton, writes:

> ... the present writer has applied what the scientific men call the best
> test of scientific knowledge, – the power of *prediction* given by the hy-
> pothesis that *Nina Balatka* is written by Mr Trollope. The critic said

to himself, 'if it is written by Mr Trollope, I shall soon meet with the phrase, "made his way," as applied to walking where there is no physical difficulty or embarrassment, but only a certain moral hesitation as to the end and aim of the walking in question,' and behold within a page of the point at which the silent remark was made, came the very phrase in the peculiar sense indicated. And of such test-phrases we could indicate a dozen or so which, as far as we know, are found in Mr Anthony Trollope's stories, and in those alone (Smalley, p. 268).

Hutton's articles on Trollope are discussed in Skilton, pp. 100–125, and listed on pp. 160–62.

11 *declined a third attempt though a third such tale was written for him*: *The Golden Lion of Granpere*, which was eventually placed in *Good Words*, edited by Norman Macleod, as a serial running from January to August 1872, and published in book form by Tinsley in the same year.

12 *dooming some Milton to be mute and inglorious*: see Thomas Gray, 'Elegy written in a Country Churchyard', l. 59:

Some mute inglorious Milton here may rest.

13 *the lines were Pindar's*: from *The Biliad, or, How to Criticise* (1846), a verse satire by Terence McMahon Hughes. Richard Payne Knight's *The Principles of Taste* was first published in 1805.

Chapter Twelve

1 *Arcadia ... Ivanhoe ... Robinson Crusoe which is the earliest really popular novel which we have in our language*: Trollope's final plan was in line with what became the orthodox view of the history of English prose fiction for a century or more.

2 *when Dickens and Bulwer died*: in 1870 and 1873 respectively.

3 *detestable trash ... Aphra Behn*: Aphra Behn (1640–89), novelist, poet and playwright. The novels that Trollope so disliked include: *The Adventures of the Black Lady* (1684); *Lycidus* (1688); and *The Lucky Mistake* (1689).

4 *they read them, – as men eat pastry after dinner*: this is one of Thackeray's favourite comparisons. See for example his letter to Trollope reproduced in Chapter 8.

5 *the opinion expressed by wise and thinking men as to the work done by novelists*: Trollope is referring principally to Carlyle, whose essay, 'Biography', of 1832 he quotes in a deleted passage. See Textual Notes.

6 *Lydia ... Peregrine Pickle ... Lord Aimsworth*: *Peregrine Pickle* (1751) by Tobias Smollett; *The History of Lord Aimsworth, and the Honourable Charles Hartford, Esq., in a Series of Letters* (1773), 'by the Author of *Dorinda Catsby*, and *Ermina*,

or the Fair Recluse'. In act one, scene two of Sheridan's play, *The Rivals* (1775), Lydia Languish hurriedly conceals the fiction which she has been reading in opposition to the wishes of her aunt, Mrs Malaprop, and Sir Anthony Absolute: 'Here, my dear Lucy, hide these books. – Quick, quick! – Fling *Peregrine Pickle* under the toilet . . . – thrust *Lord Aimworth* under the sofa – cram *Ovid* behind the bolster . . . and leave *Fordyce's Sermons* open upon the table.'

7   *Editor of Good Words . . . would have been accepted*: See note 4 to Chapter 10.

8   *fictitious Cagliostros*: Cagliostro was the assumed name of a notorious Italian imposter, Giuseppe Balsamo (1743–95), whose most infamous fraud was the offer of everlasting youth to all who would pay him for his secret.

9   *Jack Sheppards . . . Macheaths*: criminal heroes of Harrison Ainsworth's *Jack Sheppard* (1839) and John Gay's *The Beggar's Opera* (1728).

10 *the most foolish of existing mortals*: see note 5 above.

11 *Lydia Bennet . . . Earl Leicester . . . Beatrix*: immoral characters in Jane Austen's *Pride and Prejudice* (1813), Sir Walter Scott's *Kenilworth* (1821) and Thackeray's *The History of Henry Esmond* (1852) respectively.

12 *says Sir Anthony in the play*: *The Rivals* I.ii.235–9. See note 6 above.

13 *how Laura Bell loved Pendennis*: Laura is an archetypically patient Victorian heroine in Thackeray's novel.

14 *Naturam expellas furcâ, tamen usque recurret*: Horace, *Epistles* I.10.24: 'You may drive out Nature with a pitchfork, but she always comes running back.'

15 *Wilkie Collins*: William Wilkie Collins (1824–89), novelist, dramatist, and close associate of Dickens, whose works include: *Antonina* (1850); *The Woman in White* (1860); *No Name* (1862); *Armadale* (1866); *The Moonstone* (1868); *Man and Wife* (1870); and *The New Magdalen* (1873).

16 *Rebecca . . . Sir Peregrine Orme*: these incidents occur respectively in Scott's novels *Ivanhoe* and *Old Mortality*, Charlotte Brontë's *Jane Eyre* (1847), Thackeray's *Esmond* and Trollope's own *Orley Farm* (1861–2).

17 *Bride of Lammermoor*: Scott's novel of 1819.

18 *Solve senescentem mature sanus equum, ne/Peccet ad extremum ridendus*: Horace, *Epistles* I.1.8–9: 'Be wise in time and turn loose the horse which has weakened with age, lest it fail at last amid ridicule'.

19 *wiser than Gil Blas' Canon*: in Book Two of Le Sage's novel *Gil Blas* (1715–35), Gil Blas's employer, the canon, regardless of his age, persists in over-indulgence in food and drink, for which he is famously chastised by his physician, Dr Sangrado. Trollope probably knew the book from Smollett's translation of 1749.

20 *What Macaulay says . . . Hardly any popular author except myself thinks of it'*: this reference has not been located.

21 *Sapphic stanza ... the fault*: Horace, *Odes* III.11.1–4: 'O, Mercury (for taught by thee as master, Amphion with his measures moved the rocks) and thou, O shell, trained to respond with thy seven strings ...' (Loeb).

22 *no episodes in a novel*: an episode is a narrative digression, which, although springing from the main narrative, is incidental to it.

23 *'The Curious Impertinent,' and with the history of 'The Man of the Hill'*: famous episodes in Cervantes' *Don Quixote* (1605–15) and Henry Fielding's *Tom Jones* (1749) respectively.

24 *Caleb Williams ... Adam Blair*: William Godwin's novel of 1794, and John Gibson Lockhart's *Some Passages in the Life of Mr Adam Blair, Minister of the Gospel at Cross-Meikle* of 1822.

25 *distributing his type*: breaking up type which has previously been set up, and returning it to its proper compartments in the case.

Chapter Thirteen

1 *Colonel Newcome*: in Thackeray's *The Newcomes* (1853–5).

2 *Becky Sharp ... Lady Castlewood and her daughter ... Esmond ... Warrington, Pendennis ... the Major ... Colonel Newcome ... Barry Lyndon*: characters in *Vanity Fair* (1847–8), *Esmond, Pendennis, The Newcomes* and *The Luck of Barry Lyndon* (1844).

3 *The Virginians ... Philip*: Thackeray's novels of 1857–9 and 1861–2.

4 *Seth Bede, Adam Bede, Maggie and Tom Tulliver, old Silas Marner, and ... Tito in Romola*: characters in George Eliot's *Adam Bede* (1859), *The Mill on the Floss* (1860), *Silas Marner* (1861) and *Romola* (1862–3).

5 *Mrs Gamp, Micawber, Pecksniff ... well known words*: Mr Micawber appears in Dickens's *David Copperfield* (1849–50), and the other two in *Martin Chuzzlewit* (1843–4) ...

6 *Smike ... Nicholas ... Kate*: characters in *Nicholas Nickleby* (1838–9).

7 *Boucicault's plays*: among the most successful of the many popular plays of Dion Boucicault (1820?–90) were *London Assurance* (1841), *The Corsican Brothers* (1852), *The Colleen Bawn* (1860) and *The Shaughraun* (1874).

8 *The Boffins and Veneerings*: characters in *Our Mutual Friend* (1864–5).

9 *Pelham ... Ernest Maltravers ... My Novel ... The Caxtons*: novels of 1828, 1837, 1853 and 1850 respectively.

10 *Eugene Aram*: character in Bulwer Lytton's novel of the same name (1832). *Mrs Poyser*: character in George Eliot's *Adam Bede*.

11 *Corney Delaney*: character in Charles Lever's *Jack Hinton* (1842).

12 *Harry Lorrequer*: Charles Lever's novel of 1839.

13 *The Eighth Commandment*: published in 1860.

14 *pseudonymuncule*: a petty or insignificant person who writes under a

pseudonym. The dispute concerns Reade's adaptation in *White Lies* (1857) of the plot to Auguste Macquet's play *Le Château Grantier*.

15 *he inserted a dialogue . . . from Swift*: Reade inserted unacknowledged a passage from Swift's *Journal of a Modern Lady* into the narrative version of his play, *The Wandering Heir*, which appeared as the 1872 Christmas number of the *Graphic*. The matter was topical when Trollope was writing, since Reade's counterattack on his accuser, the *Punch* contributor Mortimer Collins (1827–76), was published in 1873 as a supplement to the book edition of the work.

16 *Annie Thackeray*: W. M. Thackeray's daughter (1837–1919), later Lady Ritchie, whose novels include *The Story of Elizabeth* (1863), *The Village on the Cliff* (1867), *Old Kensington* (1873) and *Mrs Dymond* (1885).

17 *speaking to her brother*: the incident occurs in *Nancy* (1873).

18 *Rhoda Broughton . . . her fault in this direction*: novelist (1840–1920), whose works include *Not Wisely But Too Well* (1867) and *Cometh Up as a Flower* (1867). Trollope's reservations here about the unladylike behaviour of Broughton's heroines are at odds with his remarks to her in a letter of 28 June 1868: 'I have just read your novel *Not wisely but too Well* and wish to tell you how much it has pleased me . . . I must tell you . . . that I have heard that your stories were written in a strain not becoming a woman young as you are – not indeed becoming any woman . . . In the story which I have read there is not a word that I would not have had written by my sister, or my daughter – if I had one' (*Letters*, p. 434).

19 *Vivian Grey . . . twenty three years old . . . Dickens was . . . younger when he wrote The Sketches by Boz, and as young when he was writing The Pickwick Papers*: Disraeli was in fact marginally younger than Dickens was when each published his first book in 1826–7 and 1835–6 respectively.

20 *buhl*: ornamental inlay.

21 *Jack Sheppard . . . the same direction*: see note 9 to Chapter 12.

22 *Lady Corisande*: character in *Lothair* (1870).
Venetia or Henrietta Temple: eponymous heroines of Disraeli's two novels of 1837.

Chapter Fourteen

1 *Facilis descensus Averni*: see note 17 to Chapter 4.

2 *a critic of the day . . . the manuscript of a book recently published . . . by the same author*: F. X. Roellinger shows that this critic was almost certainly E. S. Dallas, principal literary critic of *The Times*, and the manuscript that of Dickens's *Our Mutual Friend*. Trollope's friend, Kate Field, told the story of

the gift in an article in *Scribner's Monthly* (vol. 8) in 1874, the year before
Trollope started *An Autobiography*. See F. X. Roellinger, 'E. S. Dallas in Trollope's *Autobiography*', *Modern Language Notes* 55 (1940), 422–4.

3 *a straining at gnats*: Matthew 23.24: 'Ye blind guides, which strain at a gnat,
and swallow a camel.'

4 *the great thunderer of some metropolitan periodical publication*: *The Times* was
commonly nicknamed 'The Thunderer'.

5 *Ponatur ... deinde labores*: identified in MS as Juvenal, Satire IX, 40–43:
'Thus he makes a reckoning with his lusts. Well, set out the counters, call
in the lads with the reckoning board, count out five thousand sesterces all
told, and then enumerate my services' (Loeb).

6 *Mentor*: in the *Odyssey* Mentor is the faithful friend of Odysseus, in whose
care the latter left his son Telemachus and his household. The goddess
Athena takes the form of Mentor when helping Telemachus.

7 *tanquam ex cathedrâ*: as though with the authority of the Church, because
uttered from the Pope's chair (Latin).

8 *on the tapis*: on the table-cover, i.e. as a subject for conversation (French).

Chapter Fifteen

1 *An old groom*: see note 10 to Chapter 5.

2 *One of these has been six years finished*: the three unpublished manuscripts
were *An Eye for an Eye* (written 1870, published 1878–9), *Is He Popenjoy?* (written 1874–5, published 1877–8) and *The American Senator* (written 1875, published 1876).

3 *the enterprise was not altogether successful*: John Sutherland speculates that the
publication of the *Last Chronicle* in sixpenny weekly numbers was an attempt to capitalize on the success of Captain Mayne Reid's *The Headless
Horseman* (1865), which had broken with the custom of issue in shilling
monthly parts. He further points out that 'when Trollope induced James
Virtue to repeat the sixpenny experiment in 1868–9 with *He Knew He Was
Right*... the publisher promptly slid into insolvency'. See John Sutherland,
Victorian Fiction: Writers, Publishers, Readers (London: Macmillan, 1995), pp.
102–3.

4 *the poor old dean dying at the deanery*: presumably a reference to the death at
Barchester deanery of Septimus Harding, who in fact turns down prefer-
ment to the deanery at the end of *Barchester Towers* in favour of his pro-
spective son-in-law, Dr Arabin.

5 *And so I did*: this, possibly the most celebrated anecdote concerning Trollope's working practices, is not to be taken literally. At the time when these
two clerics were supposedly speaking (during the composition of *The Last*

Chronicle in 1866), neither the Archdeacon nor 'the old Duke' (of Omnium) were in any Trollope novel currently running, the former having last appeared in *Framley Parsonage* (1860–61), and the latter in *The Small House at Allington* (1862–4). Neither is Mrs Proudie anywhere to be found in Trollope's fiction of that year, although there is a single passing mention of Bishop Proudie and his domineering wife in Chapter 2 of *The Claverings*, which was coming out in *Cornhill Magazine* during the relevant months of 1866.

6 *the first volumes of the series will now very shortly be published*: the *Chronicles of Barsetshire* were brought out by Chapman & Hall in 1878, including *The Small House at Allington*. Trollope clearly made a later decision on this omission, since a textual note to the present edition records that 'The Small House at Allington' is cancelled from the list of the *Chronicles of Barset* in the MS.

7 *Mr Scudamore*: Francis Ives Scudamore (1823–84), Trollope's highly qualified junior in the Post Office. Hall tentatively suggests that Trollope's being passed over for promotion may have been because he was the only Post Office Surveyor to question officially the rejection by the Post Office Board of a pay claim made by the Surveyors in April 1864. (See *Letters*, p. 259.)

8 *pillar letter-boxes . . . of which accommodation . . . I was the originator*: for details of this innovation see R. H. Super, *Trollope and the Post Office* (Ann Arbor: University of Michigan Press, 1988), p. 259.

9 *the great thing which Sir Rowland Hill had done for the country*: the introduction of the Penny Post in 1840. See note 1 to Chapter 8.

10 *Mr James Virtue*: James Sprent Virtue (1829–92), highly successful printer of the mid-nineteenth century, and publisher of specialist art books.

11 *Mr Goschen . . . Dutton Cook*: George Joachim Goschen (1831–1907), statesman who contributed two articles to the first two numbers of *St Paul's* (October and November 1867); Captain Henry Brackenbury (1831–90), Professor of Military History at Woolwich, and writer on military subjects; Edward James Stephen Dicey (1832–1911), journalist engaged by Trollope as subeditor on *St Paul's*, subsequently editor of the *Observer* (1870–79); Percy Hetherington Fitzgerald (1834–1925), barrister and author; Austen Henry Layard (1817–94), politician and archaeologist of renown, who contributed an article to the second number of *St Paul's*; William Allingham (1828–89), journalist and later editor of *Fraser's Magazine*; Leslie Stephen (1832–1904), man of letters, subsequently editor of the *Cornhill* from 1871 to 1882; Eliza Lynn Linton (1822–98), novelist and journalist, who contributed to the second number of *St Paul's*; Frances Eleanor Trollope, *née* Ternan (?1834–

1913), novelist and writer, and Thomas Adolphus' second wife; Sir Edwin Arnold (1832–1904), man of letters; Henry Austin Dobson (1840–1921), poet and miscellaneous writer, subsequently contributed volumes on Fielding, Richardson and Burney to Macmillan's *English Men of Letters* series, for which Trollope supplied a biography of Thackeray (1879); Richard Anthony Proctor (1837–88), celebrated astronomer; Juliet Creed Pollock (d. 1899), miscellaneous writer; Charles Mackay (1814–99), editor of the *London Review*; Frederick Hardman (1814–74), novelist and journalist; George Macdonald (1824–1905), Scottish poet and novelist, now best known for his children's stories *At the Back of the North Wind* (1871), *The Princess and the Goblin* (1872) and *The Princess and Curdie* (1888); Margaret Oliphant (1828–97), Scottish novelist, whose *The Three Brothers* ran in *St Paul's* from June 1869 to October 1870; Leone Levi (1821–88), jurist and writer on economic matters; Edward Dutton Cook (1829–83), journalist and miscellaneous writer.

12 *the thorn in his pillow of which Thackeray complained*: see 'Roundabout Paper' no. 5, 'Thorns in the Cushion', (*Cornhill Magazine* 2 [July 1860], 122–8) in which Thackeray laments the constant bombardment of letters from impecunious authors desirous of publishing in the magazine: 'At night I come home, and take my letters up to bed (not daring to open them), and in the morning I find one, two, three thorns on my pillow. Three I extracted yesterday; two I found this morning. They don't sting quite so sharply as they did; but a skin is a skin, and they bite, after all, most wickedly.'

Chapter Sixteen

1 *an uncle of mine, who was himself a clerk in the War Office*: Henry Milton (1784–1859), Trollope's maternal uncle.

2 *that bourne from whence he was not likely to return*: see *Hamlet* III.i.78–80: 'death/The undiscover'd country, from whose bourn/No traveller returns'.

3 *drags and holdfasts*: brakes and clamps.

4 *the late Charles Buxton*: Charles Buxton (1823–71), Liberal politician and devotee of hunting. Buxton's eldest brother, Sir Edward (d. 1858), had been MP for Essex South from 1847 to 1852.

5 *the liberal member for Newark*: Grosvenor Hodgkinson, MP for Newark 1859–74, successfully proposed a radical amendment to Disraeli's Reform Bill, whereby some half million non-occupiers were enfranchised.

6 *will not be at a loss to find it*: W. S. Hind, a local solicitor.

7 *Sir Henry Edwards ... a young man of fortune in quest of a seat*: Sir Henry

Edwards (1812–86), MP for Beverley from 1857 to 1869; Captain Edmund Hegan Kennard (1835–1912), MP for Beverley (1868–9), and later MP for Lymington (1874–85).

8 *all leather and prunella*: words of Alexander Pope, commonly interpreted to mean the material of shoes, and hence unimportant things; see *Essay on Man* IV.204–5

> Worth makes the man, and want of it, the fellow:
> The rest is all but leather and prunella.

In fact Pope uses 'leather and prunella' metonymically to designate the callings of cobbler and clergyman, prunella being the woollen stuff from which a cleric's gown was made.

9 *the Ballot*: the secret ballot was not introduced until the Suffrage Bill of 1868.

10 *the Permissive Bill*: a Temperance measure to which Trollope, in defiance of dominant Liberal opinion, was opposed.

11 *to swallow such gnats*: see note 3 to Chapter 14.

Chapter Seventeen

1 *I had to deal with two men*: the American Postmaster General, Alexander Randall, and his Senior Clerk, Joseph Fanwood.

2 *a certain American publisher, he who usually reprinted my works*: Harper of New York.

3 *Since this was written the Commission on the Law of Copyright has sat and made its report*: the Commission reported 24 May 1878.

4 *their great ring-robberies*: the formation of cartels in order to defraud the public.

5 *two old gentlemen . . . irresistible comedy*: not identified.

6 *an American woman*: Mary Katherine Feemle Field (1838–96). Kate Field, as she was known, was the successful American lecturer, journalist and advocate of women's rights, with whom Trollope formed a long-standing (probably platonic) attachment, after meeting her in Florence in 1860.

7 *I created the scheme of the book during a visit to Ireland*: Trollope visited Ireland in late September 1866. *Phineas Finn* appeared in *St Paul's Magazine* from October 1867 to May 1869 inclusive, and was published in two volumes by Virtue in March 1869.

8 *in the Graphic in 1873*: *Phineas Redux* was serialized from July 1873 to January 1874 inclusive, and was published in two volumes by Chapman & Hall in 1874.

9 *terrible condemnation and scorn pronounced by the great man in Paternoster Row*: see Chapter 6 (p. 74).

Chapter Eighteen

1 *the Editor of the periodical*: E. S. Dallas. See note 12 to Chapter 5, note 10 to Chapter 7 and note 2 to Chapter 14.

2 *one of Victor Hugo's modern novels, L'Homme qui rit*: Victor Marie Hugo (1802–85), French poet and author whose works include: *Notre Dame de Paris* (1831); *Les Voix intérieures* (1837); *Les Misérables* (1862); and Trollope's bugbear here, *L'Homme qui rit* (1869).

3 *the Gentleman's Magazine*: although formerly a periodical of some importance, the *Gentleman's Magazine* was now of low repute.

4 *laches*: in legal Latin, *laches* means negligence or delay in seeking legal remedy. There may also be a play here on the French *lâché*, or 'slipshod work'.

5 *like painted sepulchres*: Matthew 23.27: 'Woe unto you, scribes and Pharisees, hypocrites! for ye are like unto whited sepulchres, which indeed appear beautiful outward, but are within full of dead men's bones, and of all uncleanness.'

6 *make him break up the type*: the novel in question, which came out in three instead of the two volumes Trollope intended, was *The Belton Estate*.

7 *John Blackwood*: Blackwood (1818–79) had in 1852 succeeded his father, William, as head of the Edinburgh publishing company. He also served as editor of *Blackwood's Magazine*, from 1845 to 1879.

8 *William Lucas Collins*: Revd William Lucas Collins (1817–87).

9 *that most futile book by the late Emperor of the French*: *L'Histoire de Jules César*, by Emperor Napoleon III, 1865–6.

10 *thanked me for my 'comic Caesar'*: the friend was Dean Charles Merivale (Hall, p. 357. Hall notes R. H. Super's suggestion that Trollope misread 'Comm.' as 'comic'.)

11 *Ne sutor ultra crepidam*: 'the cobbler is not to judge of things above the sandal' (Latin). The phrase derives from Pliny's *Natural History* XXXV.36.85, in which Apelles is recounted as allowing a cobbler to criticize his representation of a sandal, but not his rendering of the leg.

Chapter Nineteen

1 *a series of articles . . . duly paid for*: ten letters to the editor of the *Daily Telegraph*, published from 23 December 1871 to 28 December 1872, above the signature 'Antipodean'.

2 *Kenelm Chillingly*: the novel *Kenelm Chillingly: His Adventures and Opinions*, by Bulwer Lytton, was published posthumously in 1873.

3 *Young*: Brigham Young (1801–77), American Mormon leader, and governor of Utah Territory from 1850 to 1857.

4 *the 'Baron' and Mr Selby Lowndes*: Baron Meyer Amschel de Rothschild (1818–74); William Selby Lowndes (1807–86), Master of the Whaddon Chase hounds. Hall reveals the likely source of Trollope's dissatisfaction of hunting with Lowndes: when deer-hunting with the Baron, '[t]he deer were brought in carts and released for the hunt, so those taking part were sure of a gallop and their game; the fox-hunter, however, had no such certainty' (*Letters*, p. 579).

5 *Singula de nobis ... poëmata*: correctly identified in the MS as 'Horace, 2 book of Epist 2nd epistle' (lines 55–7), and the translation as 'Conington p. 163' (from John Conington, *The Satires, Epistles, and Art of Poetry of Horace Translated into English Verse*, 1874).

6 *Vixi puellis ... habebit*: identified in the MS as 'Horace 3d book, 26 ode' (lines 1–3). A more literal translation reads, 'Until recently I lived fit for young women and served not without glory. Now my arms and my lute, whose campaigns are over, will hang here on this wall ...' In these celebrated lines the poet makes play with military campaigning as a metaphor for sex. Trollope's translation is a *jeu d'esprit* which is characteristic of classically educated men of the period, and, like the previous quotation and translation, it appeals to group or class fellow-feelings, by the reversion to the public school exercise of verse translation. See D. Skilton, 'Schoolboy Latin and the mid-Victorian novelist: a study in reader competence', *Browning Institute Studies* 16 (1988), 39–55.

Chapter Twenty

1 *Mr Ruskin*: John Ruskin (1819–1900), the highly influential English author and art critic, became increasingly concerned, as his career progressed, with the social ills of capitalism, a preoccupation not to the taste of the clubbable literary set to which Trollope belonged: his *Unto this Last* (1862), a critique of market forces, was dropped from the *Cornhill* by Thackeray (1860) after just four numbers; a similar fate awaited his next work of social criticism, *Munera Pulveris* (1872), which was dropped from *Fraser's Magazine* (1862–3) after six numbers. His series of papers 'To the Workmen and Labourers of Great Britain', *Fors Clavigera*, was published from 1871 to 1884, during part of which time Trollope was composing *An Autobiography*.

2 *wailing and gnashing of teeth*: Matthew 13.42, 50.

3 *Apician dinners*: Marcus Gabius Apicius was a celebrated gourmand in the reigns of Augustus and Tiberius.

4 *Burke and Fox*: Edmund Burke (1729–97), Irish statesman and philosopher; Charles James Fox (1749–1806), English statesman and notorious libertine.

5 *the highest place in the council of his Sovereign*: i.e. the office of Prime Minister, or (more correctly) First Lord of the Treasury.

6 *I know to be a good critic*: Trollope was mistaken in his implicit attribution of
   this review (*Spectator* xlix, 22 July 1876, 922–3), to Richard Holt Hutton. It
   was in fact written by the *Spectator*'s Political Editor, Meredith Townsend,
   who was not generally favourable towards Trollope.

7 *the mainstay of another story*: Trollope returned to Plantagenet Palliser in
   The Duke's Children, written in 1876 and published in 1879–80.

8 *Voltaire . . . Varro*: François Marie Arouet de Voltaire (1694–1778), prolific
   French philosopher and author of the Enlightenment; Marcus Terentius
   Varro (116–27 BC), Roman scholar and author, whose works included
   the *Disciplinarum Libri IX*, an encyclopaedia of the liberal arts, and the
   Imagines, a collection of 700 Greek and Roman biographies.

9 *Nulla dies sine lineâ*: 'no day without a line'; Pliny's *Natural History*
   XXXV.36.84, in which Apelles is described as keeping in practice by drawing a straight line every day.

10 *constancy in labour will conquer all difficulties*: see note 1 to Chapter 7.

11 *Gutta cavat lapidem non vi, sed sæpe cadendo*: 'the drop of rain maketh a hole
   in the stone, not by violence, but by oft falling' – Latimer, *Seventh Sermon
   before Edward VI* (1549). Latimer (with a possible glance at Lucretius, *De
   Rerum Naturæ*, I.313) is adapting Ovid, *Epistulæ ex Ponto* 4.10.5: 'Gutta cavat
   lapidem, consumitur anulus usu, atteritur pressa vomer aduncus humo'
   ('Drops of water hollow out a stone, a ring is worn thin by use, the hooked
   plough is rubbed away by the soil's pressure' – Loeb.)

12 *a record of my inner life . . . Rousseau probably attempted it*: a reference to Rousseau's famous claim at the opening of Book One of his *Confessions* (1782) to
   have revealed his inner being exactly as it will be known on the Day of
   Judgement.

Individual works by Anthony Trollope are indexed alphabetically in the main sequence, and those by other authors are indexed under the names of those authors. Fictional characters are distinguished by an asterix, thus: *Proudie, Mrs.

READ MORE IN PENGUIN

In every corner of the world, on every subject under the sun, Penguin represents quality and variety – the very best in publishing today.

For complete information about books available from Penguin – including Puffins, Penguin Classics and Arkana – and how to order them, write to us at the appropriate address below. Please note that for copyright reasons the selection of books varies from country to country.

In the United Kingdom: Please write to *Dept. EP, Penguin Books Ltd, Bath Road, Harmondsworth, West Drayton, Middlesex UB7 0DA*

In the United States: Please write to *Consumer Sales, Penguin USA, P.O. Box 999, Dept. 17109, Bergenfield, New Jersey 07621-0120*. VISA and MasterCard holders call 1-800-253-6476 to order Penguin titles

In Canada: Please write to *Penguin Books Canada Ltd, 10 Alcorn Avenue, Suite 300, Toronto, Ontario M4V 3B2*

In Australia: Please write to *Penguin Books Australia Ltd, P.O. Box 257, Ringwood, Victoria 3134*

In New Zealand: Please write to *Penguin Books (NZ) Ltd, Private Bag 102902, North Shore Mail Centre, Auckland 10*

In India: Please write to *Penguin Books India Pvt Ltd, 706 Eros Apartments, 56 Nehru Place, New Delhi 110 019*

In the Netherlands: Please write to *Penguin Books Netherlands bv, Postbus 3507, NL-1001 AH Amsterdam*

In Germany: Please write to *Penguin Books Deutschland GmbH, Metzlerstrasse 26, 60594 Frankfurt am Main*

In Spain: Please write to *Penguin Books S. A., Bravo Murillo 19, 1° B, 28015 Madrid*

In Italy: Please write to *Penguin Italia s.r.l., Via Felice Casati 20, I–20124 Milano*

In France: Please write to *Penguin France S. A., 17 rue Lejeune, F–31000 Toulouse*

In Japan: Please write to *Penguin Books Japan, Ishikiribashi Building, 2–5–4, Suido, Bunkyo-ku, Tokyo 112*

In South Africa: Please write to *Longman Penguin Southern Africa (Pty) Ltd, Private Bag X08, Bertsham 2013*

BY THE SAME AUTHOR

Trollope is a supreme portraitist of the professional and landed classes of mid-Victorian England. His early novels depict, with irony and wit, the comfortable world of the English gentry, contrasting the apparent stability of rural life with the harsh, disturbing rhythms of London. In his later work Trollope's rural order has given way to the values of industrial society, and his tone acquires a more sombre note.

The Barsetshire novels:

The Warden
Barchester Towers
Doctor Thorne
Framley Parsonage
The Small House at Allington
The Last Chronicle of Barset

The Palliser novels:

Can You Forgive Her?
Phineas Finn
The Eustace Diamonds
The Prime Minister
The Duke's Children

and:

He Knew He Was Right
The Way We Live Now
Rachel Ray

also published:

The Penguin Companion to Trollope